D0407844

NATIONAL UNIVERSITY
LIBRARY   SAN DIEGO

Revolutionizing Workforce Performance

A Systems Approach to Mastery

Jack E. Bowsher

Jossey-Bass
Pfeiffer

San Francisco

ASTD

Copyright © 1998 by Jack E. Bowsher

ISBN: 0-7879-0798-7

Library of Congress Cataloging-in-Publication Data
Bowsher, Jack E.
Revolutionizing workforce performance: a systems approach to
mastery / Jack E. Bowsher.
     p. cm.
     Includes bibliographical references and index. ISBN 0-7879-0798-7 (acid-free
     paper)
     1. Performance technology–United States. 2. Employees–Training
of–United States. I. Title.
HF5549.5.P37B69 1998
658.3'124–dc21   97-21087

All rights reserved. No part of this publication may be reproduced, stored in a retrieval
system, or transmitted, in any form or by any means, electronic, mechanical,
photocopying, recording, or otherwise, without the prior written permission of the
publisher.

Printed in the United States of America
Published by

Jossey-Bass
Pfeiffer
350 Sansome Street, 5th Floor
San Francisco, California 94104-1342
(415) 433-1740; Fax (415) 433-0499
(800) 274-4434; Fax (800) 569-0443

Visit our website at: http://www.pfeiffer.com

Outside of the United States, Pfeiffer products can be purchased from the following
Simon & Schuster International Offices:

Jossey-Bass/Pfeiffer
3255 Wyandotte Street East
Windsor, Ontario N8Y 1E9
Canada
888-866-5559; Fax 800-605-2665

Prentice Hall Professional
Locked Bag 507
Frenchs Forest PO NSW 2086
Australia
61 2 9454 2200; Fax 61 2 9453 0089

Prentice Hall/Pfeiffer
P.O. Box 1636
Randburg 2125
South Africa
27 11 781 0780; Fax 27 11 781 0781

Prentice Hall
Campus 400
Maylands Avenue
Hemel Hempstead
Hertfordshire HP2 7EZ
United Kingdom
44(0) 1442 881891; Fax 44(0) 1442 882074

Simon & Schuster (Asia) Pte Ltd
317 Alexandra Road
#04-01 IKEA Building
Singapore 159965
Asia
65 476 4688; Fax 65 378 0370

Acquiring Editor: Larry Alexander
Marketing Manager: Matt Holt
Director of Development: Kathleen Dolan-Davies
Senior Production Editor: Dawn Kilgore
Editor: Rebecca Taff

Printing 10   9   8   7   6   5   4   3   2

This book is printed on acid-free, recycled stock that meets or exceeds the minimum GPO and
EPA requirements for recycled paper.

This book is dedicated to CHARMIAN. In my adult life there has been the constant love and support of my wife, who has encouraged me to write my books and who has contributed hundreds of hours to my projects through her editing and word-processing skills. Those who purchase this book will be making a contribution to the advanced education of our grandchildren, Elizabeth and Kevin.

Contents

Acknowledgments

This book is based on my work over the past thirty years, during which time I have had the opportunity to interact with literally hundreds of educators, trainers, and performance specialists, as well as many professors of instructional design. Over the years, writers and editors of training magazines and journals have also been a great source of information for me. The speakers at ASTD, ISPI, SALT, and Training Conferences have added much to my knowledge of best practices. In addition, I have been fortunate in my career to work with many chief executive officers and senior executives who provided me with insight on how to manage large organizations successfully. I thank all of you for what you have taught me.

Numerous clients in the past eight years have enabled me to review the success of best practices in almost every industry. Certainly, an association with over two hundred directors of training in the ASTD Chief Training Officer Workshop has influenced my thinking on what works and does not work in most organizations. In that workshop, I had the support of Gretta Kotler and Kristy Husband from ASTD and the creative assistance of Reinhard Ziegler and John Splavec from Andersen Consulting.

Most of all, I would like to express appreciation to my fellow chief training officers, who have so willingly shared their knowledge and experience over the years, particularly to the fifteen members of the Business Training Consortium.

I owe a special thank you to a group of senior executives and CEOs who helped develop the executive summary in the final chapter of this book.

I would also like to thank Bob Craig, *ASTD Training and Development Handbook* editor-in-chief; John H. Rosenheim, Universal Training's retired CEO; Jerry Tucker, GTE's chief training officer; and Charles Bowsher, my brother, the retired Comptroller General of the United States, who provided me with positive ideas on how to enhance the manuscript.

One person in particular made this book substantially more readable than it would otherwise have been: Rob Bowsher, who did an outstanding job editing both the book proposal and first draft. My friend, Jane Mangold, also provided her talent for the graphics.

This book would not exist without the endorsement and special help I received from Nancy Olson, ASTD publications vice president, and from my agent, Sidney B. Kramer. The entire editorial staff at Jossey-Bass deserve special recognition for their contributions, especially Larry Alexander, Kathleen Dolan-Davies, Dawn Kilgore, and Matthew Holt.

Introduction

Much like the U.S. Department of Education's 1983 report, "A Nation At Risk" (U.S. Department of Education, 1983, p. 5), this book will sound alarms. This report described the deplorable conditions existing in the American public school system. In that report, the National Commission on Excellence in Education stated, "If an unfriendly foreign power had attempted to impose on America the mediocre educational performance that exists today, we might well have viewed it as an act of war. As it stands, we have allowed this to happen to ourselves" (U.S. Department of Education, 1983, p. 5). Ever since that report was published, almost everyone has concluded that the number-one educational crisis in the United States is the public schools' poor performance.

Audiences are shocked when I tell them that, from an economic viewpoint, that honor belongs to employee-training programs. Nearly every corporation, not-for-profit organization, and government agency has inadequate training and support programs. Not only are they underfunded but, too often, the existing courses have almost no impact on overall organizational performance. Moreover, program results are so poorly measured that many organizations do not even realize that they have a problem. Unfortunately, the crisis is real: Millions of employees, including managers and executives, go to work every day untrained or only partially trained to do their jobs. America has a workforce at risk. This situation led Dr. W. Edwards Deming to state, "The greatest waste in America is failure to use the abilities of people."

In late 1994, The Conference Board issued a report (Csoka, 1994, p. 7) titled "Closing the Human Performance Gap." The report said, in part, "Despite major investments in technology, downsizing, restructuring, and reengineering to cut costs and to improve their competitive advantage, 98 percent of companies responding to the survey report a need to gain more productivity and higher performance from their workforce" (p. 7). It also pointed out, "The competitive advantage is people. The human resource is the constant that ultimately determines a company's fate in the global marketplace. Consequently, the quality of workforce performance has become a key business issue" (p. 7).

Despite good economic conditions, business headlines provide a constant stream of depressing news about downsizing, layoffs, loss of market share, elimination of product lines, and going out of business. Good, high-paying jobs disappear with each announcement. The typical reasons given are streamlining, being more responsive to customers, realigning for greater shareholder value, or whatever. The excuses go on and on as American workers adjust to lower standards of living because their jobs are eliminated.

Fortunately, it is not all bad news. Some American companies are looking for the missing link leading to growth and increased profits. They have discovered that a competitive, well-trained workforce remains as one of the best organizational strategies for distinguishing companies from their competitors. Organizations such as Motorola, Federal Express, the FBI, GAO, Arthur Andersen, Andersen Consulting, GE, Xerox, Ford, Nordstrom, Southwest Airlines, Delta Airlines, GTE, McDonald's, The Southern Company, and a few leading-edge financial-service companies have invested in performance-based employee training and support systems in order to fully train and develop their workforces.

It is not just allocation of resources, however, that makes these companies so successful at training employees. They have *management systems* that enable their training and support staff to adjust quickly to new business objectives and new strategic directions. These organizations know that a well-trained workforce is more productive, has a lower error rate, and requires less supervision than a workforce with little or no training. Their aim to have a well-trained, low-cost, and *competitive workforce* that knows more and does more than the other companies in their industry. These organizations have demonstrated that American companies can still have workforces that are the envy of the world.

Most organizations have only a *workforce with some training*. They offer generalized employee and management-development courses that have little impact on financial performance. Senior and line executives have not defined what they want their employees to know and be able to do within each major job category. Course curriculum and support systems simply do not exist, and ways to measure whether lessons are being learned or being applied on the job are inadequate or nonexistent. Everyone comes to work with good intentions, but inadequate training renders them second- or third-class performers who make too many errors, which requires layers of management to audit performance. Worse yet, senior executives view employees as a variable expense and seek to reduce costs by eliminating employees or transferring jobs to lower-wage environments. Under such conditions, morale is low and attrition high, leading to rising recruitment and training costs.

Too many organizations do not know their cost of people, which includes total payroll, total benefits (including retirement), and total support (buildings, utilities, office furniture, workplace fixtures, tools, telephones, FAX machines, personal computers and copiers) for both full-time and part-time employees. In nearly every organization, the costs associated with people are the number-one expense. Certainly, it is at least the number-two expense. On average, the overall cost of a full-time employee varies between $25,000 to $60,000, with high-technology companies being at the upper limits. When senior management focuses on the cost of people, there is a renewed interest in the system that trains and supports their workforce. After all, there are no inexpensive employees, managers, or executives. Therefore, the lessons and messages in this book address the issues that greatly influence the number-one or number-two expense item of an organization. Only when top executives make training those people a priority will their investment pay off. The typical organization in the United States spends an estimated 0.9 percent of their payroll expense on training, according to ASTD (1997). This amount is shockingly low when one considers that the top-performing companies in many industries spend ten times that. Investing in workforce performance rather than reducing training expense should be every organization's focus for achieving better operating measurements as well as improved financial statements.

Why do organizations underspend on training? Unfortunately, senior executives simply do not know how to develop a well-trained, competitive workforce. The subject is not covered in business schools or in most executive-development programs. Although annual reports often state that "Our employees are our most valuable assets," in practice executives eliminate employees who are struggling to perform as management leaps from crisis to crisis. Training directors also are quite often not trained to develop a competitive workforce, measuring themselves by how many classroom seats are filled, student-satisfaction ratings, and how well they stay within budget, rather than on performance improvement.

Every organization that has a workforce with some training needs to replace the traditional performance-management system that produces a bell-shaped curve with a system that achieves mastery of learning and performance. To be industry leaders in quality and customer service, an organization needs all employees to be at the far right on the curve—A and B performers. When this critical fact is recognized, training can be seen not as an expense but as an investment necessary to reach both strategic and tactical organizational objectives.

The primary objective of this book is to transfer the best practices from a dozen or more successful organizations with well-trained, low-cost, and *competitive workforces* to thousands of organizations that have only a *workforce with some training*. No one organization has a complete and perfect system. However, the top-performing organizations all have some form of *management system* for training and performance that achieves the following results:

- Increased productivity.
- Lower operating expenses.
- Additional revenues and market share.
- Enhanced employee morale and job satisfaction.
- Reduced attrition rates and employment costs.
- Decreased supervisory costs.
- Improved quality levels.
- Higher customer satisfaction levels.
- Greater earnings.

This book presents a new systems approach to workforce performance that companies can use to remedy their training deficiencies in order to develop a competitive workforce. Rather then just raising an alarm, this book offers specific solutions to the crisis in workforce training and performance. It provides "how to" guidelines for restructuring a training department to focus on breakthroughs in workforce performance. Everyone buys the concepts of increased efficiency and tying training programs to business objectives. However, very few people know how to transfer these concepts into reality.

Sections of the Book

Part One begins with some comparisons between a *competitive workforce* and a *workforce with some training*. Chapter One describes why a *workforce with some training* causes so many operational problems. The good news in Chapter Two covers how leading-edge organizations are achieving their goal of having only above-average performers in their workforces, essential to meeting and overcoming intense competition in the marketplace.

Part Two describes the Systems Approach for Workforce Performance, a new management system that integrates the best practices of organizations that have achieved strategic advantages through their workforces. This approach, shown in Figure 1, can succeed in small, intermediate, or large organizations in any industry. Corporations, partnerships, government agencies, and not-for-profit organizations can use it in either centralized or decentralized environments.

Parts Two and Three provide a detailed explanation on how to implement the Systems Approach. Chapter Three describes in detail the Systems Approach for Workforce Performance; Chapter Four covers how to choose the right leader to implement training and performance systems; Chapter Five discusses how to develop a working partnership between the training organizations and lines executives; Chapter Six explains how to achieve maximum benefits from quality programs, continuous improvement programs, new strategies, directions, and reengineering programs; and Chapter Seven describes how to develop performance requirements for each major job category.

Chapter Eight explains how to design and develop a performance-based curriculum with courses for each major job category;

Figure 1. Systems Approach for Workforce Performance.

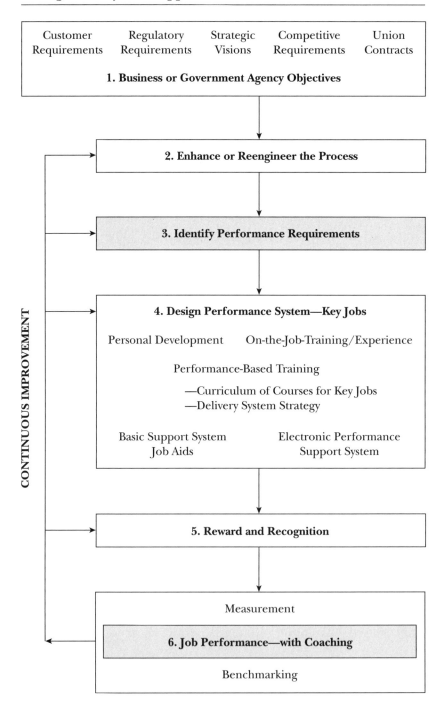

Chapter Nine shows how to utilize and justify cost-effective delivery systems. Developing structured on-the-job training assignments is discussed in Chapter Ten; and how to develop basic support systems such as job aids and knowledge systems to reinforce performance-based training programs is the topic in Chapter Eleven. Chapter Twelve describes the need to investigate electronic performance support systems to achieve a major competitive advantage; developing and implementing reward systems is the topic for Chapter Thirteen; how to implement an entirely new approach to evaluating job performance is covered in Chapter Fourteen; and implementing measurements that ensure students like the courses, learn the lessons, and increase their job productivity is discussed in Chapter Fifteen.

Chapters Sixteen and Seventeen in Part Four describe how an organization can justify new performance-based training and support systems and discusses the cost of incompetence and poor performance. As the old joke goes, "If you don't like the cost of education, try ignorance." Unfortunately, the price of ignorance and poor performance——enormous in many organizations——is rarely calculated. In this part of the book, it will be shown that the training and performance department may need to double or triple its budget through trade-off planning, lower operating expenses, and greater revenues to develop a performance system for every major job category.

In Part Five, Chapter Eighteen describes how to organize a training and performance department to achieve maximum results with the Systems Approach for Workforce Performance. The chapter also features key lessons on how to develop the staff to achieve organizational objectives within a restructured training department.

The final chapters describe the leadership needed from senior management to reengineer the training division successfully. The need for bold action rather than fine-tuning is emphasized, along with the fact that training is not a one-time event but a process that requires continual updating to reflect the latest strategic directions and tactical decisions in an organization.

This book can also be used as a reference manual to develop a plan of action during the months spent restructuring a training organization to focus on workforce performance.

Benefits of Reading the Book

Most training directors want the senior executives in their organizations to appreciate the importance of training. Fortunately, senior executives in a few organizations are asking the right questions, such as the following:

- Does the training department fully understand the strategic directions of the organization?
- Does the training department react to new strategic directions and tactical decisions in a timely manner?
- Does the training organization have a working partnership with senior and line managers?
- Does the organization have the right courses and support systems for each critical job?
- Does the training department measure whether employees are learning what they need to learn, whether they are applying their lessons to the job, and whether their new knowledge and skills are having a positive impact on operating results?
- Do we utilize cost-effective delivery systems?
- Do we use instructional-design methods to minimize course length and maximize learning?
- Do we operate training programs as efficiently as we run other functions such as manufacturing?
- Do we have outstanding programs within the training function to attract, retain, and develop outstanding personnel?
- How do we compare to others in our industry? Is our workforce competitive?
- Which jobs require integrated electronic performance support systems, and have we started pilot programs?
- Are training and performance systems part of our reengineering studies?
- What is our overall reputation for providing life-long learning to increase workforce performance?

Very few training directors could answer these penetrating questions positively. After completing this book, senior executives will know what questions to ask, and training directors will have the appropriate answers. No organization can achieve real breakthroughs in workforce productivity without this management system.

This book was written for the training department and the executive team, both essential to workforce training and development. Recently, a major insurance company's CEO stated, "We have been looking at learning as an outcome when learning is only a by-product. Performance is what we want. As business managers facing a tough and unknowable future, we cannot afford the luxury of learning when it is not accompanied by performance" (Malcolm, 1992, p. 22). This attitude needs to permeate all executive offices.

The field of *workforce performance* has the same challenges that *quality* had in the 1980s. Like quality, workforce performance is taken for granted in almost every organization. When people first heard about Dr. Deming and his quality message, they thought it applied only to companies that had severe quality problems—certainly not IBM, Motorola, or Xerox. People did not understand that Deming had developed a management system that would not only increase a company's overall quality performance but would reduce its operating expenses as well.

The Systems Approach for Workforce Performance is another management system that will also achieve breakthroughs by reducing operating expenses, which will convince senior and line executives to focus on workforce performance as they did on quality, creating even greater payoffs than quality did.

This book represents the culmination of many years of research and practice on the best ways to restructure the training functions within corporations, government agencies, and not-for-profit organizations. It is based on studying organizational best practices, including those of twenty-five clients I have worked with during the past eight years since retiring from thirty-three years with IBM. Input from more than two hundred executives who have attended the ASTD Chief Training Officer Workshop has greatly influenced my views. Serving as the chief training officer of one of the world's largest training programs enabled me to test the lessons in this book in more than one hundred education centers that were located in over one hundred countries.

There is no reason for an organization to learn by trial and error. We know what works and what does not. When training was decentralized at IBM, we tried almost every method within every subject. Other companies have had similar experiences. Over the years, it has been painful to watch so many people and organizations reinvent everything as they struggle to improve their training programs. Enormous resources have been invested to learn the same lessons. In the current world of intense competition, companies do not have the luxury of time or money to experiment. We must learn from others and from the past.

Although this book provides an overview of how to restructure and manage the department responsible for training and support systems, readers still need to study a number of other sources to obtain a more in-depth knowledge in the subject. The bibliography at the end of this book should not be considered all-inclusive, but it does give an overview of the subjects to be studied.

The American workforce is at risk of a lower standard of living. Although salaries and benefits are high, productivity and customer-service levels must improve to maintain or improve our current standard of living. A highly paid workforce is justified only by outstanding performance.

All organizations must aim for new workforce performance levels. Every individual and work team must demonstrate distinguished levels of competence and productivity. Systems that increase performance must be developed, implemented, and measured.

Yes, we need to restructure the American public school system, but it is not causing our productivity and performance problems. Remember, millions of American employees go to work each day untrained or only partially trained to do their jobs.

In the ASTD *Training Data Book* (Bassi, Gallagher, & Schroer, 1996) it says, "Empirical literature on the adoption of performance improvement systems is sparse. In other words, no single activity or set of activities is the defining characteristic of a performance improvement system." This may have been true in the past, but the reader will discover in this book a well-defined management system that produces a performance system for every major job category within an organization. In this book, there is a science to both learning and performance improvement that achieves mastery of learning and performance.

An organization can achieve a well-trained, competitive workforce by implementing the Systems Approach for Workforce Performance, beginning by establishing a working partnership between senior executives and the management team responsible for training and performance. The key messages within this book are directed at these two audiences.

The author realizes that this book will initially be read by members of the training organization. In many instances, the typical reaction will be, "If only we could convince our senior executives to read this book." To facilitate this, the final chapter "Essential Messages for Executive Management" is an executive summary of the book for members of the training organization to present to senior executives.

A number of chief executive officers and senior executives were asked to read Chapter Twenty prior to the book's final draft. All agreed that the executive summary's messages stimulated their interest in workforce training and performance. All read additional chapters and said that they would ask their human resources vice president and training director to give them a presentation on how the organization could implement a management system like the Systems Approach for Workforce Performance. Every CEO said he or she would ask line executives to do a fast read of the book to generate a greater working partnership between the line organizations and the training department.

Therefore, if you want your senior executives to be your partners in workforce training and performance, you only have to send a short note to them with a copy of the book. Here is an example of such a note:

> I've read this recently published book on breakthroughs in workforce performance. It has many new ideas and a new management system that we should consider implementing in our organization. Please read the executive summary in Chapter Twenty. I've scheduled a meeting with you (date and time) to discuss a plan of action.

For years, managers and training directors have said, "If only I could get the CEO and other executives involved in training, we could really make progress." Well, there are no excuses left for not having senior and line executives as your partners on this important subject. It only takes a few minutes to ask your CEO or any other senior executive to read the executive summary, which can be read in under thirty minutes.

It has been said that as technology, systems, products, and quality become more equal, and they will, the only real competitive advantage will be the performance of the workforce. The UNCF College Fund has a great slogan, "A Mind Is a Terrible Thing to Waste." I wish that I could hang a plaque in every senior and line executive's office that reads, "An Employee Is a Terrible Asset to Waste."

Westport, Connecticut   Jack E. Bowsher
August 1997

Part One

From Mediocre to Superior Workforce Performance

Organizations can be separated into two groups. The vast majority of companies and government agencies have a *workforce with some training,* which results in second- or third-class performance at higher costs. A much smaller number of organizations have a well-trained *competitive workforce,* which often leads the industry in productivity and lower operating expenses. The key is to transfer "best practices" of organizations that have well-trained, low-cost competitive workforces to those that have workforces with inadequate training and support systems.

Chapter One

Common Practices in a Workforce with Some Training

Ninety-nine percent of American companies and government agencies have an unstructured, unmeasured, and inadequately resourced training organization. Millions of Americans go to work every day only partially trained to do their jobs, which is why many corporations are struggling with intense competition and low productivity.

Until recently, almost every corporation, partnership, government agency, and not-for-profit organization had a workforce with some training; very few companies had a well-trained, competitive workforce. The focus was on training as an end in itself, not as a means to improve the performance of the workforce. Performance was usually considered the responsibility of line management, not the training department.

Today, although a majority of trainers will say that their courses are tied to business objectives and are focused on the performance of the workforce, the facts do not support them. Over 99 percent of all organizations continue to have a workforce with some training. Their management systems continue to focus on issues such as the following:

- How large is the course catalog?
- What percentage of the seats are filled?
- Is the training department within budget?
- Do the students enjoy the courses and instruction?

Why have so few training organizations restructured themselves to focus on workforce performance? First, the four basic goals listed above are easy to fulfill. Second, most executives do not know how to convert their traditional training organization into a performance-enhancement department. Third, the directors and managers of training also do not know how to refocus their efforts on business objectives and workforce performance. Unless they receive a direct call from the executive suite, they conduct "business and training as usual" year after year. Training remains a "nice to do" activity that leaves the workforce only partially trained.

Indicators of a Workforce with Some Training

This section describes the danger signals and the common practices of a *workforce with some training* and discusses the negative results that this type of workforce produces.

Training Is Reactive

The training department waits to be called into a task-force meeting. Someone explains that there is a problem, such as the company is not achieving its revenue objectives or the programmers never complete a project on time. The trainers suggest a sales-training course or a project-management course to fix the problem. This is the corporate version of "Take two aspirin and call me in the morning." Not surprisingly, new training lessons are rarely implemented on the job. Adding a few more courses to the course catalog simply does not fix the company's problems.

In this situation, the line executives view training as something to do if you have a major problem. Training becomes a dramatic and expensive gesture when business objectives are not being achieved.

Training Is Not Focused on Organizational Objectives

Too often, the training department's main objective is to survive and grow during the annual budget cycle when all departments plead for more money. The trainers tell the executives and financial personnel that the students love their courses and that morale will fall next year if the number of classes is reduced.

Many training managers cannot articulate the organization's broad goals and its strategic directions. Even if they have read the annual report and the strategic plan, they leave the same courses in the catalog year after year. After all, the instructors like to teach those courses and the students like the courses. The executives have not issued any direct orders to revamp the course catalog, so why change?

Job Training Is Incomplete

Very few directors and managers of training can list their organizations' *key jobs*. They may be able to list quite a few jobs, but they rarely conduct studies that determine the key jobs within their organizations, the ones that increase revenues, increase market share, enhance customer satisfaction, reduce operating expenses, and determine the organizations' profitability levels.

This is because the training department does not have a day-to-day working partnership with the line executives or the top performers, as they remain focused on having a series of successful training events. Managing the logistics of an education center, selling the seats in the classes, producing the catalog, recruiting instructors, and so on is a full-time job that leaves little or no time to meet with line executives and above-average performers.

If the key jobs have not been identified, there usually is no curriculum of courses or on-the-job-training events for each job. Notice how course catalogs are organized. Rarely are courses listed by key job. With few exceptions, the training department has not met with either the line executives or the above-average performers to answer the following questions:

- What do you want the employees and managers within a key job category to know and be able to do?
- What measurements will be implemented to reinforce the lessons of the course?
- What job aids are required to achieve optimum performance on the job?
- Are there any other barriers to superior job performance, such as performance-management systems, incentive-pay programs, recognition programs, or poor hiring methods?

Not knowing the answers to these questions results in inadequate job training within most organizations.

Too Many Resources Devoted to General-Purpose Courses

The course catalogs in these organizations are filled with classes on time management, stress management, diversity, financial information for the nonfinancial person, effective communications, and so on. These courses, which consume the majority of training funds, are essential, but they do not have a direct impact on revenues, customer satisfaction, operating expenses, and earnings, so they should be offered with a minimum of expense through new cost-effective delivery systems.

In many large corporations and government agencies, there is a lot of duplicate effort. It is not unusual to find five different time-management courses, seven different courses on stress management, or ten different communication courses. In one computer company, there were thirty-five different courses on basic electronics. The titles varied, but 80 to 90 percent of the content overlapped.

Whenever employees say they have no time to take training courses, it is almost certain that the catalog is filled with general-purpose courses. It is only logical that if the employees needed the lessons from a course to do their jobs, they would find the time to take the course.

Greater time pressures in this period of downsizing forces supervisors and employees to ask, "Do I really need this course?" If the course focused 100 percent on the requirements of the job, there would probably be a waiting list for it. For example, if the course is called, "How to Sell More Insurance Policies," there will be a higher demand for it than for one entitled "Selling Fundamentals." If the employees know that they will be evaluated based on what they learn in "How to Sell More Insurance Policies," they will undoubtedly attend the course.

A high rate of canceled enrollments and canceled classes is also an indicator of a workforce with some training, although the training department offers such explanations as "Managers don't view training as very important" or "The executives don't support training."

Executive Training Limited to Awareness Lessons

Executive-development courses have been debated for years. Many senior executives are encouraged to attend an advanced management course at one of the prestigious graduate schools of business. The selection of courses is frequently based on what school the executive wants on his or her resume, so executives within an organization may attend five or six different graduate schools and take many different courses. When these executives return to their organizations, they go back to "business as usual" because there is no reinforcement of the lessons learned.

In some companies, people assume that executives are completely educated and trained before they become vice presidents, so no more formal training is deemed necessary. Of course, this attitude makes no allowance for the continually changing nature of the business and political worlds.

In companies and government agencies that do have formal executive-development courses, most of the time is spent on awareness lessons that have little or no impact on job performance. High-paid, well-known, and proven performers from universities, consulting firms, and speakers' bureaus are hired as the faculty. The in-house trainer usually becomes a coordinator whose sole purpose is to ensure that the coffee and speakers arrive on time. The executives of the organization often speak at these sessions. Their messages are usually fascinating to the students who come from the field organization, but boring and familiar to the students from headquarters.

Many people assume that executive education simply cannot focus on job skills because there is no real structure to an executive position. This assumption simply is not true. Chief information officers need to learn the best practices for managing their functions. Chief financial officers need courses on new issues and the latest practices in the financial world. In most organizations that have a workforce with some training, the executive-education program increases the expense of training but has minimum impact on other business objectives.

As more and more organizations downsize, lose market share, sell off poor-performing divisions, and leap from crisis to crisis, the fundamental question has to be asked: Could organizations hold their executive-development programs to the same standards as their nonexecutive job training? What do we want our executives to know and be able to do? To address the leadership crisis in our country, most organizations need to restructure their executive-development programs.

Little or No Training for Middle Managers

Most organizations offer a mixed bag of programs for middle managers, varying from no training to about forty hours of training a year. Very few companies and government agencies have ever asked: What do we want the middle managers to know and be able to do? Unfortunately, as organizations downsize, many middle-management programs have been eliminated along with middle managers themselves.

Middle managers are responsible for implementing strategic directions and tactical decisions made by executives, and they usually are blamed when an implementation program is not successful. Some of the better training programs have educated them on cross-functional and divisional activities of their organizations, because once middle managers understand the overall organization, they implement new and revised tactical programs more effectively. In-depth training on change management is also helpful to these managers, but companies rarely provide it.

Voids in Supervisory Training

Supervisory training programs became popular soon after World War II as various entrepreneurs established themselves as management-development experts. They knew the theory of management, but most had never been managers. They invented games and activities that entertained new supervisors.

Many supervisory programs are strong on people management but weak on functional information such as how to be a good manager within manufacturing, operations, or sales. There needs to be a balance of lessons on both people management skills and functional management skills.

Another major void within supervisory training has been teaching them how to develop and train employees to achieve mastery of learning and performance. Most supervisors are weak at motivating their employees to reach their optimum performance. Fortunately, in recent years, a number of practical courses have been developed for employees who are trying to make the great leap into supervisory positions.

Course Content Is Outdated

If there is no formal working partnership between trainers and line executives, the content of courses will not be current. Instructors will continue to teach the same lessons because they know what entertains the students and leads to positive responses on evaluation sheets. Most companies do not have a formal system in place to update course content.

Instructors rarely attend meetings in which strategic directions and tactical decisions are discussed. Businesses make changes every day, but their training courses may be updated only every few years. Ironically, many updates result from a student telling the instructor that his or her lessons are completely out-of-date because of new methods or policies that were approved months ago.

In a meeting of training directors that the author attended recently, one person said that the only way to kill an unnecessary course in his organization was to kill the instructor. Everyone laughed and agreed that this statement was also true for their organizations. Some courses remain only because the course and the instructor are entertaining. There is usually no pressure from senior executives to update the courses.

Years ago, WICAT, a course-development company, ran a cartoon in a learning magazine that showed the senior executives gathered in the board room. The aggravated CEO stated, "What do they mean our training program is outdated? We all went through it!"

Measurements Are Ineffective

The vast majority of training departments measure themselves on quantity, not quality, measuring student hours and course completions. They know their expenses compared to budget; they even know the occupancy rate of classrooms. What they do not usually know is what effect, if any, the training has on performance.

Quality is usually measured by the students' feedback forms, often called "happiness sheets." Experienced instructors know how to manipulate the students to achieve high ratings. There is no way to tell whether the student learned the lessons or will apply the lessons on the job. Furthermore, there is rarely a follow-up survey to determine if the training sufficiently influenced the performance of the workforce or had an impact on organizational objectives.

Does Not Include Mastery of Learning and Performance

The education world lives by the bell curve. The assumption is that there are smart students, average students, and dumb students. Our nation has been raised on the grades of A, B, C, D, and F. This system exists in elementary schools, junior high schools, high schools, colleges, graduate schools, and in most training departments that have a grading system.

Most performance-management systems also use the bell curve. About fifteen years ago, Dr. Deming, commenting at a seminar about the quality movement said, "Throw away your performance-management systems and your bell-shaped curve." He told the leaders of business and government to aim for mastery of learning and performance, which is the basis for his theory of total quality management (TQM). With TQM, every employee is expected to do every task right the first time. This approach was heresy to HR vice presidents who had spent decades implementing performance-management systems based on the bell-shaped curve. Many refused to change their performance management systems.

Quality programs have failed in almost every organization that has a performance-management system and a training system based on the bell curve. Total quality management cannot succeed in an organization that is not willing to give up the bell curve. In practice, there are really three types of performers:

- The very outstanding, *superior performer* who is going to evolve to be either an executive or a leader within a certain area of the organization. Superior performers make up 5 to 10 percent of employees.

- The *very good performers* who will be an asset to the organization for many years. Over 90 percent of the workforce should be in this category.
- *Mediocre workers* who should be counseled out of their positions if they cannot improve their performance.

In today's intensely competitive world with its high cost of labor, organizations can only afford to have superior and very good performers. Mediocre performers cannot be tolerated.

Training Costs Are Poorly Managed

Few organizations know the total cost of their training programs because the training function is spread all over the organization. Some managers use training as a reward for good work. They say, "Take a few days off and go to San Francisco for a course on stress management." Some vice presidents hold training events at resorts, with as little as 5 or 10 percent of real training lessons on the agenda. Unstructured training can exist in any operating unit of an organization. The stated cost of training within an organization is often 25 to 50 percent lower than the actual cost, according to a series of cost studies done over the past ten years.

Training is very expensive. Half the cost is usually for the education centers and half for the employees' or students' salaries. If the senior executives knew the true cost of training, they would immediately demand that training be managed like any other important cost center in the organization.

When there is a workforce with some training, there is usually a de facto delivery system of classroom training. Every large- and intermediate-size organization should have a delivery system that includes individual study in learning centers. Cost-effective delivery systems increase the quality of training and simultaneously reduce the cost of training.

Too often, however, there is very little focus on cost containment because most executives believe that training and education (like research and development) cannot really be managed. These executives select a budget amount and allocate resources for training, hoping that the workforce will perform better afterward.

Some organizations allocate funds for training equal to a certain percentage of payroll or revenues. What a mistake! The training budget can be as precise as the manufacturing or operating budget. There is no need to guess at the amount of money required to train the workforce.

Frequent Downsizing Decisions

Many famous corporations have made downsizing decisions during the past fifteen years. This downsizing can be very expensive for the company as well as the employees, and it can have a real impact on customer satisfaction. In the April 1996 issue of *ASTD Training and Development Magazine* (pp. 41–43), Bob Nelson (1994) said that only 46 percent of the companies surveyed by a pension and profit sharing company had achieved their expense reduction goals after downsizing. Only 33 percent met their profit objectives, and only 21 percent had enhanced shareholders return-on-investment.

When there is no management system or an ineffective system for workforce performance, downsizing may be a quick answer for near-term financial problems. One computer company has spent billions of dollars with a series of downsizing decisions that removed almost 200,000 people from the payroll, and now is spending millions of dollars hiring 26,000 new employees in 1996. Many organizations need a new system to avoid these wild swings in hiring and downsizing.

Executive Involvement Is at a Minimum

When there is a workforce with some training, the senior and line executives rarely participate in employee training. They know that training is going on, and they just assume that it must be doing some good. These executives could never answer the question, "How do you justify training in your organization?"

Many executives assume that the people who work for them know what to do and need no training to perform well on the job. This assumption is usually misguided, as many employees guess at what they should be doing and, as a result, create idiosyncratic work procedures and methods. They learn their jobs on a trial-and-error basis, making many frustrating mistakes, especially at the entry level, whatever their rank. New mail-room personnel and new vice presidents use these same ineffective methods to learn their jobs. Of course, the cost of learning through trial and error is much greater for the higher positions.

Executives rarely work with the training department to define measurable performance requirements for key jobs that report to them. Only a few executives live by the following statements:

1. Every job in my area of responsibility must be well defined as far as what the employees must know and be able to do. There must be detailed, measurable performance requirements for each job.
2. Every employee should aim for mastery of learning and performance. There must be a performance-measurement system for each job in order to achieve this goal.
3. Job performance should be evaluated to achieve continuous improvement and be based on best practices.

Very few executives review the major lessons of the various courses to be certain that using these lessons in the workplace will achieve the organization's objectives. Most managers have no idea if the right employee is sitting in the right class at the right time.

Many executives do not realize that a well-trained workforce is more productive, has a lower error rate, requires less supervision, has higher morale and lower attrition rates, and has a big impact on achieving organizational objectives. Naturally, their ambivalence about the value of training leads to inadequate allocation of resources for training and support programs.

Results of a Workforce with Some Training

In almost every organization with the problems listed above, there will be an *increased cost for people,* including payroll, benefits, and basic support, because of low productivity.

The *cost of supervision* will also be greater because untrained or partially trained workforces make more errors. It is an easy cost to determine: Simply look at the number and the salaries of the organization's supervisors.

The *cost of rework* grows when people learn by trial and error. Rarely measured, this cost can be shocking. In manufacturing, it is often referred to as the cost of scrap.

With a high rate of errors comes a *lower rate of customer satisfaction,* which can be measured with surveys and interviews. Recent studies have shown that the cost of losing established customers and the cost of obtaining new customers can be extremely high (Schohl, 1991, pp. 19–20).

Untrained or partially trained employees have *lower morale* and *job satisfaction.* Not knowing how to do a job is very frustrating, and new jobs are always stressful unless there is a training and support program to achieve mastery of learning and performance in a relatively short period of time. Employee frustration leads to *higher attrition rates* and an *increase in the cost of recruiting and hiring new employees.*

Organizations that have a workforce with some training are usually *slow to change* after their executive management has decided on new strategic directions or made major new tactical decisions. When the changes are not translated into new performance requirements that bring new or revised training and support programs, the employees continue with "business as usual." This failure to respond to change is the primary reason why most quality-enhancement and reengineering programs fail. In addition, this often *creates competitive disadvantages.*

All of these problems can lead to a *migration of jobs* to countries with lower labor costs and, in turn, a *decrease in job security.* At one time, only manufacturing jobs were moved overseas, but with computer networks and other recent breakthroughs in communication systems, administrative and white-collar jobs can now be filled in other countries as well. Millions of foreign employees are willing to do the same work for less money. They are even willing to learn a new language to take steady jobs with American corporations. Companies that have well-trained, competitive workforces within the United States rarely subcontract to low-wage countries, but organizations with partially trained workforces are doing it more and more. If American employees are properly trained and supported by their companies, they will almost always be more valuable, based on greater productivity.

Poor performance by a workforce in any industry always leads to a *reduction in market share and revenues*. Customers simply will not tolerate poor performance in today's world. In most situations, this does not mean that the employees are lazy; it just means that they are receiving ineffective training and leadership.

Poor performance also leads to *massive downsizing*, which is now accepted as standard operating procedure when an organization does not meet its objectives. Employees are viewed as a variable expense. The finance function tells the CEO that next quarter's profit can be fixed by eliminating 10 or 15 percent of the workforce. No one in the boardroom can defend the workforce. Performance is not measured, so it cannot be defended. No vice president stands up to quantify how much work will not be accomplished with a diminished workforce, and therefore how far revenues and profits will decrease. As a result, most companies that start down the path of downsizing usually stay on that road for several years with one layoff after another.

Downsizing is necessary only when there are excess employees who are noncontributors to the organization's objectives. It is certainly true that many corporations and government agencies have had bureaucratic and wasteful numbers of employees who created nothing but increased expenses, so it is important to review the contribution that each employee and department makes to organizational objectives to ensure that the cost of people is optimized. A famous mayor of New York City once stated that a reduction of 20 percent of the city's workforce would increase service to the taxpayers and decrease taxes, if the city government could eliminate the poor performers and the wasteful departments. Corporate America has certainly found that it could reduce the size of its headquarters without hurting revenues, customer service, or earnings.

Unfortunately, however, downsizing has moved far beyond the goals of being efficient and competitive. Corporations are downsizing their workforces to achieve financial objectives. Many companies have been severely damaged by this strategy. For a period of time, downsizing has adversely affected their global reputations and their financial performances. They have less market share, lower revenues, and lower earnings as they leap from crisis to crisis. In a few situations, such as Pan American Airlines and RCA, industry leaders have gone out of business because they failed to remain competitive.

In each of these great companies, there were serious performance problems that the executives never addressed. In some companies, the sales force failed to perform; in others, the manufacturing division was not performing well. In a few companies, the operational workforce failed to meet organizational objectives.

Too often, poor performance was tolerated because the executives believed that the organization was too large to change course. In other situations, they blamed their problems on government regulations. Some called it a shift in the marketplace or cited global competition as a reason. All of these reasons were actually excuses for weak management that could not identify and correct serious performance problems. Performance problems are like quality problems. Most of them are caused by a lack of training and support systems, rather than by the poor attitude of individual employees.

It is hard to believe that companies and government agencies spend about $50 billion annually for training, yet achieve such a dismal record of accomplishment. Adding in the salaries of the students doubles the figure to $100 billion. How can this be? It is because most companies and government agencies simply do not have management systems for training that achieve breakthroughs in workforce performance. Their management systems just record how much money they are spending and how many employees are being trained. This book was written to illustrate how this problem can be corrected in a relatively short period of time.

Fortunately, a number of government agencies and companies do focus on the performance of their workers. In fact, they believe that high workplace performance can provide a strategic advantage. The next chapter shows how these organizations have achieved well-trained, low-cost, competitive workforces.

Chapter Two

Best Practices for a Competitive Workforce

The business world is evolving into two major groups. The first treats its employees as a reducible expense, aiming for shareholder value at any cost. "Trashing the workforce" drives up the value of their stock; downsizing is practically an annual event. These companies invest very little money in research and product development. The only goal is to have a successful financial statement next quarter.

Leading-Edge Organizations

Fortunately, the second type of company values outstanding workforce performance. Those companies believe that employees are their most important assets, and their goal is to have a highly trained, competitive workforce. They want their people to know more and be able to do more than any other organization's employees within their industry. They provide support systems, including job aids and databases (knowledge systems) to increase workforce productivity. They invest major resources in training and support systems that are tied directly to organizational objectives. A few government agencies, such as the FBI and GAO, also belong to this small and exclusive group. Probably only twenty-five to fifty organizations in the United States have achieved a competitive workforce as defined in this book. Some of them are described as follows.

Arthur Andersen and Andersen Consulting

Andersen Worldwide is the leading provider of professional services in the world. With more than 91,000 people in seventy-nine countries, its global practice is conducted by member firms in 381 offices through two business units, Arthur Andersen and Andersen Consulting:

- Arthur Andersen is a multidisciplinary professional services organization that provides client service through audit and business advisory services, business consulting, tax, legal, and business-advisory services.
- Andersen Consulting is a global management and technology consulting organization whose mission is to help its clients change to become more successful.

In 1956, the organization had worldwide revenues of $20 million. Forty years later, its revenues have risen to over $8 billion. This explosive growth is unusual for an organization that provides professional services rather than products. Clients pay professional fees for audit, tax, and consulting services. Simply put, it is a people business. Andersen accomplished this primarily through internal growth, rather than mergers.

The commitment to employee training began with founder Arthur Andersen, who was a professor and chairperson of the Accounting Department at Northwestern University. He knew the value of professional development in helping clients continually seize new opportunities.

Since the company's inception, the training program has paralleled the organization's growth. In 1913, Arthur Andersen initiated continuous learning at his first office. By 1940, the firm had instituted the first central training program in the profession. In 1971, the organization purchased a central training facility, located in St. Charles, Illinois, the first in the profession to do so. Since that purchase, the firm has expanded and enhanced its Center for Professional Education to meet the overall growth and development needs of the organization. The goal was and is simple: Hire the best people and train them rigorously to deliver outstanding client service. The strategy has been a great success story. Currently, the Center for Professional Education, located on 151 acres, is the largest conference center in the world, accommodating more than 1,600 residents and having a capacity for more than 2,000 students daily. The Center logs more than 68,000 guests annually.

Training is tied to career advancement and is continuous. It takes place not only at the Center for Professional Education in St. Charles, but also regionally, in local offices and at client sites worldwide. Training is designed and delivered in a variety of ways, including leading-edge interactive multimedia technologies and on-demand computer-based training, as well as problem-based learning approaches, self-study courses, seminars and workshops, and business television. Andersen provides professionals with specialized industry training, comprehensive technical training, simulated client engagement, and customized training.

On average, Andersen partners invest 6 percent of revenue (currently more than $500 million a year) to train their professionals. Additionally, they contribute to the education process as subject matter experts, instructors, coaches, facilitators, and guest speakers.

Learning is the catalyst for communicating the corporate culture, with an emphasis on quality and consistency worldwide. The CEO and senior partners of Andersen Worldwide believe that training is a differentiator and a key factor that has enabled the company to lead, not only in growth, but also in record earnings each year.

Federal Express

Federal Express has also enjoyed explosive growth over the years to realize approximately $10 billion in revenues with over 100,000 employees working in nearly two hundred countries. The company has been an innovator in many ways. Today, it has over five hundred airplanes carrying parcels to centralized distribution centers.

Federal Express air crews have always been expected to achieve mastery of learning and performance, because their failure to perform would cause fatal accidents. In recent years, the concept of "first time right" was also applied to the personnel who pick up and deliver packages. First, the company installed a computer system that kept track of every package at every point in the delivery cycle. Then Federal Express developed and implemented a multimedia training and support system at a cost of over $40 million for the people who handle the packages. New, cost-effective, and high-technology systems were used to train thousands of employees. With these systems, Federal Express achieved a strategic advantage that its competitors are now attempting to copy.

Training at Federal Express is considered as critical to the success of the business as computer systems, jet planes, and distribution centers. It is integrated into the organization's overall business processes.

McDonald's and Starbucks

One of the great success stories during the last half of the century has been the world-wide growth of McDonald's fast food restaurants. McDonald's is as serious about training as any "high tech" organization. They have the world-famous Hamburger University in Oak Brook, Illinois, which is a state-of-the-art education center where all managers and owners must attend courses to certify that they are qualified to do their jobs.

Once again, training is one of the key strategies that has enabled McDonald's to achieve explosive growth. It has provided the company with a strategic advantage within its industry, although competitors have tried to erode its market share with lower prices. With its well-trained, competitive workforce, no other organization has been able to equal McDonald's financial performance. Every key job in the organization has an in-depth training program with a focus on job performance. Today, there are almost 20,000 McDonald's restaurants around the world achieving over $30 billion in sales.

Other national chains have adopted the McDonald's models. For example, Starbucks in Seattle, Washington, had eleven stores in 1987, and now there are over 1,000 across the nation. New hires receive twenty-four hours of training, divided into six classes over several weeks. The courses are taught by store managers, who are certified as instructors. All this training is set up by a national training department.

One of Starbucks' objectives is to have a low attrition rate. They offer health-care insurance to part-time as well as full-time employees. There is a stock option plan for anyone who works five hundred hours per year. All of these programs are important, but none of them would be successful without an outstanding training program. Starbucks' goal is to instill in workers a sense of purpose, commitment, and enthusiasm. Training makes this vision a reality.

Home Depot and other franchised organizations also have first-rate training systems. No organization could have the explosive growth that these new national chains have realized in such a short time without a formal training program aimed at achieving mastery of learning and performance for each key job. Their revenues, operating expenses, and earnings are directly dependent upon the success of their training and support programs.

Motorola

From the basic jobs of McDonald's and Starbucks to the "high tech" jobs of Motorola, the goal remains the same—mastery of learning and performance. This goal is one reason why Motorola won the Malcolm Baldrige National Quality Award in 1988, an amazing turnaround given that Motorola had a workforce with some training until 1980. In 1979, the CEO, Bob Galvin, asked the human resource department to develop a five-year plan to restructure the company's training function. Galvin also hired Bill Wigginhorn, former head of training at Xerox, to lead the effort.

The new education function, Motorola University, had a board of directors consisting of the CEO, two executive vice presidents, and a senior executive from each operating unit. They decided to use training to accelerate the implementation of strategic directions and tactical decisions. Their first major strategic thrust was quality. Without the new training and support programs, Motorola would not have won the Baldrige award.

Motorola's annual investment in training has grown from $7 million to more than $150 million. They invest over 4 percent of their payroll in training, which is four times the average amount invested by other companies. In the field of advancing technology, employees require constant training. Motorola offers courses ranging from basic skills for employees who need to improve their reading or writing, all the way to executive-development courses. Customers and vendors also receive training. Training is a strategic advantage to Motorola.

Motorola is an example of how a company can grow world-wide once training and support systems are in place around the world. Today, Motorola operates in Europe, India, mainland China, Eastern Europe, and other Asia-Pacific countries. The company has enjoyed years of growth and record earnings. Motorola's executive team agree that Motorola University was essential for the company's superior financial performance in recent years.

Xerox

The Xerox Corporation is a leader in the field of workforce training. They have a large central education center at Leesburg, Virginia. Virtually every employee goes to Leesburg at one time or another for training. The education center has also played a major role in the implementation of Xerox's corporate culture and values. Their management team believes strongly that training provides them with a strategic advantage within the competitive marketplace. The senior executives also use training to accelerate the implementation of new strategic directions and tactical decisions.

Automobile Companies and Other Manufacturers

American automobile manufacturers have historically spent large sums of money on employee training and management development, but their efforts resulted most often in a series of unstructured programs. Consequently, they ended up with a workforce with some training.

The Japanese automobile companies provided a wake-up call to the American corporations with their emphasis on "first time right" quality. The Japanese aimed for nothing less than mastery of learning and performance within each job category.

When the Japanese companies exported new luxury cars to the United States, they hired the same training firm in Detroit that had been providing training to General Motors. But their requirements were quite different. Lexus and Infiniti insisted on in-depth performance-based training for all dealer personnel. Their goal was to achieve the number-one rating for customer service in the first year of business, which they accomplished.

Ford has restructured its training organization to go from an attendance-based system to a system that focuses on job performance. They received the top ASTD award for an outstanding training program a few years ago. Chrysler has appointed a new executive to reengineer its training function. General Motors continues to have a decentralized organization of training, and Saturn is the bright spot for GMC training.

Too many manufacturers have neglected employee training. For this reason, relatively few have successfully implemented Total Quality Management (TQM). In fact, the quality movement in the United States is floundering. Too often, TQM programs have just been awareness training on quality rather than in-depth job training to achieve mastery of learning and performance. Quality training became the "flavor of the month" in too many organizations with quality banners, quality coffee mugs, and quality pep rallies. Although everyone became more aware of the quality objective, employees and managers did not create or implement new training programs to achieve the mastery of performance goals. By contrast, Motorola went from three days to twenty-eight days of quality training when it became serious about TQM.

Airlines

The major American airlines have been leaders in converting unstructured training programs into performance-based training systems. After all, the performance of pilots and mechanics is a life-or-death matter. Many of the training and support systems in the airline industry have evolved from military systems that strive for mastery of learning and performance. For example, the airlines use multimillion-dollar flight simulators as part of their performance-support systems. Commercial airplanes are some of the most complex and technically advanced products manufactured. Boeing, which has outstanding training programs, is also a leader in providing training and support systems to both its customers and employees. Regulatory agencies and airline corporations govern the quality of their training.

Quality is often defined by statisticians and industrial engineers as Six Sigma, which means six standard deviations from a statistical performance average. This translates into 3.4 defects per million opportunities, or performance that is 99.99966 percent defect free. Thus, when a passenger flies on an airplane, he or she is flying in a Six-Sigma system.

Even among all this exceptional training and performance, one airline stands out. Southwest Airlines flies more passengers per employee; they have the smallest number of employees per aircraft; and their costs are usually the lowest in the industry. Their flight turnover time is just fifteen minutes, compared with an average of one hour for other major airlines. Their outstanding training system and executive leadership make this superior performance possible. Every major function, reservations, provisioning, operations, flight activities, customer service, and mechanics, has a separate training department that focuses on job skills and performance.

Financial Service Firms

The administrative functions of banks, savings and loans, insurance companies, investment banks, and securities firms have been highly mechanized for years. Training within this industry is slowly evolving from a workforce with some training to a more structured program, although too many unstructured programs still exist. Numerous mergers also have created integration problems for the institutions' training and support programs.

Public Utilities

Nuclear power plants require highly structured training programs. As the power industry evolves from regulation to deregulation, training and support programs must be enhanced. The Southern Company, which provides electricity to Alabama, Georgia, Florida, and southeastern Mississippi, has implemented the Southern Company College. They provide management-development courses on "What it takes to be successful in the electrical utility industry." They want all employees and managers to embrace the company's vision. The company also provides technical training for the key jobs within its operating companies.

Telephone Companies

Some of the Bell operating companies have refocused on training. At Ameritech, the CEO has restructured the entire organization. Rigorous training, coaching, and evaluation systems were implemented as the company identified each major job category.

Sprint also made an executive decision in 1990 to restructure and centralize its training organization to increase the performance of its workforce.

In 1993, GTE made a major commitment to use education and training as a strategic tool to transform the company from the "old telephone company" into a world-wide competitive telecommunications company. By all measures (financial, speed to market, and growth), this commitment to restructuring the organization and capabilities of the workforce through training has been a major success, showing how essential training and performance measurement are to implementing major new strategic directions.

General Electric

General Electric has always been a leader in training. The company established one of the first corporate management-development centers at Crotonville, New York, in 1955. The original purposes of this famous school were to disseminate the virtues of decentralization and to teach the basic subjects of management. The curriculum was similar to a graduate school of business.

When Jack Welch took over as CEO in 1981, he implemented a radical change. He delegated technical and basic management training to the company's operating units and used the Crotonville center to accelerate the implementation of new strategic directions and tactical decisions. He also directed the center to work on real business problems and issues. Welch believes that much of the increase in productivity at GE can be attributed to tying training to the organization's strategic vision.

General Electric still aims for "best practices," and benchmarks various areas of the business to achieve that goal. The company designs training and support systems regularly to implement these best practices.

Disney and Ritz Carlton

Disney was one of the great American corporations when its founder ran the business. After Walt Disney's death, the company fell on hard times, but it has become one of the great comeback stories under new management. In 1963, Disney University was launched to train all Disney employees on the tasks required for their jobs, with the goal of delivering exceptional customer service.

The university today continues to orient new Disney "cast members" to the histories and traditions of the company. Employees receive in-depth job training focused on superior performance, which is continually reviewed within the Disney organization. A continuous-improvement program exists for all training courses.

The Ritz Carlton hotel chain is another service organization that has been honored by ASTD for outstanding training programs. Again, they focus on job performance within every major job category.

Intel and Microsoft

The personal computer industry's two superstars have invested major resources to train their employees. Intel uses Intel University to train all employees on its corporate culture and values and on individual jobs. Like other successful organizations, Intel not only states its corporate values, but also trains its employees to achieve value statements on quality, customer satisfaction, risk taking, and other results.

Microsoft has achieved breakthroughs in its software engineers' performance. In many computer companies, these employees are renowned for being late on projects, and for producing computer programs with errors (bugs). Microsoft's systems approach to performance has proved that complex jobs can be vastly improved with a management system that focuses on job performance.

No one company or government agency has a perfect system, but many top-performing organizations engage in what are commonly referred to as best practices, as described below.

Executive Involvement and a Working Partnership

In a few organizations, the executive in charge of training has rung the alarm bell and educated the senior executives on what must be done to achieve a well-trained, competitive workforce. In most cases, the CEO or another senior executive demands that the training organization be restructured to focus on the performance of the workforce rather than on the size of the course catalog. A number of CEOs and senior executives have learned about the subject of education firsthand by being involved in the American public schools' reform movements.

No matter who rings the alarm bell, the senior executives and CEO are almost always involved when a training organization moves from being an attendance-based system to one that focuses on job performance. Senior executives are quick to recognize that a well-trained, competitive workforce does more work, makes fewer errors, requires less supervision, has higher morale, and has a lower attrition rate. They also know that a well-trained, competitive workforce provides a strategic advantage within the industry and a higher level of customer service and that performance-based training results in higher revenues, lower operating expenses, and increased earnings.

Part Five of this book contains some penetrating questions that the CEO should ask the training department. The CEO should manage training the same as any other important functional area in the organization. Taking on this responsibility requires very few hours each year, but it makes the difference between a second-or third-class workforce with some training and a first-class well-trained, competitive workforce.

When a company restructures its training function, there must be a formal working partnership between line executives, subject-matter experts, and top performers for each major job category and the training department. This working partnership rarely exists, even though it requires very little time from upper management.

Training Tied to Organizational Objectives

Almost all training organizations think that their courses are tied to business objectives or a government agency's goals. In reality, the ties are quite loose. A formal procedure is presented in the next chapter that will help organizations tie their training to organizational objectives. Courses that are just "fun" or reflect what the instructors like to teach cannot be continued, given the high costs of training. All courses should be "must do," from the senior executive's point of view.

Training Focused on Job Performance

Much of the early work in organization development (OD) and performance technology focused on a thorough analysis of performance problems. This resulted in some insights and gains, and yet very few organizations today focus their training and support programs on job performance. Most organizations are still in the business of offering training events.

The management system described in this book is an entirely new approach, proactive with respect to opportunities and organizational objectives. Performance enhancements are continuous, based on new strategic directions and major tactical decisions. Parts Two and Three in this book serve as a road map on how training and support systems can be used to raise job performance, revenues, and earnings.

Adequate Resources for Job Training and Performance Systems

Almost every company and government agency is inadequately funded in the area of training. The resulting weakness in workforce performance increases operating expenses, decreases earnings, and reduces customer service.

The management system presented here is a formal, systematic approach to determining the training and support systems needed to maximize job performance *at the lowest possible cost*. An organization's training and support function can determine as precisely as can its manufacturing function what resources are required. Not one dollar more than is absolutely necessary should be spent on these systems.

Areas of Training and Performance Systems

The responsibilities for training and performance systems must be broken into manageable areas. Figure 2.1 shows how a number of organizations have developed a way for all employees and all jobs to be covered by performance systems that include the required courses.

This matrix can be utilized by any industry by inserting the proper titles. Figure 2.1 shows areas of performance systems for a manufacturing company, but if it were for a hospital, the job areas would include medical staff, nursing staff, pharmacy staff, or whatever titles apply.

In some companies, courses are modified or customized for customers to attend, especially if products and services depend on advanced technology or for major vendors to get the training they need to provide quality products and services.

Basic Skills Must Be Provided

When the famous U.S. Department of Education report, "A Nation at Risk," was published in 1983 detailing the inadequacies of America's public schools, most organizations assumed that only fast-food restaurants and motel chains had a problem. Very few organizations believed that their workforces had fundamental problems with reading, writing, arithmetic, and basic communication skills.

Years ago, Motorola conducted a study within its manufacturing organization to determine if its personnel had the reading and mathematic skills to implement new technologies and methods. Motorola discovered that 60 percent of its workforce could not do simple arithmetic. They needed a workforce that could operate and maintain new sophisticated equipment and procedures to a zero-defect standard, but most of their employees could not calculate decimals, fractions, or percentages. This deficiency was compounded by many employees who could barely read English. Today, Motorola requires three basic skills of its manufacturing employees: Reading, writing, and math skills at the eighth-grade level.

Motorola's study woke up other organizations to potential deficiencies in their own workforce. Unfortunately, most organizations have employees with problems in basic reading, writing, and math skills. Billions of incremental dollars have been invested in dozens of quick-fix and feel-good solutions for the public schools during the past fifteen years. Still, roughly 50 percent of students are not at grade level, meaning that they have not learned all the lessons

Figure 2.1. Areas of Training and Support.

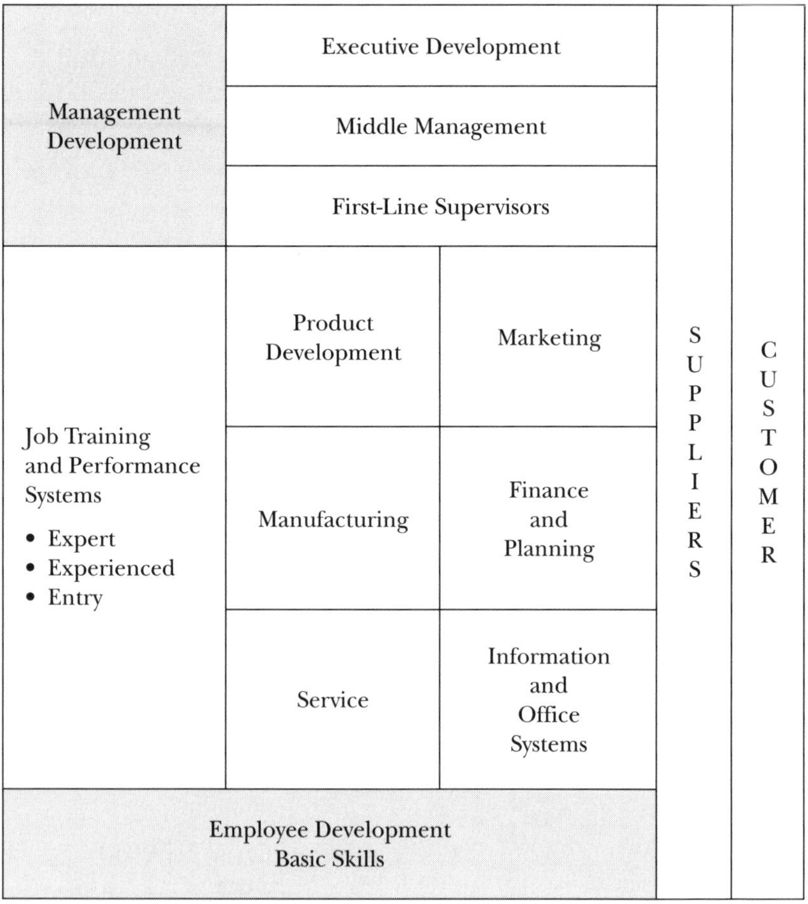

Management Development	Executive Development		SUPPLIERS	CUSTOMER
	Middle Management			
	First-Line Supervisors			
Job Training and Performance Systems • Expert • Experienced • Entry	Product Development	Marketing		
	Manufacturing	Finance and Planning		
	Service	Information and Office Systems		
Employee Development Basic Skills				

from their previous years of schooling. Thousands graduate from high school without learning all the lessons needed due to a practice of "social" promotion. Because of this, education in basic skills will be a workplace requirement for decades.

Employee-Development Courses

Twenty to forty employee-development courses should always be offered to all employees, whether secretaries, programmers, accountants, sales personnel, engineers, or clerks. The need for the courses crosses functional lines and operating units. They are job related, but not focused on one job. These start with an orientation to the company and end with a preretirement seminar.

They include basic communication subjects such as writing business letters, effective presentations, listening, negotiation skills, plus financial systems for the nonfinancial employee. Because these courses do not have a direct impact on operating expenses, revenues, or earnings, organizations should try to use outside vendors for them rather than develop courses internally.

Recently, courses such as computer literacy, word processing, graphics (for presentations and publications), setting up databases, using spreadsheets, and using electronic mail or the Internet have become necessary because almost every job category includes some application of a personal computer.

The progressive organizations maintain records on who has completed the various courses. Employees who want to improve their knowledge, skills, and promotability benefit from them. More and more organizations are not paying wages for the time spent in such training, but they are providing other rewards and incentives to employees who complete the courses.

Focus on Job Training

Job training is the greatest challenge in most organizations because line executives have not completely outlined what employees in each major job category should know and be able to do. Therefore, voids exist in training that have the greatest impact on revenues, operating expenses, and earnings.

To achieve maximum workforce productivity, a performance system must be developed for each major job category. The performance system concept for every major job category is new. Parts Two and Three of this book are devoted to this important new subject.

Management-Development Courses Keep Pace

Major changes have taken place in management development due to the flattening of organizational pyramids. Executive development is more important than ever because strategic and tactical decisions must be made so much faster. Executives need training on creating and managing change, developing visions, reengineering, implementing TQM, developing cost-containment programs, understanding 360-degree feedback, creating people-management systems, and developing a competitive workforce, to name a few.

In the past, some executive jobs were really caretaker positions, and executive education was composed mostly of awareness subjects such as the economic health of the nation that had little or no impact on an organization's operating results. Today, it is a world of white-water rapids rather than calm seas. Businesses and governments need outstanding leadership more than ever. Unfortunately, there appears to be a real shortage of successful executive talent in these demanding times.

Some people claim that the leadership crisis is really an executive-development crisis. On-the-job experiences do not produce executives with the talents required. It is time to eliminate the outmoded executive-education programs of the past and develop programs that are based on what organizations really need an executive to know and be able to do, with an eye on how marketplace trends can be converted into strategic initiatives.

If an organization has middle managers, it should train them on cross-functional systems that serve all operating units. They also should be trained on how to implement change, which has become one of their primary responsibilities. Middle-management training needs to be concentrated on creating and alignment and commitment between strategic directions from the executive group and with their implementation by front-line employees. This is the pivot point for achieving competitive goals—alignment of all workforce levels.

The role of the first-line manager or supervisor has changed in most organizations. Span of control has grown from five or six employees to twenty or thirty, making management skills ever more important as they oversee varied projects and do many tasks themselves. In addition, they probably supervise temporary employees and "permanent temps." In many cases, they are so busy that they expect their employees to supervise themselves, meeting first-time-right objectives somehow. However, employees can be empowered to supervise themselves only if they have received the proper training and if they have adequate support systems. To this end, first-line managers need to be retrained to help their workforces evolve into self-managed, high performance teams.

Another challenge for supervisors is the virtual office. At one time, all employees worked within walking distance of the supervisor's office. Today, millions of employees do not have an office, a desk, or a work station. They often work out of their homes or automobiles, using cellular telephones, copiers, facsimile machines, personal computers, and pagers. Computer networks allow employees to do their work at any time or place. This freedom creates the need for even better training and support systems. Sending empowered employees out without a support system is like telling athletes, "I want you to win the game, but I'm not telling you how to play the game."

Transition to Mastery of Learning and Performance

For generations, educators have supported the concept that intelligence quotient (IQ) is the number-one predictor of performance, and people have been placed on the bell curve to compare them with one another. That may work within the academic world, but evidence suggests that the vast majority of employees can be successful if the recruitment process works and people are properly trained. Students in training courses should be given one of three ratings:

- Completed the course and far exceeded requirements (enabling the organization to recognize superior performance)
- Completed and mastered all requirements of the course (true for the majority of employees)
- Failed the course (Usually, there is less than a 1 percent failure rate in a well-designed course, and most failures are due to severe personal problems rather than a lack of intelligence.)

Organizations need to shift from thinking of employees on a bell curve to using mastery of learning as a training goal to complement the quality goal of "first time right." See Figure 2.2.

Figure 2.2. The Great Transition.

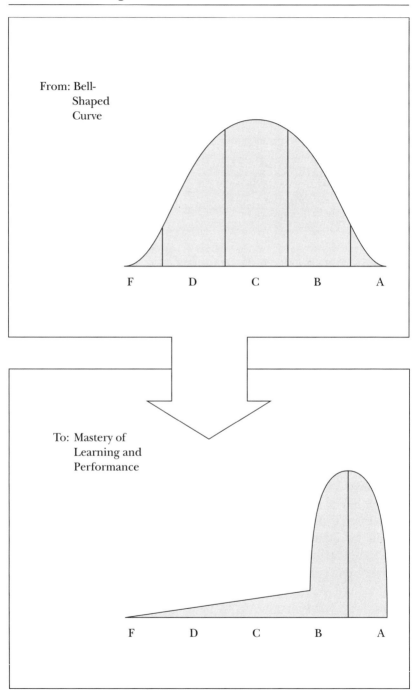

Implement a Course-Development System

The two major costs in producing a corporate training program are (1) the costs to develop, modify, or buy a course and (2) the cost to deliver the lessons (which will be discussed in Chapter Nine). Very few organizations know how to minimize the cost of course development or acquisition because each instructor spends money in an unstructured way, and there is almost no quality control in the process.

How to implement a high-quality system while controlling costs will be discussed later in this book. Suffice it to say that many courses are filled with information, but they do not lead to improved job performance, revenues, operating expenses, or earnings. In the future, most companies will want to have performance-based training and support systems.

Implement Quality Measurements

Training directors should be able to tell their senior executives whether students liked the class and the instructor; learned the lessons; and are applying the lessons on the job. Ideally, they also should know whether the training has had a positive impact on the organization's operating results.

Implement a Cost-Containment Program

A well-managed training organization needs to have a formal program for cost containment to keep waste from creeping into the system. Executives must be convinced that the training and performance department is as concerned about controlling expenses as the other units of the organization. The number-one cause of cost-containment problems is the absence of a management system, which is discussed in Chapter Three.

Recruit and Develop Training Personnel

Leading-edge training and performance organizations have a formal program for recruiting and developing outstanding people. After all, training personnel are the multipliers of great performers. Too often, service departments such as training do not receive enough attention from the HR department. No one writes job descriptions or develops career paths for trainers. This can lead to lower compensation levels for trainers. Worse yet, the training department usually does not have a structured training program for its own staff.

Apply a Systematic Approach for Justification

Two major reasons why organizations allocate inadequate resources to training are a lack of quality measurements and an inadequate system to justify the investment.

Too many directors of training sit back and hope that the CEO will someday provide executive endorsement for training, but why should they do this when most training is not measured nor tied to the organizational objectives? Yet the number-one excuse given for inadequate training is lack of support from the CEO and senior executives. An investment in training should be like an investment in plant and equipment. The return on this investment drives up revenues, lowers operating expenses, and increases earnings.

Compare with Benchmarking Information

The companies and government agencies that profit the most from training and performance often benchmark their performance against other top-performing companies. The American Society for Training and Development (ASTD) has made a major commitment to benchmarking over the past several years. They have enlisted the following organizations to invest time and resources in the ASTD Benchmarking Forum:

Aetna Life & Casualty
Albemarle Corporation
Allstate Insurance
American Express
  (Financial Advisors)
Ameritech Services
AMP
Arthur Andersen
AT&T

Ford Motor Company
Freddie Mac
General Motors
Georgia-Pacific
GTE
Hallmark Cards
Honda of America
  (Manufacturing)
IBM

Bank One
Boeing Commercial
  (Airplane Group)
Boeing Information
  & Support Services
Carrier Corporation
Chase Manhattan Bank
Chevron
Corning
CRA Limited
Cummins Engine
Delco Electronics
Digital Equipment
Federal Express
Fiat Group
Florida Power & Light
Ford Credit

Johnson & Johnson
KPMG Peat Marwick
Long Island Lighting
MCI
Motorola
NYNEX
Pacific Telesis
Polaroid Corporation
Qualcomm
Southern California Gas
Sprint
Tektronix
Texas Instruments
UNISYS
U.S. West Communications
The Vanguard Group
Xerox

Ironically, although several members of this benchmarking forum are winners of the Baldridge National Quality Award, the Deming Prize, and ASTD's Corporate HRD Award, not all of them have well-trained, competitive workforces.

The ASTD Benchmarking Forum offers a survey instrument for collecting data that includes questions on training costs, staffing, administration, design, development, and delivery, all for $100. This is by far the most ambitious benchmarking project within the training industry.

The task was far more challenging than most people realized at the start. First, they had to agree on common definitions and on how to obtain consistent data, as training methods and practices vary widely among organizations. It took the group four years to obtain consistent data.

One finding from the study was that few organizations systematically measure whether students learn their lessons or whether the training has a positive effect on the organization's objectives. As the training and performance function becomes identified with the organization's goals, benchmarking is needed more than ever to ensure that they are moving in the right direction toward the right strategic goals.

Results of a Well-Trained, Competitive Workforce

The results from a well-trained, competitive workforce are almost the opposite of those from a workforce with some training:

- Reduced labor costs.
- Lower supervision costs.
- Less cost for rework and fixing errors.
- Increased revenues.
- Greater market shares.
- Enhanced customer-service reputation.
- Higher employee morale.
- Lower attrition rate.
- Reduced expense for recruitment and employment.
- Faster implementation of strategic directions and tactical decisions.
- Increased job security.
- Increased job enrichment.
- Enhanced cross training across jobs.
- Improved job performance.
- Full use of advancing technology.
- A more competitive strategic advantage.

Conclusion

These best practices result from common sense and practical management methods. The challenge is to implement them; very few organizations actually practice them. Remember, most companies and government agencies have nothing more than a workforce with some training. They are light years away from having a well-trained, competitive workforce. The good news is that the leaders of every organization can obtain this competitive strategic advantage by implementing the lessons outlined in the rest of this book.

Part Two

Systems Approach for Workforce Performance

First Steps

To achieve a breakthrough in workforce performance that has an impact on operating and financial results, five important steps must be taken:

1. Appoint a proven change leader to the executive position of *Chief Training Officer.*
2. Develop and implement a *management system* that integrates the best practices of organization development, training, performance technology, reengineering, and HR programs.
3. Develop a formal *working partnership* between *executive management* and a *restructured training and performance organization.*
4. *Enhance or reengineer the basic processes* of the organization.
5. *Identify key jobs* within the organization and the performance requirements for each major job category.

Chapter Three

Develop and Implement a Management System

A management system is defined as a process for managing resources (people, facilities, and funds) to achieve business objectives. If the training and performance department is going to be a mainstream function within an organization, there must be a management system. The challenge is to develop a management system that includes the best practices discussed in the previous chapter. This big systems-integration task must be accomplished by the leaders of the training and performance organization.

Why a Management System Is Essential

Without a management system, there is usually an inadequate working partnership between the training organization and the line organization. This definitely turns training into a "nice to do" activity because the courses do not relate directly to the key jobs' performance requirements. All this leads to a lack of support from the senior executive team. No wonder executives believe that a 10 percent cut in the training budget will have little or no impact on operations, except to reduce expenses and increase profits.

Without a management system, the executive team often holds this view of training:

- 25 percent of the courses are outstanding
- 25 percent need to be fine-tuned

- 25 percent need major improvements
- 25 percent are a waste of time and money

With this view, organizations usually do not budget adequate resources to sustain the training and support systems they need. Also, there usually is little justification for using cost-effective delivery systems except for a few hobby shops of innovation.

Without a management system for training, most organizations drift along with traditional performance-management systems, never taking the leap forward to mastery of learning and performance. They also receive low marks for implementing new strategic directions and major tactical decisions. An inefficient management system also explains why most organizations botch new quality systems and experience disappointing results with their reengineering projects.

The quality measurements of applying training to the job and determining its impact are usually missing, so the company or government agency never comes close to being a learning organization.

Without a management system, organizations rarely achieve an optimum cost of people (labor) and desirable customer-satisfaction levels. Instead, expenses rise, revenues disappoint, and earnings decline. Only a few organizations have a truly effective management system for their training and support function, the key word being "effective." Over 99 percent of all organizations are managing with hard work, good intentions, and an outdated requirements system

Essential Elements of an Effective System

Effective systems abide by the KISS theory, "Keep it simple, stupid." Too many systems become too complex and wind up gathering dust with other strategic plans. Successful management systems must be understood, endorsed, and advocated by the senior executive team, line executives and their staffs, the HR executive and the HR functional staffs, all training personnel, middle management, supervisors, and all other employees.

Winning the support of all of these groups is a big challenge. In some organizations, only the trainers understand their management system. In others, senior executives and the training executive understand it, but no middle managers or employees have ever heard of the system that will increase the performance of the workforce.

To be easily comprehended and endorsed by employees, a management system should be no more than one page, easily explained verbally in ten minutes. The system should be so simple that it seems like common sense to everyone to implement it.

The management system outlined in this chapter works in every industry, whether in large- or intermediate-size or small organizations. It has been used in organizations with 100 employees as well as those with over 400,000 employees. The system has been successful in commercial companies (corporations, partnerships, sole proprietorships), government agencies, and not-for-profit enterprises. Equally important, it works whether the organization is centralized or decentralized, so an organization has no reason not to develop a basic management system for its training and support function. The steps to take for implementation are described below.

Start with a Mission Statement

Many of today's training departments have mission statements, although many are only a generalized set of words that commits to nothing but good intentions. Each organization should develop its own customized mission statement. Here is an example of a more meaningful mission statement:

> Based upon business and performance requirements identified by line and staff management, our mission is to assess, develop, deliver, and evaluate effective training and support systems. These performance systems must empower our entire workforce to rise above the competition with a performance level that will contribute significantly to our leadership position within the industry.

This mission statement shows a CTO who is definitely moving his or her department into the organization's mainstream. It focuses on workforce performance instead of training events and mentions support systems as well as courses of instruction.

The mission clearly places the responsibility of determining business objectives where it belongs: On the line and staff management's shoulders. These managers must also articulate what their employees must know and be able to do within each job category. Once they establish these requirements, the training and performance function can create programs that transform the employees and managers into a competitive workforce. Line management will continue to be responsible for supervising employees and for inspiring them to enhance their performance.

This is the type of mission statement that makes a great impression on senior and line executives. To accomplish this mission, there must be a comprehensive management system.

Overview of a Management System

Shown in Figure 3.1 is an outline of the Systems Approach for Workplace Performance, which has been developed over a ten-year period, with many organizations and individuals contributing to its vision. It represents best practices of organizations that have achieved breakthroughs in workforce performance. As indicated by its title, the Systems Approach is a systematic approach to achieving superior workforce performance. Each element of the system is a key link in the process of managing performance to achieve organizational objectives.

Six basic steps comprise the Systems Approach. The first step is documenting the business or government agency objectives. The inputs to business or government agency objectives are shown at the top of the figure. There are five potential inputs:

1. *Customer requirements* are extremely important to commercial organizations, and listening to customers has become a way of life for most successful companies. Even government agencies are listening more and more to taxpayers. Customer satisfaction surveys and focus groups are the primary sources for this information.

2. *Regulatory requirements* are the main source of input for government agencies. In regulated or semiregulated industries, requirements are laid down by law and guidelines, for instance, all organizations must abide by certain rules on environmental and workplace safety. Public utilities, medical facilities, financial insti-

Figure 3.1. Systems Approach for Workforce Performance.

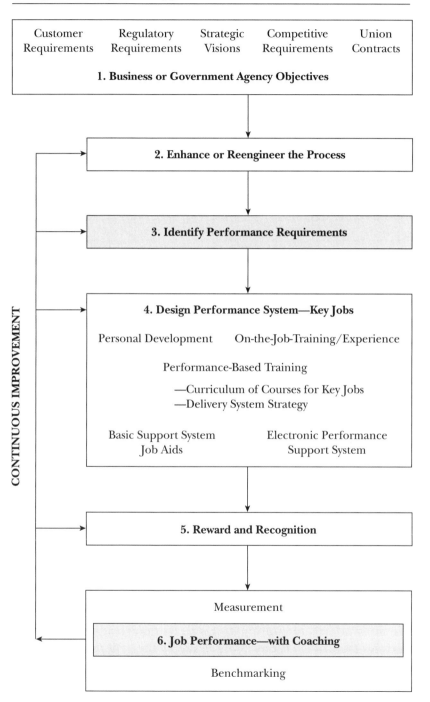

tutions, transportation companies, and manufacturers all have many regulations.

3. *Strategic visions* apply only to a select group of organizations that are blessed with outstanding senior executive leadership. For example: American Airlines created the concept of reservation systems and frequent-flyer programs; Federal Express invented the concepts of overnight delivery and computerized package tracking at all times; IBM invented the System/360 that dominated the computer industry for decades; Xerox had a grand strategic vision for years with the copier that spawned an entire industry; and Andersen Consulting's strategic vision enabled it to go from last to first place in revenues within its industry.

4. *Competitive requirements* are a major input for almost every commercial organization, and copying the competition has become a way of life. A review of most organizations' strategic directions would reveal the strategies of top-performing companies within those industries.

5. *Union contracts* provide many inputs from labor unions in both commercial companies and government agencies. Union contracts often influence business requirements in nonunion companies also, because management wants to perform at or above the level of workforce standards established in the contract of their industry.

Line and staff executives must translate all five of these inputs into *business objectives,* Step 1 of the management system. In government, these objectives are referred to as "agency objectives." In some organizations, these inputs become part of the strategic and operating plans. Almost every large- and intermediate-size organization does this work, and it is relatively easy to determine the organizational objectives. For example, a company can set an objective of growing by 5 percent or reducing expenses by 8 percent. Another organization may create an objective of introducing four new products or offering two new services.

Step 2 of the management system is for the organization to *enhance or reengineer processes,* based on the objectives established in the first step. Too often, an organization's methods and procedures are not updated in conjunction with its new strategic directions and the tactical decisions being made by the senior executives. It is shocking to see how many training programs and support systems are outdated because the basic processes have not been enhanced or reengineered, or the training has not been updated for revised processes.

Step 3 is for the training organization to work with line management to use the objectives from Step 1 and revised procedures from Step 2 to *identify performance requirements*. They must find out what the line executives want employees within each major job category to know and be able to do. Most organizations never address this question. Too often, they talk about empowering employees or they speak generalizations such as "work smarter, not harder." To become a world-class workforce, employees must be told what training they need and what tasks they must be able to do.

Defining the performance requirements of jobs is hard work, requiring strong leadership on the part of line management. Equally important, the training organization must lead line executives through this process with methodologies such as front-end analysis, needs analysis, or task analysis.

After line executives have documented these performance requirements, they need to determine *how* their employees will gain the necessary knowledge and skills to become A or B performers. There are five ways to develop employee knowledge and skills, a process referred to as a *performance system* (Step 4 in the figure).

Personal Development Assignments. The management team can ask an employee to attend selected meetings, read assigned publications, and complete appropriate employee-development courses, for example, a course on time management. Sophisticated companies and government agencies maintain outstanding libraries for their employees, a big help for personal-development assignments as well as for research. Many of these libraries even have on-line retrieval systems. A training organization should create a low-cost and effective library system when it includes the required books from its overall performance system. This is the way a company maintains cost control over the required knowledge systems.

On-the-Job-Training and Experience. The most common approach to learning a job in organizations that do little or no training is this hit-and-miss approach that leads to many errors. The employees often learn by making costly mistakes that adversely affect customer satisfaction. Fortunately, some organizations have a positive mentor and tutoring system, a cost-effective way to develop knowledge and skills. On-the-job training and experience is essential in every job category and will be covered in Chapter Ten.

Performance-Based Training Curriculum. By doing a needs and task analysis, companies can convert performance requirements into a performance-based training curriculum that achieves mastery of learning and performance. The output from such an analysis is detailed specifications for training required, from which a curriculum must be designed and developed.Unfortunately, most organizations assign this work to untrained instructors during their "spare time" between classes. Courses should be developed to incorporate instructional-design methods. Once the curriculum design is completed, the courses may be developed by internal or external personnel. They may also be modified or purchased from a course-development company. It is a classic make or buy decision. This process will be discussed in detail in Chapter Eight.

The training and performance department must choose how to deliver the lessons to the students and where this instruction will take place. There are two fundamental delivery systems: self-paced, individual instruction or classroom instruction. The courses can be delivered at any of the following types of site:

- Central education centers
- Local education centers
- Learning centers
- Work stations

Delivery systems are covered in detail in Chapter Nine.

Basic Support Systems. For decades, there have been job aids to help employees become outstanding performers, although most companies have underutilized them. With the widespread use of the personal computer, more and more companies are now providing support systems and knowledge systems through technology, which will be covered in Chapter Eleven.

Electronic Performance Support Systems. This new paradigm for enhancing workforce performance uses multimedia tutoring systems tied to networks. Employees learn and perform tasks with electronic supervision, eventually achieving mastery of learning and performance. This new breakthrough system will be discussed in Chapter Twelve.

Step 5 of the Systems Approach for Workplace Performance is *reward and recognition,* which must be included if there are to be breakthroughs in performance. Too many companies fail to integrate them into their overall process. This will be covered in Chapter Thirteen.

Measurement and benchmarking with job performance are the next step, as shown in the figure. Chapter Fifteen will provide new insight on how to measure the success of training, personal-development assignments, basic support systems and electronic integrated support systems. Measurement and benchmarking allow the training to improve continuously for each major job category. By applying quality measurements to training and support systems, companies can create a built-in formal change-management system that ensures optimum performance. The line executives and chief training officer should be able to say that all employees (except for new hires) are fully trained to achieve maximum performance objectives. This, of course, means lower operating expenses.

In the final step of the management system, management evaluates employees' job performance. Prior to any *performance evaluation,* supervisors and managers need to know what performance level should be expected and how to coach their employees to achieve that level. As employees are evaluated throughout the year, managers should determine if there are any gaps or major deficiencies that keep an employee from being at an A or B level. If there are, then managers must determine if these gaps represent system problems. If not system problems, gaps must be considered to be individual-performance problems. Employees with performance problems not caused by the system should be coached to an acceptable performance level, reassigned, or terminated. Long-term performance problems should not be tolerated. If they are tolerated, management has its own performance problem, which needs to be addressed.

Once a workforce is competitive, it should remain at that level year after year if the organization uses a benchmarking process that annually compares the performance of every key job category with its counterpart in other top-performing organizations.

This management system requires a comprehensive administration-enrollment and skills-inventory system. Fortunately, numerous systems are available on the market, although choosing one is not a trivial matter, as in many organizations the training and support function's administrative area represents about 25 percent of the budget.

The skills inventory should tell management how many employees are at the entry level, experienced level, and mastery level within each major job category, rather than just maintain records on the courses that an employee has taken. The task of keeping track of skills accurately can become so complex and expensive that executives view it as a waste of time. Many skills-inventory systems die because they are too big of a burden. On the other hand, top-performing organizations *always* maintain a skills-inventory system on their employees.

How the Management System Can Work

Years ago, secretaries answered the telephone, handled the mail, arranged meetings, typed documents, and took dictation. Their world, like so many others, has changed dramatically because of technology. Personal computers arrived, copiers were installed, FAX machines were plugged in, and secretaries received very little training on each new piece of equipment. Frustrated secretaries struggled to master their new tools, disappointing supervisors with their declining productivity. Their learning curves were so long that many organizations that expected an increase in efficiency from the new equipment just added the equipment costs to the cost of people, which resulted in increased operating expenses and lower earnings.

What would have happened if companies had used the approach outlined in Figure 3.1? Here is what might have happened: Line executives decided to purchase new hardware and software for their secretaries, expecting them to be able to handle word processing, spreadsheets, graphics, databases, and electronic mail, and still answer the telephone. New performance requirements (Step 3) should have been based on the managerial decisions made in Step 1. Performance requirements should have been converted into training requirements, personal-development assignments, and on-the-job assignments (Step 4). Most of the courses could have been purchased from course-development companies. Most of the training could have taken place in learning centers or at employee work stations, enriching the secretaries' work and their satisfaction. Equally important, the organization could have realized gains in productivity, decreases in operating expenses, and positive contributions toward earnings.

Here is another example: Remember when all the CEOs said that they wanted to implement Total Quality Management (TQM)? In most organizations, this implementation amounted to a round of awareness courses, posters on bulletin boards, articles in the company newspaper, and great disappointment because employees continued to do "business as usual."

If the Systems Approach for Workforce Performance had been utilized, the new strategic direction would have established the business or government agency objectives for TQM in Step 1. The basic processes within the organization should have been enhanced to include TQM, which is Step 2. Then the line executives would have decided what their employees within each major job category needed to know and to be able to do by establishing the performance criteria in Step 3. The training requirements would have included both awareness and performance-based training, plus all the required support systems (Step 4). Every employee with new performance requirements would have been evaluated (Step 6) on how well they were implementing their course lessons on quality. Total quality management would have been institutionalized due to the continuous-improvement process.

Advantages of a Management System

The Systems Approach for Workforce Performance can significantly improve any organization's operating and financial performance. An effective management system can minimize the cost of people (labor); reduce operating expenses; increase revenues; increase market share; enhance customer satisfaction; improve workforce morale; lower the attrition rate and cost of recruitment; reduce supervision costs; enrich jobs; increase job satisfaction; lower training and support costs; provide adequate resources for training and support; move training into the organizational mainstream; accelerate the implementation of new strategic decisions; build a competitive workforce; enhance job security; and improve earnings.

Needless to say, every company and government agency should have a management system for its training and support systems so it can have these advantages. It does not have to be called the Systems Approach for Workforce Performance, and each organization should feel free to develop its own customized management system. Remember, this model works in all industries and in all large- and intermediate-size organizations. It is a basic outline for every organization.

How Management Systems Relate to Other Systems

Almost every company and government agency has a planning system consisting of the following:

- Goals to reach over a three- or five-year period
- Strategic plans designed to achieve those goals
- Annual action programs and budgets

These planning systems should go one step farther and determine what the training and support requirements will be. This vital step is missing in most organizations, which is why so many action programs are never completed on time, within budget, or at the desired performance level.

The Systems Approach for Workforce Performance needs to become a key part of career planning and individual employee-development planning, items that receive a lot of good words in most organizations, but lack real structure due to the absence of a management system in the training department.

However, when an effective management system is in place, succession and career planning become more realistic. The management system also influences the compensation system by helping to create more realistic job descriptions. Most important, an effective management system improves the recruiting process and decreases costs.

Benefits of a Learning Organization

Too often, executives view training as a series of random events. The management system outlined in this chapter clearly shows that training and performance systems require a continuous process that aims to enhance workforce performance. No organization will achieve a competitive workforce at minimum cost until it implements this type of system.

An effective management system focuses continuously on improving workforce performance. Such a system can turn any company, not-for-profit group, or government agency into a learning organization. Too many places of employment call themselves learning organizations because they have a training department, when in fact they are nowhere close to becoming a learning organization.

Too many organizations manage by fear as they leap from crisis to crisis. In opinion surveys, employees express a deep mistrust and low opinion of their executive leadership. All of this ill will can be alleviated with the Systems Approach for Workforce Performance because it forces a working partnership among the executive team, managers, and employees.

Too many organizations are ripping out middle management before replacing it with an effective training and support system. It is no wonder there are so many debacles in today's business world. A flat organization must adapt the system because it is based on senior executives translating their decisions into action with front-line employees with no help from middle management, which has been eliminated.

The Systems Approach ensures that all employees have an equal opportunity to achieve mastery of performance within each major job category. Women and minorities are attracted to organizations that have a formal system for training and developing employees. Because this approach can be explained to new and potential employees within a few minutes, it provides a strategic advantage for hiring outstanding personnel.

The management system also enables the training and performance function to be managed as efficiently as any other major functional area.

The rest of this book explains how to implement a management system, a process that begins with the appointment of a proven leader of change for the training and performance department.

Chapter Four

Appoint a Chief Training Officer

Restructuring or reengineering a traditional training organization into a function that focuses on workforce performance is often a greater undertaking than anticipated by executives, whose initial reaction is typically "no big deal." In practice, however, failures are common and successes are rare. Comparing the successes to the failures, the quality of leadership for directing the change effort usually determines how successful the restructuring will be.

In some organizations, training is managed by people who have "peaked and parked." They are caretaker executives who are satisfied with the status quo while they wait to retire. In other organizations, the director of training is a high-potential employee who serves in a career-development position for eighteen to twenty-four months. Often, he or she is impressed with the "happiness sheets" that imply that current courses are "right on target and run like a Swiss watch." Satisfied that no major changes are required, they too become caretaker executives as they serve their time and plan their next promotion.

If CEOs or senior-management teams want to achieve a strategic breakthrough in workforce performance, they need to hire or appoint a leader who has a proven record for creating and managing change. This new executive position can be given the title of Chief Training Officer (CTO), Chief Learning Officer (CLO), or Chief Performance Officer (CPO). (The latter title could lead to the inevitable "performance" jokes that relate to the research done by Dr. Ruth and other human-sexuality experts.) The CEO may also reject this title because he or she does not want the line executives to feel that they are no longer responsible for workforce performance.

Some companies use the descriptive term Training and Performance Department, but all executive titles are three words. Because the first and last letters are always C and O, the choice for the middle word becomes "learning" or "training." It really does not matter which is used as long as the company selects the right person for the job. The Chief Training Officer (CTO) title is used throughout this book because executive management easily relates to this title.

It is exciting and rare when a company creates a new executive position. Skeptics will ask why a new executive position is needed at a time when companies and government agencies are trying to reduce the size of their corporate staffs. The answer is quite clear: Virtually every successful organization (Big-Six accounting firms, Motorola, Sun Microsystems, Intel, McDonald's, Southern Company, Sprint, GTE, Coca-Cola, GE) has an executive in charge of training who reports directly to the senior management team. The concept has proved to be successful over the past ten years. The title varies, but the job description does not. The CTO is responsible for transforming a traditional training organization into one that drives up workforce performance through leading-edge performance systems.

A leader of training and support systems is required whether the organization is centralized or decentralized. Line executives simply do not have the time to become experts on needs and task analysis, instructional-design methods, course-delivery systems, education technologies, measurement systems, authoring systems, performance-management systems, and communication networks. Line executives should be responsible for stating what employees need to know and be able to do within the major job categories, but a separate department has to create the systems to achieve these performance requirements. Someone has to lead this effort, and that executive must have specialized knowledge.

This position is analogous to the chief information officer position that emerged thirty years ago when companies and government agencies needed a better way to install computer programs successfully.

Requirements of a Successful CTO

The following indicate what a CTO must be in order to be successful.

Leader

Leadership skills are essential for a chief training officer. To be successful, the CTO must be able to establish a working partnership with the CEO, COO, CFO, CIO, senior HR executive, and the line executives. The methods for establishing these relationships are discussed in Chapter Five. The CTO must be well-respected by the senior management team and be able to influence their decisions. A solid working partnership ensures that the CTO participates in discussions on new strategic directions and major tactical decisions when they are first brought to the table, rather than after the fact. The CTO must be viewed as an executive first, and a trainer second.

The CTO must drive up workforce performance with leading-edge training and support systems. The CTO must have an in-depth knowledge of his or her business or government agency and must have the leadership skills to empower the training department's employees and managers in order to achieve the organization's objectives.

Creator and Leader of Change

The CTO must be a student of change systems and a successful practitioner of the subject and must know how to apply change methods based on current research. Too often in the past, reengineering efforts have been based solely on trial-and-error methods. Senior executives must view a successful CTO as a change accelerator.

Developer and Implementor of a Management System

If you ask today's directors of training how their management systems achieve organizational objectives, most of the responses will disappoint you. This area is a real weakness in almost every training department. The CTO must develop a vision and communicate it to the entire organization.

Developer and Implementor of Best Practices

The CTO must continually review the generally accepted practices of training and support systems in order to improve the current management system to meet performance goals. These reviews ensure continuous improvements, not just a one-time effort to enhance job performance. The best practices should be documented and regularly updated in guidelines for the training and performance department.

Developer of Performance Systems

The CTO must insist on a curriculum of courses and support systems for every major job category within the organization. Today, performance systems for each major job category only exist in about twenty-five organizations.

Manager of Education and Learning Centers

A CTO must deliver cost-effective courses that incorporate the benefits of advancing technologies and educational research. Methods for moving from traditional classroom courses with few measurements to courses that achieve mastery of learning and performance will be discussed in a later chapter.

Implementer of Measurements

Today's training departments rarely have adequate measurements, a situation that must change if the department is to achieve its goal of improving workforce performance. In order to obtain the adequate resources that a well-trained, competitive workforce needs, the CTO must implement quality measurements that achieve the following goals:

1. The students like the course and instructors.
2. The students learn the lessons and skills.

3. The students apply the knowledge and skills to the job.
4. The employees' enhanced performance has a positive impact on the organization's objectives.

Manager of Talented People

The CTO must implement basic HR systems such as job descriptions, career paths, compensation programs, recognition programs, training programs, and employee-development plans. In addition, the CTO must hire, develop, and retain outstanding personnel in the training and performance function.

Manager of Financial and Operating Controls

The CTO must develop and implement financial controls that enable the training and performance function to operate within a budget. In large- and intermediate-size organizations, the CTO must play the role of a business manager overseeing a multimillion-dollar budget. Financial controls require numerous operational systems and reports; fortunately outstanding administrative software systems are available to help a CTO establish these controls.

How Challenging Is the Job of a CTO?

The job of the CTO is not easy. As with training systems, there are more failures than successes, usually because of a lack of leadership skills. Chief training officers often do not see themselves as members of the executive team; too often they merely respond to the demands of senior executives, rather than guiding the senior and line executives toward the strategic programs that lead to a well-trained, low-cost, and competitive workforce.

An under-skilled workforce continues to threaten our global competitiveness. Therefore, senior executives must select a true leader for the CTO position, one who can trim the fat out of current operations while developing and selling a vision that excites all of the organization's employees, managers, and executives. Most important, the CTO must win over the training organization to accept the changes his or her vision will bring.

Today, only 55 percent of Americans get either formal or on-the-job training related to their job tasks. Only 16 percent of the workforce receives any formal training for their jobs. This means that millions of Americans go to work every day only partially trained to do their jobs. Unless companies and government agencies appoint real leaders to their training and performance functions, the workforce will remain at risk. It is imperative for every major corporation and government agency to appoint a chief training officer.

Sources for Chief Training Officers

According to a March 1995 ASTD survey, trainers who responded came from one of twenty different academic backgrounds, ranging from agriculture to theater arts. Thirty-four percent of the trainers surveyed have business backgrounds and 32 percent have degrees in education, with most being former public school teachers who did not like teaching or never started to teach in that environment. Sixteen percent come from a social-science background. Only one-tenth of 1 percent have HR degrees. The smallest group (a fraction of 1 percent) had master's degrees in instructional design.

Companies can acquire CTOs in four basic ways. One way is to *promote someone from within* the training organization. Although many managers and directors of training are former instructors, senior executives rarely select a chief training officer from the training department. They do not want their new CTO influenced by the old school of training; they want him or her to focus on job performance. This will change when managers and directors of training departments implement new systems to focus on workforce performance.

The second source for CTOs is to *promote a successful executive from another area of the organization* who has a proven record in creating and managing change. Today, most corporations and government agencies tap this source, as they did with chief information officers in the 1960s and 1970s. Senior management concludes that it is easier to teach a proven executive how to manage training than it is to elevate a proven trainer to an executive post. In the past fifteen years, Arthur Andersen has selected three chief training officers from line managing partners after hiring a professor from the University of Texas to start the process. The Southern Company selected one of its proven executives of change to be CTO.

The third source is to *hire a proven chief training officer* from another company or government agency. This approach works well if a highly qualified person is available. However, based on input from executive search firms, there are probably no more than twenty highly qualified, proven performers in this field. Coca-Cola recently hired its CTO from Coopers & Lybrand, and KPMG Peat-Marwick hired one of their CTOs from IBM.

General Electric is one of the few companies that has had success with the fourth source: *Hire a college professor.* The last three chief training officers at GE were Jim Baughman, Noel Tichy, and Steven Kerr, who have all had academic backgrounds. Some professors fail in the CTO job because they come from the unstructured world of education where there are no measurements other than those for grading students. Typically, they last two or three years in the position and then return to the academic world.

People often ask me who the number-one CTO in the country is. In my opinion, that honor now belongs to Motorola's Bill Wiggenhorn, who started his career as a Xerox sales representative and later became the company's head of sales training. Motorola's CEO had tried twice to revitalize training inside the company and finally concluded that he needed to hire someone who had a proven record for restructuring a training organization. Wiggenhorn had such a record at Xerox. In 1981, Motorola hired him and gave him a $7 million training budget.

Today, Wiggenhorn is the president of Motorola University and the senior vice president of training and education. His annual budget is now several hundred million dollars, which proves that a well-qualified CTO can obtain adequate resources from executive management. As senior vice president, Wiggenhorn has earned the respect of his fellow executives and has built a working partnership with the company's line executives. Today, Motorola has job-training programs designed from the manufacturing floor all the way to the executive offices. Motorola University, located in a new building close to corporate headquarters and attached to a company museum, communicates the company's history, traditions, practices, and beliefs.

Compensation for CTOs

Ten years ago, *Training Magazine* published a story on "Six-Figure Trainers." At the time, only eight executives belonged to that exclusive group making over $100,000 a year. On February 4, 1996, the *New York Times* published an article about chief learning officers, stating that these new executives were earning annual salaries between $300,000 and $700,000. Today, at least fifty executives in charge of training functions are earning in excess of $100,000. This is a dramatic change in under ten years. The trend is clear: As more CEOs realize how vital it is to have a proven leader in charge of training, CTO's salaries will rise dramatically.

Training and Development for CTOs

With the growing number of job opportunities, CTO candidates need appropriate training and development courses for themselves. In association with Andersen Consulting, ASTD commissioned a Chief Training Officer Workshop in 1992. The workshop was developed primarily by instructional designers as a performance-based course. To date, approximately two hundred managers and directors of training have attended this four-day seminar. The author was fortunate to be a key member of the course-development team and one of the workshop instructors. This book features many of the lessons taught in this CTO workshop.

For over ten years, *Training Magazine* has offered a Training Directors Seminar, which several hundred training managers attend annually. The agenda is designed to allow training managers to present their proven methods to one another.

A few universities are now offering courses on this subject, and it seems likely that training programs will emerge for future CTOs who have proven leadership skills that will enable training managers and directors to be promoted to this new executive position.

Training managers and directors can read numerous books and articles from professional journals such as *Training and Devel-*

opment. These articles do an excellent job of communicating best practices. Training directors also discuss best practices when they meet formally and informally. From 1987 to 1995 there was a Training Directors Consortium; fifteen of the most advanced companies met annually to exchange ideas on management issues. It is to be hoped that, in the future, some leading-edge companies will organize again, because chief training officers have much to learn by exchanging best practices.

Chapter Five

Develop a Working Partnership for Key Jobs

Many executives show a genuine interest in the fields of education and training. They have attended grammar school, high school, universities, employee-training programs, and executive-development courses. They often serve on school boards and school reform task forces. They also donate considerable sums of money to educational institutions.

But, despite their interest and frequent involvement in education outside of their companies, too many executives make the assumption that the employees who work for them have been adequately trained to do their jobs. They know little about training, job aids, and support systems within their own organizations. To understand the effectiveness of the training functions in their organizations, executives must ask themselves these five questions:

1. Have jobs been clearly defined?
2. Are employees trained to do their jobs?
3. Are there adequate support systems for the jobs?
4. Are the employees being coached and supervised?
5. Are there meaningful measurements for job performance?

To train employees adequately, the training department must establish a working relationship with the company's senior and line executives.

The Working Partnership

Why is the working partnership so important? First, the *senior executive team needs to view training as a mainstream function such as finance or HR*. This will never happen unless the executive team helps the training organization create and implement its mission and its management system. Executives need to be involved in the process that will restructure the organization's training and performance function.

Second, it is imperative that *line executives play a significant role in identifying the major job categories*. After all, the vast majority of employees report to line executives who are responsible for their performance. Therefore, line executives should want to help the training department enhance the performance of their workforce.

Third, once the major job categories are identified, *line executives must help choose the curriculum of courses, development programs, and support systems* that will increase the performance of the workforce. They must help in the design of the performance system. Line executives must agree on course objectives and key lessons and provide subject-matter experts during the needs and task analysis as well as during the course-development phase. Remember, line executives are essential to determining how job performance can be enhanced.

Fourth, the *director of training should review the quality measurements and cost-containment efforts with line management* to convince them that the training and performance function is being managed just as efficiently as any other mainstream organizational function.

Fifth, *line executives should be involved in determining who should attend the training programs*. Getting the right person in the right class at the right time cannot be accomplished solely by the training and performance department. It should be noted that many leading-edge training groups also secure the participation of senior executives as guest speakers in a few selected courses. In some situations, the line or senior executives send written invitations asking employees to attend the more advanced courses.

Sixth, a number of training and performance organizations have advisory committees made up of *senior and line executives who meet at least twice a year to review the performance of the workforce,* as well as the training and performance systems. This review is essential if the organization wants to focus on continuous improvement and a competitive workforce.

Seventh, *the training and performance organization must be knowledgeable about strategic directions and major tactical decisions* as soon as the executives determine them. In the best of situations, a representative from the training and performance organization attends all of the key meetings leading up to major new strategic directions and tactical decisions. The training and performance organization can accelerate change by retraining the workforce on new products, new services, or strategic directions. Unfortunately, these improvements will not happen if there is not a close working partnership between the senior management team and the training organization.

Eighth, *the line-management team needs to be responsible for reinforcing the lessons taught in the training courses.* Lack of reinforcement of lessons is often what reduces the value of training to near zero. Remember, the training and performance department is not responsible for performance on the job. That clearly is the job of line management.

Ninth, and most important, *the training and performance organization must have adequate resources.* That includes the right number of outstanding employees, proper facilities, effective information systems, and sufficient funding. Therefore, every hour spent in building a working partnership with the line and senior executives is a worthwhile investment that will complement the training and performance department's efforts.

Developing a Working Partnership

How do you actually develop this working partnership? If you have a mission statement, a management system, and a list of activities that you want an executive to participate in, then it is a simple four-step process.

Schedule a meeting with the senior or line executive. Assume you want to meet with the vice president of operations. Tell his or her secretary you need forty-five or sixty minutes to discuss how you plan to restructure the training organization and to hear the vice president's input. During the meeting, review the current strengths and weaknesses of the training programs, asking the executive whether he or she agrees. Involve the executive in your plan of action. Executives are usually flattered to hear that someone in the training and performance department values their opinions.

Share the mission statement for the department. Quite often, an executive will help fine-tune the wording. Review the proposed management system, the Systems Approach for Workforce Performance. The executive will probably give some advice on how to improve the management system. Finally, state that the training and performance organization cannot work in a vacuum and that you will need the line executive and his or her staff to help in such areas as:

- Identification of critical job categories.
- Subject matter experts (SMEs) for needs and task analysis.
- Review of curriculum and courses by SMEs.
- Help in course development by SMEs.
- Help in teaching the courses by SMEs.
- Assistance in having the right person in the right course at the right time.
- Executive participation in selected courses.
- Feedback on strategic directions and tactical decisions.
- Reinforcement of lessons by line management.
- Participation in an advisory board.

Stress that the training and line organizations must work together to increase the performance of the workforce and reduce operating expenses. The executive will quickly realize that you are working for the good of the organization and will probably ask you to present your ideas at a staff meeting.

The second step in developing a working partnership occurs at the line executives' staff meeting, which typically requires a more formal presentation. The executive who met with you before is now your inside mentor. This person will now tell the group how he or she helped you develop your mission statement and management system. The executive will also assign staff to the project. The theme of the meeting usually becomes how the restructuring can happen, rather than whether or not it should happen.

Now a formal process is necessary for being continually updated on the organization's strategic and tactical decisions. An Advisory Board that meets twice a year or quarterly can serve this purpose. Sometimes the manager of training will attend all the important staff meetings to be certain that training remains up-to-date. Sometimes, in order to update everyone, the vice president of operations and the other line executives make an annual presentation to the training managers.

An annual review of training and performance to determine strengths and areas requiring improvement must be implemented. Of course, a continuous relationship will already exist between line executives and the training department, who perform such routine tasks as analyzing needs and tasks, developing courses, teaching the lessons, and looking for breakthroughs in performance by enhancing the curriculum and support systems.

Another benefit of having a continuous working partnership between line management and the training department is the opportunity for line executives to hear direct feedback from frontline employees by attending selected classes or seminars. This eliminates the problem of bad news being filtered before it reaches the executive offices. The long-term partnership is, of course, built on a continuous series of meetings and events.

All this seems so simple. Why then do so few training organizations have a working partnership with their senior or line executives? Some reasons include the following:

- Too few training organizations are focused on workplace performance. They measure themselves on the quantity of training events and good "happiness sheets."
- Only a few training organizations have a mission statement and a management system that is exciting to senior and line executives.
- Most executives view training as a variable expense, because no one has shown them that training and performance systems actually lower operating expenses.
- Many training directors avoid contact with senior executives because they are afraid of a budget cut or penetrating questions on how to justify their expenses.

- Executives quite often view training as an expense that cannot be measured. They are not aware of the four levels of quality measurements.
- Many training directors operate in a reactive mode, waiting for executives to call them, rather than being proactive.

Typical Views of Training

Remember, without a working partnership with the training department, the executives in most organizations will continue to think that 25 percent of training courses are a waste of time; 25 percent need to be improved; 25 percent are fairly good; and 25 percent are outstanding. This model is based on hundreds of executive interviews within corporations, not-for-profit organizations, and government agencies. With rare exception, executives have a low opinion of education and training programs, and they know very little about performance systems.

The executives come to this conclusion based on their own educational experiences in public and private schools. Their courses at colleges and universities fit this model. Even their own courses in management development fall into these four categories. This is the bell-shaped curve that has been institutionalized in education and training organizations for over a century.

Frankly, in the world of six-sigma quality-management systems, the bell-shaped curve is unacceptable. Executives will continue to have no problems reducing the training budget by 10, 15, or 20 percent if they hold this view of education and training programs.

Therefore, it is important to educate your executive team on the potential for improving performance by investing in a restructured training organization focused on the performance of the workforce! Aim for mastery of learning and performance! And you *must* have a management system!

Identifying Key Jobs

More and more trainers agree that no course should be offered without business and performance requirements. Almost all of them agree that training should focus on performance, but somehow training departments remain focused on "nice to do" courses, long lists of skills, and competencies. They never get around to focusing on the key jobs that drive up revenues and control costs. It is rare to find a company or government agency that lists the key jobs of their organization and plans their training and support systems to meet the performance requirements of those key jobs, which is one of the most critical success factors for restructuring the training organization. Listed below are the major benefits a company will obtain by identifying those key jobs.

Strong Relationships with Executive Management. The senior executives cannot understand long lists of skills and courses, nor are they impressed with large catalogs of classes, which they see as excessive expense for training. Their penetrating question is: Are the employees in my area fully trained and supported to meet the performance requirements of their jobs?

Senior executives pay attention when you discuss the critical jobs that report to them because these are the employees who "make or break" the executive's performance record. Most executives have five to ten key jobs reporting to them. The chief training officer should build and enhance his or her relationship with these executives.

Proof that Employees Apply the Lessons. If the curriculum is not planned by key jobs, then employees will rarely apply the lessons learned. That is why only a few organizations can prove that the students apply the lessons from their training courses to their jobs.

Results of Training Tie to Business Results. If a substantial sum of money is invested to develop a curriculum, then there should be a tangible return on that investment. This return is feasible if you can measure performance on the job prior to a new or revised performance system and again after the new performance system has been used for a period of time. Lower operating expenses, lower cost of errors or rework, higher customer satisfaction, and more sales can be measured and support the need and the resources for adequate employee training and performance systems. Measurement is only feasible if the key jobs have been identified, and the training, as well as the support systems, have been designed specifically for each job.

Management Convinced That Training and Performance Is Tied to Business Requirements. The belief that certain courses can be eliminated often results in a 10 to 15 percent cut in operating funds for training, especially in years of uncertain economic conditions. Once courses are tied to workforce performance, a major misconception will be eliminated, and the annual threat of a budget reduction will disappear. This understanding leads to a renewed management commitment to support the training and performance department.

Minimum Time Away from the Job. Many line managers resist sending employees to classes because they do not see any benefit except a touch of rest and recreation. If they understand that objectives and key lessons within a curriculum are designed to enhance employee performance, line managers will support attendance. Of course, they must be convinced that these courses are developed to minimize time away from the job.

Increased Support of Line Management. Every training function needs the support of line management to have the right employees in the right class at the right time. Line managers seldom have time to study large catalogs, but they do have the time to read two to four pages that explain the curriculum of courses for a key job area that reports to them. After they are convinced that training and support systems increase workforce performance, they will provide meaningful support to the training function.

Continuous Improvement of Curriculum and Courses. If they are not focused on a specific job, many training classes remain available long after they are required and the lessons have become dated. When executives, line management, and employees are involved in job training and performance systems, they provide constant pressure to keep the content current and creditable. The continued updating of courses and support systems eliminates the expense of offering unnecessary and duplicate courses.

Clear Focus of Responsibility. When course designers and developers are clearly focused on what should be taught and how it should be delivered for each job category, split responsibility is eliminated; the executives and line managers do not have to communicate with several education departments to determine if courses are available for a critical job. The chief training officer has a clear focus on job training within the organization. There are no organizational excuses for inadequate training, support systems, and performance systems.

More Realistic Requirements. Line managers do not want to be criticized for having an untrained workforce. They do not want employee opinion surveys to reflect low marks for training not being available or being ineffective. When line managers see that the training curriculum and support systems are by job category, they will provide realistic requirements for courses because they want the right training to be available. Training requirements will move from being a wish list to being a list of essential courses and firm enrollments.

Increased Support and Participation by Employees. No one likes to work in a job by trial and error. Everyone from a beginning secretary or a salesperson to an experienced middle manager in a new position wants to have good training. All of this reduces the rate of cancellations and no-shows.

If employees know that the curriculum of courses has been designed to improve their performance on the job, they will enroll quickly. A two- to four-page explanation of the training and support systems that are available for a job is more motivating and understandable than a large catalog covering all of the offerings by the training department. Courses become like merit badges, and employees seek them out enthusiastically.

Additional Support for Alternative Delivery Systems. Too many organizations cannot justify the development costs of a new delivery system because time away from the job and performance on the job are not measured. When the courses are within a job curriculum, it is much easier to justify the development funds for a new cost-effective delivery system.

Adequate Resources. Executives often view the chief training officer's presentation of the annual budget as an exercise in "rattling the tin cup" for additional classes and good intentions rather than an investment in workforce performance. All this changes when the executive team becomes involved in decisions about critical jobs, lessons to be taught, how many employees will be trained, and what performance objectives will be achieved.

Once a line executive is involved in planning the courses, he or she will not allow the finance department to reduce the training department's budget. Line executives will defend what they see as the true financial requirements needed in the CTO budget. Executives committed to the need for training and support systems for workforce performance will also be committed to the need for adequate resources.

Planning by Skills and Competencies

A number of educators want to plan training by finding out what *skills* are needed for each job. If there are fifteen to thirty skills needed for each job, every company is dealing in hundreds and sometimes thousands of skills. No one can deal with that many elements. Planning by skills needed sounds logical, but it requires a massive control system that rarely works. There is nothing wrong with instructional designers doing a skills analysis within jobs, but the detail work on skills should remain within the training organization.

Other educators like to deal in *competencies*. Here is a sample list of competencies for partners in a management-consulting firm: Leadership, goal setting, delegation, teamwork, coaching, motivation, financial management, risk management, marketing, human resource management, business planning and development, quality, negotiations, selling engagements, presentations, project management, engagement management, knowledge of industry or segment, competitive knowledge, technology, performance-improvement methods, global perspective, continuous improvement, problem solving and decision making, innovation and creativity, new service development, effective writing, market knowledge, and risk taking.

When you see a list of thirty competencies, there usually are ten to fifteen courses required over a period of three to five years to teach them. Once again, it sounds like the logical thing to do, but it is usually a failure. Most students, whether employee, manager, or executive, are poor at integrating the lessons from several courses into a business process or a management system. They may not use the lessons learned in a course on effective presentations in a course on selling engagements. Therefore, most employees attend the various courses and go right back to doing tasks based on common sense rather than on best practices.

Instead, a professional educator should focus only on the *major tasks that will improve performance.* For the management-consulting position above, these might be defined as follows:

1. Develop and enhance relationships within client organizations.
2. Sell engagements to increase revenues.
3. Manage engagements to achieve revenue.
4. Develop new service lines for consulting engagements to grow the business.
5. Manage staff members in the selling and engagement processes.

All thirty competencies can be taught in three or four integrated courses that are directly focused on the five major tasks of the job. For example, lessons on effective presentations would be presented within the contexts of creating interest during the selling cycle and presenting a proposal. The lessons on effective presentation would be reinforced in the course on how to manage an engagement. Through this reinforcement, performance-based training is more likely to have a direct impact on the organization's operating and financial results.

Competencies must be focused on accomplishments required of a top performer, rather than on behaviors. Just generating a list of competencies is easy. The challenge is to convert the competencies into major accomplishments that will result in performance and profit objectives.

Rebuilding Employee Trust

In hundreds of organizations, the executive management team has lost credibility. Trust has hit rock bottom, and the workforce is afraid of the future. When trust is low, employees start to think of survival, productivity falls, and customer service declines.

One by-product of using the Systems Approach is that trust is rebuilt between employees, managers, and the executive team. Employees and managers learn that the performance system for each key job is driven by the strategic directions and tactical decisions of executive management. If the workers disagree with executive decisions, there is immediate feedback from the training sessions, which is part of the process of continuous improvement.

A sensitive executive team will quickly review the negative feedback and make adjustments, which drives up trust. In most situations, employees and managers accept the new strategic directions and tactical decisions as improvements to overall operations, and trust improves even more.

Determining Key Jobs

When determining key jobs, it is important to have a working partnership between the training organization and line management. The training and performance department should provide line management with guidelines such as:

1. Break your workforce into a manageable number of key jobs. (For example, IBM had eighty key jobs when they did this exercise; a leading CPA firm had forty-four; GE could have over three hundred because of their diversified businesses).
2. Almost every organization has approximately six key jobs in finance and accounting; five key jobs in administration; eight key jobs in HR; and seven key jobs within information systems.
3. Some areas such as service will probably be organized around the key-job concept already. Usually the challenge is greater in areas such as product development, engineering, manufacturing, and research.
4. The basic rule is: what breakdown allows the employees to have an embraceable responsibility based on a curriculum of courses and a support system.

There is always a concern that there will be an overlap between jobs. For example, systems engineers, application programmers, and systems programmers all need basic programming skills. Although these three jobs sound quite similar, their performance requirements are really quite different, except for a few entry-level courses. Without a specific job focus, there would probably be a middle-of-the-road curriculum with a bland set of lessons, plus great confusion on who should attend the various classes. With a job focus, we know that the personnel in each of these three jobs will be properly trained. The line executives should have a major voice in approval of what the major job categories are within their areas of responsibility.

Planning Training for Teams

Too many organizations have decided that training is not as important if they use teams of employees. That is a serious mistake. Each member of a team must be trained on some teamwide tasks plus what each member must know and be able to do within their own job. In many teams, each player has different job responsibilities. Most teams have some members who are well-trained top-performers. Others are simply trying to do what they think is important, but they are essentially untrained poor performers who can destroy the team's morale and productivity.

The phrase "high-performance teams" has acquired great status in recent years, but it is a theory in most organizations rather than a reality. The U.S. Department of Labor's Office of the American Workplace (*The Business of Training*, 1994) has recently defined nine characteristics of high-performance workplaces:

1. *Provide training and continuous learning* for all employees, shown by at least a 5 percent investment of payroll in training.
2. *Share information* throughout the organization, such as strategic plans, operating plans, and financial data.
3. *Build employee participation* into the organizational structure with ideas such as self-managed work teams and process-improvement groups, sometimes referred to as "empowered" employees.
4. *Maintain flat organizational structures* by reducing the number of layers between executive management and front-line workers.
5. *Encourage partnerships* between workers, managers, unions, and company management to focus on service, quality, or another area.
6. *Link pay to performance* with such things as gain sharing, profit sharing, or employee stock ownership.

7. *Shun layoffs* except as a last resort. Instead, use methods such as redeployment, job sharing, and part-time work.
8. *Offer a supportive work environment* with benefits such as flexible work schedules and child-care resources, as well as job aids and support systems.
9. *Integrate all of these practices* into an organization's long-term strategy.

Keep in mind all of these good intentions will not happen without a management system such as the one described in Chapter Three. Many teams have also failed because of insufficient coaching, unrealistic expectations, poor schedules, and poor communication.

On the other hand, some teams have been great successes. Each unique job within the team has been studied to be certain that the appropriate training and support systems have been developed. The teams that seem to achieve productivity breakthroughs are the ones that combine personnel from several operating or functional units to achieve a goal. For example, Boeing created a team of engineers, accountants, programmers, manufacturing personnel, and logistical experts to create the new 777 jet airlines.

Other Jobs

It is not economically feasible to do a needs analysis and develop a performance system for every job in the organization. Low-volume jobs such as photographer, cafeteria staff, attorney, or public relations staff do not warrant the full process. The training and performance organization should work with each group to help them select job aids, basic support systems, personal-development assignments, and workshops that will enable them to improve group or individual performance.

Performance is important to every employee. Therefore, all organizational areas need the professional support of the training and performance department, but some may receive only a half-dozen days of advice, while the manufacturing area may have a full-time team of performance consultants, instructional designers, and instructors.

Voids and Duplications

When the chief training officer starts establishing a working partnership with line executives to increase workforce performance, the training organization should expect to find significant voids in the system as well as duplicate programs. Usually, there is a void in the training department itself. Instructors, course developers, and instruction managers usually have received very little training. The support systems are not in place. There also will be many duplicate courses, delivery systems, administrative systems, and recognition programs. The same will be true for all areas of the organization.

After the working partnership has been established between the training department and line executives and executive management, there will be a need to build or modify the curriculum of courses and support systems, which is a performance system for each major job category.

Chapter Six

Enhance or Reengineer the Basic Processes

In their best-selling book, *Reengineering the Corporation* (1993), Michael Hammer and James Champy highlighted the need to focus on the basic processes within an organization, which they defined as "a collection of activities that takes one or more kinds of input and creates an output that is of value to the customer." Unfortunately, most executives and managers simply are not process-oriented. They pay attention to goals, objectives, strategies, operating plans, events, tasks, functions, or departments, but they rarely focus on their key processes.

Most manufacturing companies have an engineering process, a manufacturing process, a purchasing process, a marketing process, a selling process, and a service process. All companies have a financial process, information-systems process, human resources process, and a training-performance process, if they apply the Systems Approach for Workforce Performance. A mail-order business has a merchandising process, an order processing process, a credit process, and a catalog-distribution process. Each industry has its own set of processes.

In his 1996 book, *Beyond Reengineering,* Michael Hammer described how the process-centered organization is changing our work and lives. Hammer said that horizontal, end-to-end processes, such as product development and order processing, should become the permanent organizational structures to which all work is attached. Periodically, reengineering has been viewed as a one-time event. Some critics believe that Hammer failed to address the human side of reengineering, an aspect that the Systems Approach for Workforce Performance accommodates. It should be noted again that reengineering projects require management systems for employee performance. Processes lead to results, which is why a process-oriented organization is so powerful.

Dr. Deming (1986) has made it clear that most problems stem from the basic process, not from individual performance. When Adam Smith convinced managers to break work into its simplest tasks, managers focused exclusively on the individual tasks, such as creating the purchase order, expediting the order, or paying the invoice. But if the overall process is not competitive and fails to achieve organizational objectives, individual tasks will not be on target. The intense focus today on competition and cost-effectiveness mandates a shift from task management to process management.

Improving the Process

When management evaluates worker performance during the later stages of the Systems Approach for Workforce Performance, the solutions for improvement may lie in either *enhancing* or *reengineering* the basic business process, rather than in additional training or support systems for individuals. Basic processes must be changed frequently today to adapt to marketplace fluctuations, new government regulations, greater demands by customers, increased competition, advancing technologies, and new levels of expected performance.

Enhancing and Reengineering

In most situations, the organization fine-tunes (enhances) the existing process. The Japanese call this method "kaizen," which means continuous incremental improvement in a task or process. The quality movement is an example, with the aim for the steady incremental improvement of an organization's basic processes. The second approach is reengineering.

A number of excellent books are available on business process enhancement. Bob Mager and Peter Pipe (1984) wrote one such text entitled *Analyzing Performance Problems*. Their remedies include removing obstacles, offering on-the-job training, offering formal training, or changing job procedures. Sometimes a combination of these can improve the performance of an individual or an entire team.

Performance Consulting by Dana Gaines Robinson and James C. Robinson (1995) features a performance relationship map that enables performance consultants to design complete front-end performance assessments based on business needs. The Robinsons agree with Geary Rummler, "Pit a good employee against a bad system, and the system will win most every time." They also agree that the methodologies and procedures the employee uses on the job determine whether he or she will use the lessons and skills obtained at formal training events.

The Robinsons have determined, from studying numerous organizations, that there are multiple causes for performance deficiencies, although too many other educators believe that performance problems stem from only one cause—an unrealistic perspective. Most situations involve both individual employees with performance problems and processes that cause performance problems. Process problems can include the following:

- Lack of resources to do the job completely.
- Procedures not documented in detail.
- Insufficient feedback on completed tasks.
- Lack of complete database information.
- Inaccurate data.
- Data not available when needed.
- "Turf problems" within the organization.
- Lack of coordination with other work groups.
- No reliable method to determine job results.
- Inadequate administrative support.
- Conflicting directions, both verbal and written.

This list could go on and on. If basic process problems go uncorrected, an organization will not receive a payback from their formal training programs or support systems. Some people refer to these basic process problems as "work environment factors." Companies must identify and correct these environmental factors in order to close performance gaps. The Robinsons believe that performance consultants should conduct cause analysis to identify deficiencies in both skill and knowledge, as well as work environment. To accomplish this, performance consultants must identify external and internal weaknesses that created the work environment factors and discouraged desired performance.

In 1994, Richard A. Swanson's book, *Analysis for Improving Performance,* featured an easy-to-follow systems approach for performing diagnostic work. Swanson's method results in an accurate identification of actual and desired *organizational processes* and *individual performance levels.* His approach also specifies interventions needed to improve performance. He believes that performance diagnosis requires intellect, experience, effort, and methodologies. Clearly, bright people with extensive work experience make the best diagnosticians.

One of the most famous books on enhancing processes is *Improving Performance: How to Manage the White Space on the Organizational Chart"* by Geary Rummler and Alan Brache (1995). Throughout the book, the authors focus on three aspects of performance: the *organization,* the *process,* and the *job performer.* Within an organization, individuals perform and manage processes. Rummler and Brache believe the greatest opportunities for performance improvement often lie in the "functional interface"— the points at which departments pass the job baton to each other. For example, when engineering passes the design of a new product to manufacturing, engineering and manufacturing have a functional interface. These transition points are also referred to as the "silo phenomenon" because each department is separate from the others.

Most performance problems can be fixed by enhancing current methods, procedures, training programs, on-the-job training assignments, and support systems. It is hard, but very rewarding work. It is also essential if a company wants to move on to more extensive projects, such as implementing formal training and support systems.

Another important time to enhance existing processes is when new strategic directions or major tactical decisions are agreed to by senior executives. First, the organization should modify its basic processes to meet the new business requirements. For example, if two sales organizations are merged into one, the process of each must be modified so that one consolidated group of sales representatives can successfully achieve the annual sales quota. This may require rewriting a sales manual, implementing new recognition programs, designing new measurement systems, and creating new administrative systems. This is Step 2 in the Systems Approach for Workforce Performance.

Second, the organization needs to follow Step 3 of the Systems Approach. The people and jobs affected by the decision must be identified, along with what needs to be done differently. For example, the consolidated sales representatives may be asked to call on other types of customers. They may need training on an entirely new product line. New selling strategies may require additional training. Administrative personnel will also need training on new procedures to enable the consolidated sales force to be effective.

All this sounds so simple and straightforward that one wonders why more companies and government agencies do not undertake Steps 2 and 3 of the Systems Approach based on common sense. Unfortunately, many important strategic and tactical decisions are implemented by companies that do not enhance the basic processes or change their key jobs' performance requirements. When performance problems start to appear, quite often, large sums of money are thrown at the training organization. The executives want a crash training program or a quick-and-dirty course to "fix" the performance problems. Because of this tendency, it is essential not to skip steps but to use all six steps of the System Approach for Workforce Performance to ensure that the basic processes are enhanced and the required modifications to the performance systems are implemented.

Step 2 in the Systems Approach for Workforce Performance is the place where some people call performance technologists to do much of their work. They redesign jobs, work processes, and the work environment during Step 2 of the Systems Approach, then assume that the task is complete. An effective workforce performance analysis does not start with the observation of a company's top performers; it starts with a thorough understanding of the company's business objectives. Successful performance technologists continually look for interventions that will enhance the basic process and overall workforce performance.

Reengineering Business Processes

In the 1990s, an entirely new concept for achieving breakthroughs in productivity has been developed called reengineering. A far cry from enhancing or fine-tuning business processes, reengineering involves starting over with a blank sheet of paper and redesigning the process completely. This concept is a bold leap forward because one must forget the past and create an entirely new process. Reengineering requires great innovation and creativity, and it results in a radical change rather than a series of incremental improvements.

Enhancing a process usually involves only one goal, whereas reengineering involves multiple goals such as do it faster, cheaper, and better. The overall goal of reengineering is to achieve a strategic advantage within the industry.

There are many great stories of how organizations have achieved major breakthroughs in productivity by reengineering a basic process; there are also many stories of failures. The difference often is because organizations fail to train employees and managers on the new procedures and methods. Few reengineering books discuss training the workforce. In most cases, the authors write just a few sentences or a few paragraphs on the subject, which is why many reengineering teams fail to include adequate training and support systems with their breakthrough solutions and plans of action If they were using a management system such as the Systems Approach, they would not skip such a crucial step in the reengineering process.

In their book, *Reengineering the Corporation,* Hammer and Champy (1993) make the point that the crisis will not go away. They say that almost every basic process within every organization needs to be reengineered, not just fine-tuned, especially any work requiring cooperation and coordination of several departments. With new electronic information systems and new organizational methods available, most of today's work flows need to be reengineered.

The new methods for increasing productivity are analogous to what happened in agriculture and manufacturing. In 1800, it took nearly 90 percent of the American workforce to provide food for a nation of fewer than eighty million people. In 1995, only a little over 1 percent of Americans work in agriculture, even though the United States has grown to a population in excess of 260 million. This transformation did not take place just because of hard work and good intentions. Farming was reengineered with new knowledge, new inventions, new technologies, and a systems approach.

Today, Russian farms operate the way American farms did a century ago. Russian agricultural methods have reached the upper limits of efficiency. No matter how hard the Russian laborers work or how much money the government offers for increased production, the outputs of Russian farms will remain the same year after year. Needless to say, Russia needs to reengineer its agricultural industry.

Manufacturing went through a similar transformation. Decades ago, job shops with individual craftsmen manufactured most products. Eventually, these shops reached the "upper limits" of their productivity. The assembly line was the output of a reengineering effort that provided great improvements in productivity.

Today, businesses and government agencies are under great pressure to achieve breakthroughs in cost, quality, and service. Fine-tuning existing processes is always helpful, but it will not achieve the aggressive goals managers are setting to achieve productivity breakthroughs.

The public schools are a great example. In 1983, the Secretary of Education published the "A Nation at Risk" report stating that our school system was in serious trouble. Since 1983, there have been hundreds of reports on how to fix the public school system. Almost all of them have recommended quick-fix and feel-good solutions that would fine-tune the existing operational methods. These quick fixes have doubled the cost of education from $150 billion to $300 billion. The problem is that the current school systems use the same teaching methods that were used a century ago in most classrooms. These methods have reached the upper limits of efficiency.

Classroom methods must be reengineered. New electronic tutoring and administrative systems must be implemented. A new integrated curriculum must be designed; new learning systems must be developed. This transformation requires a massive retraining of teachers and school administrators. To achieve the learning breakthroughs that everyone wants, a Systems Approach for Workforce Performance must be applied to the public school system.

Nearly every government agency and corporation needs to be reengineered. This renovation will take many years, and the results will probably fall into three categories. The first category will include organizations in deep trouble or ones that are mandated by government regulations and laws to change.

The second category will feature companies and government agencies that are not in deep trouble yet, but their executive teams view change as inevitable. For example, today's leaders of many public utilities see the day when their industry will be deregulated just as the telephone industry was. They are already reengineering their basic processes and are starting to implement the Systems Approach for Workforce Performance.

The third category, currently 1 percent of all organizations, is those leading-edge companies and government agencies that want to remain leaders. One such company is Wal-Mart, which reengineered its basic processes to enhance its competitive position.

Organizations with a workforce with some training have a big job ahead of them. They either have to fine-tune continuously or reengineer their basic processes. As many as 99 percent of organizations need to implement a management system like the Systems Approach for Workforce Performance.

Of course, an organization can continue to use old methods and procedures while they implement the Systems Approach. A better-trained workforce with improved support systems will increase productivity and employee satisfaction, even with old processes. The ideal solution, however, is for an organization to enhance or reengineer its basic business process *before* it invests in new training and support systems.

In either case, the training and performance department has the responsibility to design training programs and support systems to achieve mastery of learning and performance. Training and performance department leaders must champion the cause of fine-tuning or of reengineering their organizations' basic processes. They have much to contribute to this work effort. The chief training officer must be a proven change leader and a respected business executive to help lead this transformation.

Creating the Future

When Gary Hamel and C. K. Prahalad (1994) published their book, *Competing for the Future,* they added another level of performance for executive leadership. Their challenge for the executive team was to stop the unrewarding and ultimately dead-end process of downsizing and to enter a new world of strategic leadership. They write about "finding the future" and "getting to the future first."

An example of this kind of leadership is Toyota. They invented the vision of "lean manufacturing" that gave them a strategic advantage for at least a decade. The concept of news twenty-four hours a day was created by CNN. Creating the future is more challenging than copying the successful strategic programs of a competitor. Senior executives must have a management system like the Systems Approach for Workforce Performance to translate the strategic vision into operating plans.

Role of Executive Leadership

A well-trained competitive workforce with outstanding performance systems also requires outstanding leadership from the ranks of executive management. In the past fifteen years, Americans have been shocked by the problems within some of the great corporations and government agencies. Too often, senior executives failed to react to the changes in the marketplace. Employees and managers continued to work hard, but large percentages of market share were lost in companies such as IBM, GM, Sears, Apple Computer, Singer, Kmart, Westinghouse, Digital, International Harvester, and Bendix. Some great companies such as RCA, Eastern Airlines, and Pan American even cease to exist. All of these companies had serious executive leadership problems. Their workforces continued business as usual when new strategic directions should have been implemented.

Too often, senior executives in large organizations feel it is almost impossible to change direction. Not true. The Systems Approach allows large- and intermediate-size organizations to be quite flexible. The vast majority of managers and employees will follow their executive leadership as it flows through Steps 1, 2, and 3 of the Systems Approach for Workforce Performance.

Recently, people have questioned the amount of compensation and stock options earned by some CEOs and other senior executives. Based on the performance of companies in trouble, managers and employees should want a successful CEO and should be willing to pay for him or her. In fact, the workforce should say, "Do anything and pay any price for the top performing senior executives because they bring growth, wage increases, training, and promotional opportunities to us all." Poor performing executives bring downsizing, layoffs, salary freezes, wage decreases, and intolerable working conditions.

Chapter Seven

Identify Performance Requirements of Key Jobs

Performance requirements for key jobs are missing in almost all organizations today. After reviewing their strategic directions and business objectives, executives need to identify what they want their employees to know and be able to do.

It sounds like such a simple thing to do. In fact, it sounds so simple that many line executives and managers believe it must have been done years ago. Workers seem to know what they are doing. After all, very few employees come into their offices asking what they should know or do. In reality, most employees and supervisors work hard every day doing business-as-usual tasks and assume that their executives want nothing more.

A well-known company's CEO asked me once, "What in the world are all those people doing every day? I hope it's helping our bottom line." Another executive told me, "Sometimes I wonder if I'm just paying people to play with their personal computers." Almost every senior executive believes that too many employees are working on nonproductive tasks. Yet, first-line supervisors and middle managers often complain about a lack of resources and point out the need for more qualified employees. Quite often, the biggest complainers get the most resources.

Responsibility for Workforce Performance

In many organizations, an HR representative works with a line manager to develop a *job description,* the primary purpose of which is to determine a level of compensation. In most situations, after

HR files the job description, neither the first-line supervisor nor the employee ever reviews it again. As a result, the job description has little impact on actual job performance.

A compensation expert assigns each job a *compensation level,* which determines minimum earnings, maximum earnings, and possible merit increases. Most employees know very little about their company's compensation systems unless they are under a union contract. Only managers and supervisors receive training on this important subject, which often has a major impact on job performance. Compensation is usually more influenced by years of service than by level of job performance.

Then a *performance-management system* is created, with procedures and forms. Usually, an outside HR consulting firm assists an internal HR expert with this, but first-line supervisors and managers ultimately administer the annual performance appraisals.

Another HR specialist develops *recognition programs,* using firmwide guidelines on who, how much, and when to recognize. Quite often, recognition is reserved only for individual heroic efforts. Teams quite often never receive the recognition they deserve.

The training department is responsible for the *transfer of knowledge and skills.* Unfortunately, they may hardly look at job descriptions and recognition programs. Sometimes they create job aids, but rarely conduct a comprehensive review of support-system requirements. They focus on training events rather than on employee performance within a major job category. In most large organizations, training and HR programs operate in costly uncoordinated worlds filled with split responsibilities.

The line supervisor is usually responsible for *on-the-job training* assignments which, in too many cases, are unstructured and not measured. Companies rarely coordinate their formal training events and their on-the-job training assignments because each supervisor develops his or her own on-the-job training program.

Sometimes, the line supervisor also creates *basic support systems.* In large organizations, corporate staffs may perform this work. However, many corporate staffs have been eliminated, so new support systems rarely exist today.

The employee is usually responsible for *personal-development tasks,* which means no two employees learn the same set of lessons. Many employees never do a personal-development task, while a few, who are ambitious about their careers, may attend a variety of courses at education centers or community colleges. They may also enroll in self-study programs and read numerous books.

To make matters worse, first-line supervisors rarely reinforce any of these lessons, so "business as usual" pervades the work environment. Split responsibility becomes no responsibility. Employees do not produce at optimum levels. Current operating objectives are unachievable because no one is assigned to do a detailed study on what the organization wants the employees within each major job category to know and be able to do.

All these tasks, programs, and people who share performance responsibility work hard every day, spend the company's money, incur expenses, and try to do the best they can. However, this system outdates itself once an organization decides to achieve mastery of learning and performance to lower its operating expenses.

In recent years, many organizations have tried to resolve this problem by telling employees that they can empower themselves to achieve optimum performance. In most organizations, the employees are just told that they are now empowered, but no one in management tells them exactly what they are empowered to do.

A few employees try to do something different once they hear that they are empowered, but management often criticizes them for being different. Managing empowered people requires an entirely different supervision style. Supervisors must relinquish certain areas of responsibility, while letting employees try new ideas on a trial-and-error basis.

Eventually, the bell-shaped curve takes over. Some employees like being empowered and make good decisions that help the organization. Others drift along doing business as usual; still others make costly errors and decisions. In short, empowered workforces rarely achieve mastery of learning and performance.

Self-directed teams represent another effort to fix the performance problems caused by split responsibility. If properly implemented, self-directed teams ask what they need to know and be able to do, then work with the various departments to create training programs, develop support systems, design job aids, create recognition programs, and design a performance-management system that matches their team's job requirements.

Otherwise, teams continue to do business as usual. The executives are not upset because they were just looking for teamwork rather than breakthroughs in workforce performance.

High-performing teams work well together with a positive attitude; they communicate well while taking great pride in their work. The team leader ensures that tasks are completed even if it means working overtime. The top-performing team members make up for the poor performers. Teams can improve an organization, but they will not bring about a workforce productivity breakthrough unless they implement the Systems Approach for Workforce Performance.

Responsibility for Workforce Performance

Clearly, line supervisors must continue to be responsible for their employees' performance, but they need help. They are not experts on needs assessments, front-end analysis, personal-development assignments, curriculum design, course development, cost-effective delivery systems, performance measurements, support systems, knowledge systems, on-the-job training assignments, and recognition programs. Besides, they already have a full-time job: supervising employees.

For this reason, every large- and intermediate-size organization needs a full-time department to focus on workforce performance. The chief training officer must create a department of specialists who work with line executives on each major job category. The department's goal is to achieve breakthroughs in workforce performance. Accomplishing this objective will reduce operating expenses, raise morale, lower attrition rates, increase revenues, increase market share, and raise earnings.

To achieve such breakthroughs, the CTO must first identify the key job categories within the organization, as described in Chapters Three and Five. Then, the CTO must appoint a training and performance department representative, a performance consultant, to be in charge of one or more job categories.

Role of a Performance Consultant

Think of the performance consultant as the architect of performance, who integrates the various elements that comprise the Systems Approach for Workforce Performance. This new position emerges when the focus of training shifts from successful training events to improved workforce performance. The performance consultant must receive training in the following areas:

Industry Knowledge. The performance consultant must know the industry extensively to command the respect of line executives and subject-matter experts. The performance consultant should know what the latest strategic directions are and the most current issues facing the industry. He or she should attend industry seminars and read industry publications.

Organizational Knowledge. The performance consultant must be a student of the business, whether it is a commercial company, a government agency, or a not-for-profit organization. He or she must understand the organizational structure and build relationships with key executives. Of course, he or she must understand all of the company's strategic directions and tactical decisions. Eventually, he or she should be included in meetings when the major decisions are discussed and finalized.

Consulting Skills. Performance consultants should receive training in diagnostic analysis, problem solving, analytic competence, questioning, listening, handling objections, negotiations, presentations, persuasion, partnering skills, and technical subjects. The most effective consultants also possess leadership skills, because performance consultants who just take orders from line management perform at a below-average job level.

Training and Support Systems. Performance consultants must have a management system in order to be proactive. Too many performance consultants work in a reactive mode, waiting for the telephone to ring. To be effective, they need to know how to do a needs and task analysis, select or modify available courses, and choose the most cost-effective delivery systems. They also need to design job aids and support systems and be considered experts at performance analysis. They are the architects of performance systems.

Create and Manage Change. With the emphasis now placed on reengineering, performance consultants must receive training on how to systematically create and manage change.

Human Resource Development Processes. Because the training and HR departments interact continually, performance consultants need knowledge and training in job descriptions, compensation programs, career planning, recognition programs, industrial relations, benefits, and management development.

Because this is an emerging field, university programs are not usually available for training, although some universities do offer courses in performance technology. Dana and James Robinson, in their 1995 book, *Performance Consulting: Moving Beyond Training,* provide some valuable information on performance consulting. Their consulting firm, Partners in Change, Inc., offers seminars on the subject. Today, every company or government agency that needs performance consultants should develop a customized training program for this new position that integrates books, seminars, courses, and job experiences.

Line managers and supervisors should view performance consultants as partners in achieving performance breakthroughs, and performance consultants should establish working partnerships with the line executives who are in charge of the job categories for which they have responsibility. Every senior line executive should have one to five performance consultants working on his or her area of responsibility to ensure that the key job categories are achieving maximum productivity.

The performance consultant is not an entry-level position; management experience should be a prerequisite. The individual must be well-respected both within the training and performance department and within the line organization. With the right candidate, this position can have a great impact on an organization's operating measurements.

In progressive companies, the performance-consulting group is replacing the requirements department, which was traditionally responsible for determining what courses should be developed and how many students should attend each course. This department was also responsible for having the right events scheduled to train the employees.

Today's performance consultants have an advantage over traditional requirements departments because they work with line executives to achieve maximum workforce performance. To do their job effectively, performance consultants determine requirements for personal-development assignments, formal training courses, on-the-job training programs, support systems, knowledge systems, and rewards or recognition programs designed to motivate the employees. Performance consultants can reduce the training and developing costs for employees to achieve mastery of learning and performance because they use a cost-effective approach to performance instead of relying on expensive classroom training events.

The concept is new, but it has one great advantage. The performance consultant is clearly the one responsible for the continuous improvement of performance within a major job category. Thus, split responsibility is eliminated. The job can be measured and rewarded. The importance of this new position within the training and performance department will grow over the years until the outstanding performance consultants will earn six-figure incomes.

Integrated Development Effort

Too many organizations develop the components of their performance system at different times. For example, one year they may develop two new courses for a major job category, then provide job aids the following year and a basic support system in another. Unfortunately, students are not great systems integrators, so the lessons never tie together into a performance system.

Because of this tendency, a performance consultant needs to be the grand architect of the overall system. This person must ensure that the system possesses all of the following components:

1. Performance requirements to be achieved by an employee or team.
2. Personal-development assignments.
3. Curriculum of performance-based courses.
4. On-the-job training assignments.
5. Basic support systems.
6. Integrated performance-support systems, if necessary.
7. Reward and recognition systems.

The Systems Approach for Workforce Performance ties together all of these components into a performance system. An integrated approach reduces the cost of training and support systems and increases workforce performance.

Determining Performance Requirements

The performance consultant begins the process by working with line executives to fully understand the business or government agency's objectives. As shown in Figure 7.1, he or she must understand the following five inputs:

- Customer requirements.
- Regulatory requirements.
- Strategic visions.
- Competitive requirements.
- Union contracts.

The performance consultant should be involved in Step 2 when the basic process is enhanced or reengineered based on the latest strategic or tactical decisions. The performance consultant cannot move on to Step 3, converting the business or government agency requirements into performance requirements, until he or she fully understands all the inputs that went into creating the objectives.

The line executives probably will not be precise on what they want their employees to know and be able to do. For example, they may want the sales account executives to call on customer executives. The performance consultant will need to convert that request into precise performance requirements, including items such as developing and enhancing their relationships with customer executives and influencing customers' buying decisions.

The list of performance requirements for each major job category could be five to twenty-five statements long. After developing a list, the performance consultant should meet with exemplary employees to determine what they do well. For example, the consultant may discover that all account executives are able to identify their customer executives. Some account executives may be able to secure an appointment for a meeting, but only a few might be capable of having a meaningful discussion with senior customer executives. Given this information, a knowledgeable consultant

Figure 7.1. Systems Approach for Workforce Performance.

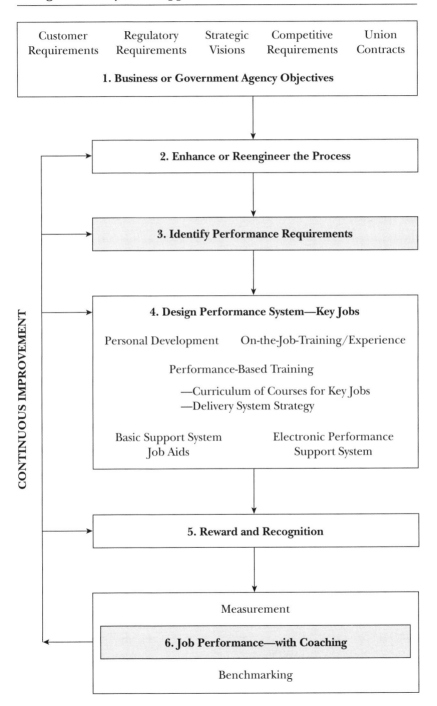

would realize that a performance gap exists in terms of influencing the buying decision.

The proposed solution for closing this gap could entail the account executives reading the books and magazines that customer executives read so the two groups can have more meaningful conversations. One company created the President's Class, a two-week course revolving around Harvard Business School case studies that teach senior-executive subjects such as strategic planning. The account executives were trained on how to call on senior executives. The account executives may also need a job aid for developing and enhancing their relationships with customer executives.

Thus, the performance consultant must do some front-end analysis to determine what the company wants its employees to know and be able to do. Robert Mager developed methods for front-end analysis and in 1970 wrote a book with Peter Pipe entitled *Analyzing Performance Problems.* Other front-end analysis books include Joe Harless' *An Ounce of Analysis Is Worth a Pound of Objectives* (1980), G. A. Rummler and A. P. Brache's *Improving Performance: How to Manage the White Space on the Organizational Chart* (1995), and H. D. Stolovitch and E. J. Keeps' *Handbook of Human Performance Technology: A Comprehensive Guide for Analyzing and Solving Performance Problems in Organizations* (1992). The new *Guidebook for Performance Improvement* (1997) by R. Kaufman, L. Thiagarajan, and P. MacGillis is also a good source. In 1997, ASTD published a new binder by Joe Harless, *Analyzing Human Performance: Tools for Achieving Business Results,* which provides the latest thinking by one of the leaders in this field. If a training department adds these books to its library, plus *Performance Consulting* by the Robinsons, it should have no trouble developing a customized program for determining performance requirements.

Once the performance requirements are determined, line managers and executives must approve them. Then and only then should the performance consultant decide how knowledge and skills will be transferred to employees. Again, there are several ways to accomplish this task:

- Personal-development assignments.
- On-the-job training.
- Formal training courses.

- Support systems.
- Integrated electronic performance support systems.

The performance consultant takes this information, which is analogous to an architect's book of specifications, and turns it over to the people who will create courses, document on-the-job training courses, develop support systems, or build an integrated electronic performance-support system.

Like an architect, the performance consultant stays involved as the subcontractors build the performance system's components. After the entire performance system is implemented, the performance consultant reviews all the measurements and job evaluations to determine how it can be enhanced. These reviews are a continuous process designed to achieve maximum performance from the employees and managers. The performance consultant is responsible for the quality, cost, and effectiveness of the performance system. The goal is simple: design and implement a performance system for every major job category that achieves maximum productivity of the workforce with a minimum number of employees to do the job and a minimum amount of resources to implement the system.

A performance consultant can handle more than one major job category. For example, one performance consultant may handle seven jobs within information systems. In the sales function, one performance consultant may be needed for the external sales personnel, and one performance consultant may be assigned to the systems engineers who support the sales personnel.

Two Worlds of Performance Consulting

As organizations evolve to this new system of performance improvement, there are really two major methods for making progress. In many cases, a performance consultant responds to small performance problems within job categories. For example, the director of administration might be concerned because there are so many errors on the invoices. The performance consultant would investigate this problem and recommend a solution within the framework of the Systems Approach.

If the recommended solution involves new methods or procedures, that would be added to Step 2 (Figure 7.1). If the solution calls for a modification to the performance requirements, it is done in Step 3. In most situations, the performance system in Step 4 will be changed or, in a few cases, the rewards and recognition programs must be modified. This systematic approach is far different from putting a patch on the procedure manual or throwing another course into the training catalog.

When the training department is reengineered to focus on workforce performance, the performance consultant will develop the performance system (Step 4) and the reward and recognition programs (Step 5) based on the performance requirements of Step 3 within the Systems Approach for Workforce Performance. It is not practical to use this top-down approach with a partnership of line executives on every major job category at once. All this must be phased in over time, with the performance consultant being a leader of the process.

Needs Assessment

Once the performance consultants determine the performance requirements, they should go one step further by doing a needs assessment to identify any gaps between the desired outputs of a job and the current output. The performance consultant then determines, by priority, how best to meet these needs. Roger Kaufman of Florida State University, an expert on this subject, wrote a book with Alicia Rojas and Hanna Mayer entitled *Needs Assessment: A User's Guide* (1993). Allison Rossett of San Diego State University also wrote a terrific book on this subject, *Training Needs Assessment* (1987).

The needs assessment will often highlight three or four key areas. First, it will tell the performance consultant and line executives if the work flow is designed to achieve optimum performance. If not, then the company must go back to Step 2 of the Systems Approach. The needs assessment also determines if problems exist within the reward and recognition programs. If so, the performance consultant will need to work on Step 5. The needs assessment will then determine if the company has a requirement for formal training events or on-the-job training assignments. Finally, the needs assessment will highlight what support systems are required.

In this emerging world of workforce performance, all tasks are not allocated the same way. Often, instructional designers (described in the next chapter) perform needs assessments. The title of the person doing the work is not as important as ensuring that the work is performed. All major job categories should have a needs assessment that is updated whenever new strategic decisions and tactical action plans are implemented.

If a company implements the steps of the Systems Approach for Workforce Performance, senior executives will not be concerned about employees doing nonproductive work. For the first time, an organization will be able to articulate the exact tasks that are being performed by every major job category; the training and support systems required to achieve optimum performance; and the true cost of people to do effective work.

In many organizations, the Systems Approach lowers both the cost of labor and the cost of training. Companies achieve mastery of learning and performance with a minimum of employees and managers. In turn, they attain optimum performance at the lowest possible cost.

The next section of this book contains descriptions of the people needed to build the essential components of the Systems Approach for Workforce Performance.

Part Three

Design a Performance System for Key Jobs

A performance system may be as simple as a guideline on how to do a job, or it might include a basic job aid or recommended reading. However, the vast majority of job categories require a combination of personal-development tasks, on-the-job training assignments, performance-based training courses, and support systems such as job aids and knowledge systems.

In recent years, integrated electronic performance support systems (EPSS) have led to breakthroughs in workforce performance. Designing any performance system, electronic or not, is a continuous process, just as a manufacturing system must be enhanced continually with new equipment and procedures.

Chapter Eight

Design Personal-Development Tasks and a Performance-Based Curriculum

After implementing the lessons from Part Two, a company must convert its performance requirements into a performance system, a massive task that requires the leadership of a chief training officer and key members of his or her staff. The architectural design was done in Chapter Seven. Now it is time to build or buy each element of the performance system, starting with personal-development tasks.

Personal-Development Tasks

Before a performance consultant rushes into developing a curriculum of personal-development courses, low-cost opportunities should be researched. The following employee-development courses are probably available in most larger organizations: Company orientation, including history and traditions, goal setting, understanding the business, speed reading, effective business writing, telephone skills, basic presentation skills, statistics, decision making, use of a personal computer, keyboarding, word processing, graphics, databases, spreadsheets, business fundamentals and basic economics, fundamentals of quality, basic electronics, finance for the nonfinancial person, project management, handling change, teamwork, conflict resolution, problem solving, business mathematics, product development, basics of manufacturing, sexual harassment, diversity, and a preretirement seminar, to name only a few. Usually, from twenty-five to thirty courses are taken by many employees.

Although orientation to the company and preretirement seminars are unique to an organization, most employee-development courses can be purchased from outside course-development companies. Almost every job category requires some of these courses as a base for learning the job.

Earlier in this book, corporate training libraries were discussed. Important periodicals for an organization and industry should be available, along with several hundred books that have been identified by performance consultants for different job categories. The library should not try to duplicate the capabilities of a public library. Usually, only the books, videotapes, periodicals, and brochures necessary to do a job should be included, although a high-tech firm may require a larger library to enable engineers, computer scientists, and programmers to do advanced research. The training and performance department should determine what information is necessary for each major job category to be certain that an organization does not spend hundreds of thousands or millions of dollars in building knowledge systems that are not used by the employees.

Assignment to a task force is another form of employee development that might be recommended by the performance consultant. Temporary assignments are often utilized in some job categories. Or the consultant might recommend that employees attend seminars or conferences sponsored by professional associations.

Performance-Based Training Curriculum

Very few job categories do not require some specific job training, perhaps only one or two courses. For more complex jobs, a series of courses over several months or even several years may be required. These could be formal classroom programs or programs offered in learning centers in which students study individually. As jobs have become more complex in recent years, the number of courses has increased. Frequent changes in performance requirements has also created a demand for more courses.

For many years, instructors worked on course development when they were not teaching a class. They viewed it as filler or part-time work, and most instructors had little or no training in course development.

The usual result of these "quick and dirty" course-development efforts was content-based courses. First, the instructors would decide how much time to allocate for each course. Would it be a one-day, a three-day, or a one-week course? Then instructors filled the time with content.

What really happens in content-based courses is that the instructor gathers all the material that was ever written on a subject—teamwork, for instance. Many articles are copied and placed in large, three-ring binders for the students. The instructor highlights the articles' key messages by using overheads or computer graphics. Between visual aids, the instructor relays "war stories" and jokes to entertain the students. For two or three days, the instructor bombards the class with awareness-level information.

Content-based courses usually contain no job aids, support systems, or on-the-job assignments. Although the students will leave the classroom with a great deal of knowledge, they rarely apply this knowledge on the job because they are not assigned to do so and their supervisors do not reinforce the lessons learned in training. In other words, the students have completed another course that will have little or no impact on their organization's operational and financial results.

Another example of content-based courses is a typical product-training course for sales personnel. The technically trained instructor inundates the sales representatives with facts, specifications, benefits, prices, and technical knowledge. The sales personnel really are overwhelmed by all the information. Usually, they leave class without knowing how to sell the new product because the instructor is not capable of teaching them how to sell. The instructor is usually evaluated on how much information has been provided. For example, in one company they provided fourteen three-ring binders of information, the course was considered to be a smashing success. After all, the sales personnel now had tons of information.

What a waste of time and money most of these content-based courses are for product training! Sales personnel need a performance-based training program that enables them to successfully sell the new products, including both product knowledge and sell-ing lessons. Quite often, there should also be job aids and support systems.

Only in recent years has there been a shift to performance-based courses, an entirely different world. Now the student is expected to learn how to do a job based on new knowledge and skills. Performance-based training is absolutely necessary for stu-dents to achieve mastery of learning and performance.

Instructional Design and Course Development

The science of teaching and learning is called instructional design. It was developed after World War II by the military services' train-ing functions. At that time, weapon systems were becoming quite complicated, and there was no room for failure, so the military ser-vices worked with several graduate schools of education to develop a new instructional system that achieved mastery of learning and performance, rather than a bell-shaped curve.

If a company or government agency is going to develop its own courses, it must hire instructional designers who have master's degrees in that subject or send instructors to a ten-week workshop on instructional design.

Developing courses is like composing music. The vast major-ity of musicians are not great composers. Similarly, only about 5 to 10 percent of instructors become outstanding course devel-opers. Instructional design requires specialized knowledge on principles of adult learning, creativity, logic, strong writing skills, and an understanding of project management methods. Course development is a full-time job in a performance-based training system.

Because the training industry is in a transitional period, job descriptions and assignments for instructional designers vary from one organization to another. In terms of education, performance consultants usually have a major in business and a minor in instruc-tional design. In contrast, instructional designers usually have a minor in business and a major in instructional design. However, many instructional designers today take on the combined roles of performance consulting and instructional design. Instructional designers will earn from $35,000 to $100,000 when they develop performance systems that achieve breakthroughs in workforce performance. Performance consultants and instructional designers are growth areas for people interested in a career in this field.

Deciding Whether to Make, Buy, or Modify

At one time, each organization designed and developed every course within its own training department. The development process became very expensive as the number of required courses grew. Fortunately, a number of course-development companies have emerged. Some of these companies produce off-the-shelf courses for employee-development classes such as listening or time management and basic skills courses on reading, writing, and mathematics. They also develop courses on being a successful supervisor or manager. Recently, they have started producing high-quality job-training courses, but only for large employee populations. These companies have large staffs of instructional designers, graphic experts, assessment specialists, and project managers. Other course-development companies produce custom-made courses for organizations that can afford them or that simply do not have the resources to produce their own unique courses.

Today, a majority of courses are purchased from course-development companies or the buyer asks the course-development companies to modify off-the-shelf courses to its unique requirements. The modification may be simple, such as putting the company's name on the binders, or it may require rewriting up to 25 percent of course materials.

In most organizations today, in-house course developers and instructional designers create only the advance workshops and the truly unique courses, such as product service and repair. Thus, after designing a curriculum a company must render a series of make, buy, or modify decisions to acquire courses in the most cost-effective manner possible.

Instructional-Design Methods

If an organization is going to have cost-effective performance-based courses that achieve mastery of learning and performance, rather than ineffective content-based courses, then it must learn to use instructional-design methods, whether the course is developed in-house or purchased off-the-shelf.

The CTO does not have to be an instructional designer, but should understand the overall methods used by instructional designers. Numerous models exist, but the most commonly used five-step model breaks down as follows:

1. *Analysis.* What do you want the students to know and be able to do after they have completed the curriculum of courses? Here, performance requirements are converted into learning objectives.
2. *Design.* The overall course is designed up to the level of teaching points or lessons.
3. *Development.* All course materials are written, including video and audio scripts. Instructor outlines are documented for classroom courses, or authoring of computer-based training (CBT) courses.
4. *Delivery.* Before the class schedule is released or the course is implemented in a learning center, initial pilot classes and validation tests are conducted to ensure that the students can achieve mastery of learning.
5. *Evaluation.* The course is evaluated on student feedback, student learning, application to the job, and impact on organizational objectives. Continuous improvement is an essential part of the model. All this goes back to Step 1, which was analysis.

Some of the leaders in the field of multimedia course development are now modifying the standard instructional systems design (ISD) model. A few of these leaders believe that the ISD model is too linear for a computer environment in which random-access and nonlinear progression can send a student off into various unrelated learning directions. After all, interactivity is not really a linear process. One thing is certain: Multimedia courses need to follow some form of an ISD model in order to be successful.

Courses can now have more behavior modeling, thanks to the CD-ROM's capacity for audio and video. Learning how to do a task by watching the incorrect way, as well as the correct way, on a video screen enriches the learning process. Advancing technology has now taken many lessons that could be taught only in a classroom and made them available on tutoring systems.

Professors and education specialists, such as Mike Allen, Bob Mager, Walter Dick, Roger Schank, and Allison Rossett, are doing extensive research on instructional-design systems and the principles of adult learning. A dozen universities are doing research projects on this subject. They all stress the need for learning to be interesting and enjoyable.

Adults want practical lessons and almost immediate feedback on how well they are doing in any course. They have no problem committing errors as long as they can make them in private. They also like to learn from subject-matter experts and master teachers. Adult students challenge almost every lesson, and they dislike wasting time. These tendencies all add up to a challenging task for course developers.

Formal Change-Management System

Every so often, an organization will commit to updating the course content, its job aids and support systems. After months of effort, the new curriculum and performance system is implemented with great fanfare. The course developers receive awards based on positive feedback given by students. Then everyone walks away except the instructors who will deliver the same lessons several times a year. What happens next? The course slowly goes out-of-date as the senior executives make new monthly tactical decisions and develop new annual strategic directions that never find their way into the course.

In addition, each instructor modifies the course to achieve better "happiness sheets" at the end of the class. Certain activities are removed, and numerous lessons are dropped. New lessons may be added, but it is a real hit-and-miss situation. Two or three years later, the course developers or instructional designers are shocked when they review the once-great curriculum and performance system.

Each curriculum and the entire performance system for every major job category needs a formal change-management system to ensure continuous improvement. The curriculum coordinator or performance consultant should be designated to review all suggested changes, some of which are valid and should be implemented as soon as possible. Other changes are way off-the-mark and need to be recognized as such. Sometimes a committee of course developers and instructors meets to review suggested course changes.

Rarely can an organization state that all of its courses, curricula, job aids, support systems, and on-the-job assignments are up-to-date. However, this goal is feasible and affordable when a company implements a management system such as the Systems Approach for Workforce Performance.

Mastery of Learning and Performance

Any company takes a giant leap forward when it progresses from a traditional bell-shaped curve to mastery of learning and performance. Organizations take this step because they want to lower operating expenses and increase earnings. They also want to achieve greater customer satisfaction, which often results in increased earnings and additional market share.

Everyone agrees that airline pilots and mechanics should receive performance-based training that aims to achieve mastery of learning and performance. The same is true for people who work in nuclear power plants or do complex medical procedures. After all, these employees perform life-or-death tasks every day.

Although it is not the same type of life-or-death situation, customers enjoy driving automobiles that do not break down. With their emphasis on quality, manufacturers of autos and other goods are moving toward performance mastery. New automobiles can now go 100,000 miles without a tune-up. Television sets last for years without repairs.

In the same vein, we would all like our doctors, dentists, lawyers, tax accountants, financial planners, and pharmacists to achieve mastery of learning and performance. Even when we take a cruise or go to an expensive restaurant, we want our service crew to perform at the mastery level. The quality movement has taught us to expect "first time right" in almost every job category. The bell-shaped curve is just not acceptable to us. All employees in every major job category within an organization are capable of achieving mastery of learning and performance—the new performance standard for the 21st century.

Other Sources for Courses

Companies and government agencies do not have to develop and deliver or purchase all of their own training programs. They can turn to other sources such as community colleges, institutions of higher learning, trade associations, unions, and government-training programs. The chief training officer should encourage the training and performance organization to fully explore the use of these other potential programs, described here.

Institutions of Higher Education

Four-year colleges and universities could play a much larger role in developing programs for job training and development. Many leading universities offer advanced management programs through their graduate business schools. Most of them also have a continuing education department that offers various courses. Although they offer some advanced courses, they rarely have a course curriculum designed specifically for a major job category.

As more organizations name chief training officers, CTOs may have an impact on university curricula. For example, the accounting profession has always had a close working partnership with all of the major accounting schools. These partnerships will probably form in other degree programs.

It is to be hoped that the colleges of education will soon develop a full curriculum and degree program for training and performance personnel; both the private and public sectors will need more performance consultants and instructional designers. If this demand rises, the deans of education will have a golden opportunity to provide more leadership in workforce training.

Trade Associations

Trade associations are always seeking new programs that benefit their members. Although some of them have offered training in the past, most of them have provided books and courses that do not aim for mastery of learning and performance. Only small organizations used their training programs because these companies could not afford any other training source.

However, trade associations have one big advantage: They have thousands of members, so their course-development costs can be divided by thousands of potential students, making the cost per student low and competitive.

Another major advantage is their understanding of what employees need to know and be able to do in order to succeed in their industry. Trade associations need to exploit this advantage by abandoning their focus on generalized employee-development training. They need to focus instead on workforce performance for each major job category within their industry. They also need to implement the Systems Approach for Workforce Performance, aim for mastery of learning and performance, and satisfy the four quality-measurement levels, which will be discussed in Chapter Fifteen.

Trade associations should also investigate cost-effective delivery systems. With members in all fifty states, multimedia tutoring systems and satellite classrooms could be more effective than traditional workshops.

Labor Unions

Some significant changes are taking place in labor unions. One big change has been the new president of the AFL-CIO, John J. Sweeney, who stated, "Our message to American workers is simple but powerful. Whether you wear a blue collar, a white collar, a new collar, or no collar, we can help you make your job better." He also stated, "I want to build bridges between labor and management, so that American business can be more successful, and American workers can share in the gains."

Given these sentiments, the union movement should support job training as a major strategy to accomplish their goals. If every company with union employees had a management system such as the Systems Approach, there would be far less downsizing. Companies would succeed more and, in turn, could afford more wage increases due to growth in revenues, market share, productivity, and earnings.

Like so many other organizations, unions have failed to understand the difference between "nice to do" generalized courses and solid "must do" job-training curricula. They have funded numerous courses that have had little or no impact on workforce performance.

In the future, unions could very well play a major role in job training. For example, in a large city, the Hotel, Restaurant, and

Services Employee Union could offer job training for its entire membership. Although the large chains may not benefit from this training, local hotels and restaurants would certainly take advantage of these meaningful training programs. The union would be helping its members acquire the training they need.

Like everyone else, unions should aim for mastery of learning and performance. This new focus would change their past image of make-work and featherbedding activities, and it would immediately signal that they want their workers to succeed in the new global business world.

Unions could also be helpful in redeploying workers from unsuccessful companies to prosperous and growing ones. They need to be a force for raising their members' performance throughout an entire industry. Workers would then want to join unions so that they could obtain this lifelong job training and greater job security.

Government Sources

The U.S. Department of Labor may emerge as a major contributor to job training and performance. The Reagan administration sponsored a report, "Workforce 2000," that alerted the country to an expected shortage of skilled American workers in the rapidly changing global economy. This led to the Secretary of Labor's Commission on Achieving Necessary Skills (SCANS) under President Bush. In 1994, Congress enacted the National Skill Standards Board. In 1995, President Clinton appointed the members of the National Skill Standards Board. Thus, in three administrations, both Republican and Democratic Secretaries of Labor have focused on how government can provide a structure for establishing standards of performance within major job categories.

The National Skill Standards Board is working with sixteen economic sectors such as manufacturing and retail. Eventually, there will be two types of certificates offered to employees who achieve the required level of knowledge and skills. A *basic certificate* will encompass either the core curriculum alone (if there are no specialist concentrations) or the core plus one concentration level. The *specialty certificate* will cover the knowledge and skills required to be a specialist in one to six areas of concentration.

Outside groups such as trade associations, accredited educational institutions, and training providers will recommend standards for the certificates. The certificates will enable employees to carry their knowledge, skills, experience, and credentials from one employer to another.

This is a classic example of when government leadership is more important than government money. The trade associations should invest their resources to create the courses and performance systems that will enable employees of a given industry to achieve certification status.

Since the 1960s, the federal government has invested $20 billion annually in 163 workforce-development programs spread among fifteen agencies. All of these programs were well-intentioned, but they caused a lot of duplicate effort. For example, sixty programs targeted economically disadvantaged people and thirty-four literacy programs targeted the same group. In addition, many state governments created job-training programs for these people.

A General Accounting Office report (Multiple Employment Training Programs, 1995) stated that people who needed training became confused on which program to take. Employers were rarely involved in the development process, which was managed by educators and social workers. The key measurements were quantity, not quality, and they never aimed for mastery of learning and performance. Only a small portion turned into real job-training courses; the rest became "nice to do" employee-development courses.

In the future, all states will play a greater role in job training as a result of block grants. They would be wise to apply the Systems Approach for Workforce Performance to their new programs. Except for literacy programs, the training should be directed to jobs that the local business community needs.

Here is an example of the real potential for a job-training program. Today, there are more meals served in restaurants than cooked at home. This situation creates the need for thousands of cooks, waiters, and waitresses. Except in some of the national chains, most of them receive little or no training, which in the end causes so many local restaurants to fail.

To enjoy a meal and learn practical lessons about job training, visit the Culinary Institute of America (CIA) in Hyde Park, New

York, ninety minutes north of New York City along the Hudson River. This culinary college was founded in 1946 with fifty students as a trade school to convert Army and Navy cooks into world-class chefs.

Today, more than two thousand students representing every state and several foreign countries enroll in the Institute's associ-ate degree programs. It takes two years to learn how to be a chef and how to manage a restaurant. The Institute has the finest facil-ities thanks to the generosity of various hotel chains, restaurants, and food companies. Julia Child, chef, author, and teacher, once said, "In practically every successful restaurant or hotel in this country that I've been in, more often than not I've encountered an Institute graduate in a leadership position." The Institute has had 27,000 graduates since 1946.

The school exemplifies mastery of learning and performance in food preparation. Guests can enjoy lunch or dinner in any of their five dining rooms, in which guests see and taste the results of good intentions, hard work, great training, on-the-job assignments, job aids, and support systems. The Systems Approach for Work-force Performance is practiced daily at the Institute.

It is a shame that every major job within each industry does not have a school like the CIA. The states could easily establish restau-rant schools in major cities, supplying basic cooks and service per-sonnel to local restaurants. Thus, real jobs would be waiting for the graduates, just as they are for CIA graduates. Not only would tax-payers feel that their taxes were well spent, but they would enjoy better food and service at local restaurants.

Trend Within Course Development

There is no doubt that a majority of courses will someday be devel-oped by third-party course-development companies; the economics favor that trend. Only the very largest corporations and govern-ment agencies will remain in the course-development business with a full-time staff of instructional designers, graphic experts, mea-surement specialists, computer programmers, authoring system personnel, and project managers. The cost of developing perfor-mance-based courses for a few students to achieve mastery of learning and performance is too high. The course-development companies can spread their development costs over thousands or tens of thousands of students to achieve a profit.

This is so different from twenty-five years ago because the basic lessons for a job within an industry are now quite common between organizations. Individual companies will continue to develop advanced workshops that differentiate their workforce from others. Every company also has some courses that can only be developed by their own personnel.

Every chief training officer should develop an approved list of education-development companies that can serve his or her organization. Some training companies will, no doubt, upgrade their services to include performance systems by major job categories within an industry. This will enable them to sell a curriculum of courses rather than one course at a time. The performance system would not only include the courses, but also include personal-development tasks, on-the-job training assignments, support systems, job aids, and training on coaching for managers.

Now that the courses have been developed, they need to be incorporated into organizational delivery systems, so the next chapter is devoted to delivery systems. Future advances in technology will have a great impact on both the cost and quality of performance-based training courses.

Chapter Nine

Develop a Delivery-System Strategy

Not long ago, companies used only two delivery systems for training: (1) classrooms and (2) reading books. The most common delivery system was the classroom because it was quick and inexpensive. An instructor could design some overheads and create a student workbook full of articles and exercises within a few days. Sometimes, in a crisis, the instructor threw a course together over the weekend.

This system worked well until quality measurements were applied. Too often, these overnight courses were high in entertainment value, but low in learning, which meant that employees rarely applied the lessons to their jobs.

Today, the demand is for performance-based courses that improve employee productivity. The students must like the course, learn the lessons, and apply the lessons to their jobs. Many new delivery systems are now significantly influencing the cost and quality of training. Technology is also affecting the delivery of training.

It is easy to become confused by all the terminology and claims of various delivery systems. Because the classroom has been the most commonly used delivery system, it is the de facto system for most organizations, but this is beginning to change as more and more companies are realizing the value of using delivery system alternatives. After all, the delivery system decision has the greatest impact on controlling costs and driving up the quality of training.

In the December 1996 issue of ASTD's *Training and Development* magazine, a graph shows training time by delivery system for over thirty companies. In one year, traditional classroom training had decreased from 78 percent to 69 percent. The shift is toward self-paced instruction, computer-based training, and advanced technology interactive classrooms. Electronic performance support systems doubled from 1 to 2 percent. The article also stated, "It should be noted, however, that these findings may actually underestimate the use of alternative delivery systems, as training time on these systems is more difficult to track than classroom time." It was estimated that traditional classrooms will be only about 50 percent of the delivery systems by the year 2000 in the more progressive training and performance organizations.

One of the major responsibilities of a chief training officer is to develop a delivery-system strategy. This chapter will provide some guidelines on formulating such a strategy.

Group-Paced Delivery Systems

Today, there are two fundamental types of delivery systems: (1) group-paced learning and (2) self-paced individual learning. Let us review these two formats, beginning with some group-paced delivery systems.

Traditional Classroom

Students are assembled in a classroom with a teacher, who lectures while the students take notes. Occasionally, the teacher writes on a chalkboard or an easel pad and may use overheads as visuals. There are usually some handouts and a few exercises, but the textbook or student notebook is the primary information source.

Every so often, the teacher asks if the information is clear. The students who understand the lessons quickly nod yes, and the students who are falling behind in the lesson usually say nothing. Nevertheless, the instructor moves on to the next lesson. When tests assess learning in this environment, a bell-shaped curve of learning arises. The resulting output is nowhere near mastery of learning and performance.

Many organizations are trying now to improve the quality of classroom education. Bob Pike and his organization (Creative Training Techniques International, Inc.) are attempting to bring more structure and quality to classroom training because it still has the following advantages:

- Provides an excellent forum for case studies.
- Enables senior and line executives to participate with students.
- Enables students to learn from their peers.
- Enables role plays to be used.
- Provides students with immediate attention and answers from instructors.
- Provides students with a role model performance by a master teacher.

However, travel costs plus room and board can make classroom education very expensive. Also, the necessary training may not be available when the employee or manager requires it. Another disadvantage is that various instructors deliver different lessons which, in turn, promotes inconsistency.

Tutored Video Instruction (TVI)

This delivery system features a master teacher on videotape who communicates to a large number of students at multiple locations, just as a distinguished professor would deliver a lecture in a large room in which no questions were permitted. A local tutor, like a graduate assistant, answers questions and helps the students with their assignments. The videotapes of the master teacher can be shown at any time, building flexibility into the schedule.

This method eliminates the cost of sending students to central education centers to hear the master teacher's lecture. Its biggest limitation is the lack of interactive learning between the students and the master teacher. The local tutor is the key to this delivery system's success.

Interactive Television Classroom (ITV)

This delivery system is sometimes called distance learning. A satellite communication system beams the master teacher to small classrooms at several remote sites. The total audience may vary from forty to four hundred students. In this delivery system, the master teacher can receive questions from remote sites so the students feel that they have an interactive session with the instructor. Only eye contact is lost, but even that feature can be maintained if the organization uses a two-way video system.

To be effective, this delivery system should have an electronic questioning system that enables the instructor to ask multiple-choice and true-or-false questions. With such a system, the students are fully engaged, and more learning takes place than takes place in a traditional lecture hall.

This system also eliminates the costs of travel and living expenses, but it requires the expense of a satellite communications system. However, a company can offer the classes at remote sites more frequently because the class size can be as small as a few people at each location.

Advanced Interactive Classroom

In this traditional classroom, each student has a keypad and the room has multimedia projection equipment. The classroom is often used for simulations and case studies. The interactivity as students answer questions provides more learning and greater lesson retention. Recently, some advanced interactive classrooms have been networked with a central education center or university for distance learning.

This method has the advantages of both classroom and computer-based training. Not many organizations utilize such a system today, but it has great potential as the classroom of the future. In most cases, the organizations that utilize advanced multimedia, self-paced individual instruction systems will insist on having the advanced interactive classrooms. Even though the time and cost to develop an advanced interactive classroom course is greater than the cost of developing a traditional classroom course, the payoff is in greater mastery of learning and performance.

Self-Paced Individual Learning Delivery Systems

Now, here are some examples of self-paced individual learning systems.

Text-Based Self-Study

The major difference between just reading a book and text-based self-study is that the latter features a workbook created by an instructional designer. Text-based self-study also has exercises at the end of each chapter or scattered throughout the workbook to test the student's knowledge of the lessons.

The main advantage of this type of training is that it is available every day, thus eliminating the wait for a class to be scheduled. It is also inexpensive to produce and deliver.

To enhance basic self-study courses, education-development companies often include videotapes or audiotapes, which give the course an entertaining case study or a master teacher to help reinforce the lessons. These tools drive up the cost, but they are worth the extra expense because they raise the motivation to learn. However, the real learning still takes place from doing lessons in the workbook.

Students learn at their own pace, which allows them to schedule time that does not interfere with their assigned work. They may even take the course home or on a business trip. The students can skip lessons on subjects they already know. The lessons are delivered consistently. The course time usually runs 15 to 25 percent shorter than a classroom course, significantly reducing the time spent away from the job. Fortunately, the problem of students claiming that they have completed a self-study course when they have actually skimmed the workbook can be avoided by administering a test at the end of the course. Later, the students can use the course materials as reference guides and job aids.

This training breakthrough has a few limitations. No interaction takes place with an instructor or a tutor, so companies should use only outstanding self-study courses. Self-study courses also take longer to develop than classroom courses. If the course content changes frequently, self-study is not feasible due to the cost of revising and distributing course workbooks, videotapes, and audiotapes. Finally, most self-study courses do not build interpersonal skills.

Computer-Based Training (CBT)

Computer-based training represents a monumental breakthrough in training. For centuries, educators have known that one-on-one or one-on-two tutoring is the most effective way to teach a lesson. The only problem with tutoring was its cost; with few exceptions, it was simply not affordable.

The invention of the personal computer led to low-cost and high-quality tutoring systems. Computer-based training has all the advantages of self-study with the bonus of being interactive. Once again, there is no cost for an education center or an instructor. If a company depreciates the personal computer over five years, the cost is about $50 a month for a simple CBT tutoring system or $100 a month for a sophisticated multimedia tutoring system. Computer-based training represents a breakthrough because the tutor is always available and is patient with the student. The computer provides positive reinforcement when lessons are learned and positive help when a lesson needs to be relearned. The computer delivers the lessons consistently day after day.

Interactivity is the key difference between self-study and CBT. A student learns faster with an interactive system, and the retention level is much greater. Computer-based training is 25 to 50 percent faster than a traditional classroom course, which reduces the cost of being away from the job.

Computer-based training has built-in assessment systems. In many organizations, the student does all of the administrative work, which also reduces the training department's costs. New color graphics have also increased the motivation for learning. In short, most students like CBT because it ensures that they will learn successfully and at their own pace.

Computer-based training has not replaced the majority of classroom courses because the up-front cost and time to develop the courses are unusually high. It is feasible to develop CBT only when several hundred or thousands of students require the course. However, many education-development companies are producing CBT courses today because more organizations are recognizing the value of using them. Course developers are also becoming more efficient at developing CBT courses because there are new and better authoring systems.

Most important, instructors are becoming computer literate. They are developing course outlines, student exercises, and visual aids with their personal computers. It is common now to see instructors using laptop computers in the classroom. Technology enables them to update their visuals and handouts even a few hours before class begins. Most instructors realize now that tutoring, in addition to teaching, represents a major breakthrough in training. They also realize that students can learn basic lessons in a CBT course prior to attending an advanced workshop on the subject. For the first time, students arrive at advanced workshops having completed all their prerequisites for the course.

Many university professors are also using technology to enhance their courses. The Harvard Business School now offers an Interactive Manager course, with fifteen hours of instruction covering twenty key management topics on CBT, including thirteen completely interactive case studies. Of course, some professors and instructors still view CBT and multimedia as the "flavor of the month." They believe that computers will never replace classrooms and chalkboards. These instructors are in for a shock, because over 50 percent of all training organizations are now using CBT. In only a few years, this figure will approach 100 percent. Computer-based training has taken a long time to gain acceptance, but the future is clear: CBT and tutoring will be a major delivery system in the next century.

Multimedia Training Systems

Multimedia training systems are an enhanced version of computer-based training. When combined with CD-ROM, they feature audio and video segments that teach the students through simulation and role plays. It is the only self-paced individual learning system that can show an employee or a manager how to do a task and how not to do it.

With these systems, service employees can learn how to fix equipment without ever going to an education center; managers can receive training on people management; and sales personnel can rehearse sales calls and even respond to objections. Very few limitations inhibit a course developer's imagination now. With multimedia training systems, mastery of learning and performance is affordable and feasible.

Ron Zemke wrote an interesting article, "The 'T' in CBT Is Still Lost Among the Cyber-Hoopla" in the May 1997 issue of the *Training Directors' Newsletter*. His main message was to have outstanding instructional design in every CBT and multimedia course. Course-development companies will need a few more years to produce a sufficient number of outstanding multimedia courses because their learning curves grow as new technology becomes available. Even now, the marketplace is rewarding those developers who create outstanding programs.

The CD-ROM is currently the lowest-cost and highest-density storage medium for personal computers. In future years, advancing technology will drive this cost down further. New CD-ROMs will hold up to fifteen times as much data as current disks. Courses will have more hours of audio and video segments, but course developers already have the elements they need to build a superior training and tutoring system today. Currently, over 50 percent of all new personal computers sold have a CD-ROM so they can be used for multimedia training. The retail computer stores are hearing from their customers and the message is clear: Customers want multimedia courses. Plain CBT courses are losing out to CD-ROM courses.

In 1987, Federal Express launched a pioneering training program for their 40,000 couriers and service representatives in six hundred locations. They used a mix of CD-ROM, interactive laser disc players, and personal computers. At the time, they had a less-than-ideal hardware system, but the company soon gained market share and a ten-year strategic advantage over companies that were still studying the hardware.

Many companies spend too much time playing with technology, instead of developing a delivery-system strategy aimed at achieving a competitive advantage. Some examples of successful efforts are given below.

Dillards is a retail chain with over two hundred locations in nineteen states. All of their sales associates are being trained with a multimedia system. Insurance companies, banks, health care organizations, travel companies, transportation companies, auditing firms, oil companies, manufacturers, and communication organizations are also shifting to multimedia courses.

Andersen Consulting, a master at measuring the costs and quality of its training, converted one of its high-volume courses from classroom to multimedia. The hours of study declined from sixty-five to forty. Andersen is now saving over $10 million annually in training and payroll. Numerous organizations are reducing the cost of their training and increasing the quality of their course offerings by using alternative delivery systems.

Another major advantage to multimedia courses is that they can accommodate different types of learning styles, visual (lots of graphics), global (start with the big picture), analytic (facts and figures), auditory (listen to instructor), kinesthetic (role play, case studies), and tactual (interact with text in a number of ways). Most traditional training courses are designed for analytic learners, who make up only 28 percent of all learners.

As noted, multimedia courses of the future will accommodate several types of learners. These courses are being developed today for the public schools. As course-development companies aim for mastery of learning and performance, they will need to appeal to all learning styles.

Another major advantage to CBT and multimedia systems that are connected to a network is the fact that the lessons can be updated quickly. Companies become true learning organizations when their systems evolve into major components of their change-management process.

Four Basic Locations for Training

Most leading-edge organizations use one of four locations for learning: a central education center, a local education center, a learning center, or a work station.

Central Education Centers

A central education center usually incurs the following expenses: Building ownership or rent, utilities, building maintenance, receptionist, education-center manager, general administrative staff, class management and administrative staff, information-systems specialists, instruction managers, and instructors.

If an education center has residential rooms and dining rooms, the company must also pay for cooks, waiters or waitresses, and maids. This adds up to a very large budget; the average daily operating cost of a central education center can be $600 per student. Thus, a five-day course for twenty students costs $60,000, not including the students' salaries while they are away from the job. For this reason, organizations are trying to offer training outside of central education centers, except for advanced courses and executive-student conferences.

Local Education Centers

If the education center is local, and students do not incur travel expenses or need room and board, the daily cost drops over 50 percent to between $150 to $250 per day. Of course, if you put five hundred students in a rent-free theater to watch free videotapes, the cost would be much lower. Many low-cost, low-quality training programs are available, but these cost figures are based on quality courses taught at education centers under average conditions.

Learning Centers

Classroom training is expensive. Recently, companies have implemented learning centers to combat these costs. A learning center is a room designed for one to thirty students, where each person studies in a cubicle called a study carrel. There may be an audiotape player, videotape player, or a personal computer in the carrel. If there are ten or more carrels in a learning center, an administrator is usually responsible for having all the course materials on hand and all equipment working properly.

The daily cost of studying in a learning center is about $100 per student. The furniture and decoration should be first-class so that students are comfortable using this alternative method. The equipment must meet the training department's standards and be well-maintained. Another advantage of learning centers is privacy. No one except for the administrator needs to know what topics students are studying. Students can tell their friends that they are going to the Learning Center. The friends assume that they are developing their knowledge and skills for the job. No one needs to know that the student is actually learning how to improve reading skills.

It is clear why large regional, national, and international organizations must have a delivery-system strategy. For example, assume that a firm has one million student days. If they are all central classroom days, the costs total $600 million. If all the student days are in a learning center, the cost drops to $100 million. With the proper mix, the firm could incur a cost of only $200 million, thus reducing their delivery expenses by more than 60 percent. In large companies, 85 percent of the training organizations now have or plan to implement learning centers.

The figures above represent only the cost to deliver education. The cost to develop, modify, or buy the courses also varies by the type of delivery system used and the development source.

Work Stations

If students learn their lessons on a personal computer at a work station, the cost of delivery will be almost nothing because the line organization pays for the computer and network. The training department usually pays for the central server and the cost to acquire the course.

Costs alone make it easy to understand why more and more companies are considering alternative delivery systems, but the other advantages are that learning is available whenever needed, the learning rate is faster, the learning is more effective, and retention levels are higher.

To achieve a well-coordinated multilevel delivery system, the CTO and the education staff must establish strict organization-wide standards for audiotapes, videotapes, computers, multimedia systems, networks, and courseware. Too many organizations have a wide mix of technology because one item is cheaper or it serves more than one function. Noncompatible systems destroy good delivery-system strategies. Strategic standardization must be the goal.

Trends Within Delivery-System Strategies

Following is a discussion of the latest developments in delivery systems.

Prerequisite Courses

When an organization designs a curriculum for a major job category, there is a trend for self-paced individual learning courses to serve as the prerequisites to the classroom courses. An individual may take two or three courses through individual learning before attending a classroom course. The curriculum and support systems for each major job category should be summarized on three or four pages so that, rather than flipping through a large catalog of courses, an employee and his or her supervisor can review a three- or four-page summary that will clearly tell them the training, personal-development tasks, on-the-job training assignments, and support systems needed to achieve mastery of learning and performance. The summary should also show which courses are self-paced for individual learning and which are group-paced for the classroom.

Self-Paced Individual Courses

A second trend is the higher utilization of self-paced individual courses. Virtually all employee-development courses are available now from course-development companies in self-study or computer-based versions that feature high-quality multimedia formats. These courses enable employees to study whenever they want, at either a learning center or at home. For this reason more courses are being converted to self-paced format.

A number of learning organizations that have had effective delivery-system strategies for years originally believed that their courses would be about 25 percent self-paced and 75 percent group-paced. A few years ago, they revised those estimates to fifty-fifty. Now, they estimate that 75 percent will be self-paced and 25 percent group-paced in the next century. One computer company has already reached 90 percent self-paced courses, with only 10 percent of the courses remaining in the classroom.

Advancing technology accounts for much of this radical change. The new multimedia tutoring systems provide high-quality instruction with simulation, role modeling, and immediate assessment of learning. The numerous high-quality and low-cost courses now available from course-development companies have also brought about this shift.

Videotape Decline

A third trend is the decline of videotapes, which are limited by lack of interactivity. As a result, the really outstanding lessons now on videotapes are being converted to multimedia courses. With the rising demand to measure the effectiveness of training, the entertainment factor of many existing videotapes is more evident than the number of lessons contained on the tape. There is also the problem of figuring out which videotape to use; for example, there are over 150 videotapes on diversity. It is time consuming and costly to determine which tapes should be selected.

Less Need for Large Centers

The fourth trend is related to the decline of videotape training. As more and more training has shifted to self-paced courses in learning centers, the need for large central education centers has dropped. Soon, every major organization will probably have just one central education center located near its corporate headquarters or in a capital city where senior executives can meet with students who are attending advanced workshops or management-development courses. Most of the centers that exist today will probably not be expanded in the future. If this trend continues, general-purpose conference centers may not be fully utilized in the future.

Distance Learning

A fifth trend is the growth of "distance learning." Attempts to cut down the expensive costs of sending employees to and housing them at central education centers has contributed significantly to the growth of distance-learning systems. Vendors now offer several satellite classroom systems. The National Technology University, just a concept fifteen years ago, now offers fourteen different master's degree programs by satellite television. Management-development courses, utilizing professors from leading graduate schools of business, have also been developed. Some institutions plan to offer undergraduate degrees through satellite systems. This trend will accelerate once instructional designers and professors start creating courses with multimedia tutoring systems.

Distance learning with interactive feedback should enjoy a prosperous future in the next century. Although better courses are needed, the technology already exists for this training breakthrough. Recently, one university offered a master's and a doctorate degree in instructional technology and distance education, with virtually all of the learning taking place in the students' homes. For the three-year doctoral program, only three eight-day summer institutes at the main campus were required for academic and hands-on activities. All other learning occurred at the students' homes.

Learning at Home

A sixth trend is the growing number of people who work at home and want to learn there as well. The home office is not just a passing fad. With technology, it is becoming more and more feasible. More institutions are encouraging their employees to learn at home rather than during the traditional business hours of 8 AM to 5 PM. This policy blends well with the fact that employees need to be responsible for their own training and development, in case their company downsizes. Furthermore, if the employee is paid hourly, the company or government agency must compensate him or her for overtime if the student is learning on the job. Millions of employees do not receive overtime pay for learning at home, a fact they accept as a way of life.

Virtual Office

A seventh trend is the "virtual office," which could be the automobile, a client's office, an airplane, a hotel room, or an airline terminal. Millions of Americans work long hours all over the country, and they want to learn while they travel. Laptop computers have made learning feasible at almost any location.

Outside Vendors

An eighth trend is the utilization of outside companies to develop courseware for computer-based and multimedia training systems, which was covered in the last chapter.

Networks

The ninth trend is the improvement of communication systems and networks. More courses are being stored library-fashion on central servers and mainframes. When a student needs to take a course, the instruction software (sometimes called courseware) is quickly transferred to the multimedia personal computer (tutoring system) from the library. New low-cost network computers have been announced by several computer companies that will enable this trend to continue using the new Java programming language. The new network computers will cost only $500 to $800. These network computers will have all the functional capability of a $4,000 multimedia personal computer. Low-cost bandwidth, the capacity of a communications carrier to deliver audio, video, and text to a workstation, is required to enable multimedia courses to be downloaded to workstations from central servers. Expensive servers and networks can do the work today. It is only a matter of time before the low-cost bandwidth is available. Sun Microsystems has organized over one hundred companies, including IBM, Apple, and Netscape, to use the promising new Java programming language that allows programmers to write a single software version that will run on any computer system. It is too early to tell if this design for a lower-cost training system will replace existing CBT systems, but it shows how far communication systems have been increased in capabilities and reduced in cost.

Community Colleges

There has also been a trend to utilize community colleges for basic job training and employee-development courses. The big attraction for this alternative has been lower costs. The competition for these colleges in the future will be inexpensive learning centers with multimedia tutoring systems. The tutoring systems will ensure learning by using sophisticated assessment systems. To stay competitive, community colleges will need to increase the quality of their instruction by hiring instructional designers and implementing new assessment systems, because companies and government agencies will insist on mastery of learning in the future.

Embedded Training

The final trend is that software developers such as Microsoft are embedding more training programs into their software products, which enables them to differentiate their products in the marketplace. It makes a lot of sense to learn how to use a software application on a personal computer, the world's most effective and efficient tutoring system. For some products, the training will be an option with a separate price, but it will still be available. The old method of teaching computer applications, such as word processing, in a classroom will disappear. Students can learn on their personal computers when they have the time or the immediate need to learn. In the next century, just-in-time training will be a way of life in most organizations.

Convergence of Technology

There is also the coming grand merger of television with the personal computer. NBC and Microsoft have created MSNBC to create programs for this new video and personal computing world. Intel has created Intercast; NBC is offering NBC Interactive; Sony is now both in television and computer markets. Everyone believes in convergence, and there are many visions for the future. One thing is certain: Whatever system emerges, there will be a major impact on training and education.

Internet and Intranet Delivery Systems

In 1969, the Defense Department developed a network called ARPANET to connect incompatible computers at research universities doing military projects. The Internet evolved in the 1970s to connect ARPANET to other networks involved in research work. The government paid for the early version of the Internet, creating the image that this network, designed only for data, was free. Now, it is being promoted as all things to all people. Some view it as a free communication system available to any organization that has a modern personal computer with communications capability.

The Internet has potential as a delivery system for training. First, it provides low-cost electronic mail, so students can receive lessons, course materials, and tests directly from the course coordinator. The instructor and student can interact, facilitating self-study. Second, students can communicate with each other through the use of electronic bulletin boards, although some bulletin boards are better than others. Third, an instructor can use the

Internet for real-time conferencing, which is analogous to having a classroom session with students who are at a remote location. Fourth, a course can be updated quickly because the materials are stored on a server. If certain software standards have been utilized, the course can be used by either Apple or Microsoft systems, which eliminates the need to maintain two separate courses. This is a big cost advantage for any course developer and is also helpful to any company that has failed to establish standards for personal computers. Fifth, the central training department can display course descriptions, class schedules, and enrollment information to prospective students by putting its course catalog on-line.

According to the Gartner Group, Inc., in the March 6, 1995 issue of *BusinessWeek* ("Do You Know Where Your PCs Are?," pp. 73–74), many organizations have lost track of their personal computers and other desktop devices. A performance consultant could be helpful with this problem. As part of their responsibilities to design a performance system for every major job category, they could also determine the true requirements for all this technology.

The Gartner article states that the typical corporate PC, complete with software, costs about $4,000 to purchase. But it costs ten times that to operate a PC for five years. If you multiply $40,000 by the number of personal computers in an organization, the number becomes important. In their article, the Gartner Group also states that $20 billion annually is wasted by the mismanagement of desktop computers.

In summary, training on the Internet is very similar to CBT and multimedia courses in a learning center. The course is always available, assessments can be implemented with the course, and the students learn interactively. The Gartner Group, Inc., in Stamford, Connecticut, predicts that more than half of all large organizations will do some training through the Internet in the next few years.

Disadvantages do exist. First, the quality of the course does not have to be good for it to be on the Internet. As a result, many low-quality courses can be quickly implemented. An organization that believes it is on the leading edge of training may actually be behind the times. Second, cost estimates are not precise as yet. In some situations, costs are less because the student does not have to travel or incur the expenses of room and board. If a self-study course or a CBT course is implemented on the Internet, the cost may actually become greater because the free services of the current Internet may not be free in the future.

Third, the mushrooming volume of Internet users and applications is causing the system to become slower and, in some situations, to fail. As more servers and bandwidth are added, more people use the system. Fourth, too much trash exists on the Internet. Few web sites have many repeat users. With little or no quality control, the Internet is already experiencing a backlash from sophisticated users, who describe it as a library with no filing system. Fifth, the current Internet was not built for many of the missions that it now has. Security is weak and the network was never designed for voice and video.

These problems have motivated organizations to build their own networks, called Intranets. Some experts predict spending on internal networks will soon be six times greater than the money invested in the Internet. One advantage is that Intranets will be managed professionally, while the Internet will continue to be managed by a very large and ineffective committee.

The Internet will, of course, help many employees who are doing research and personal-development projects, especially because the costs to use it are still very reasonable. The Internet will definitely play a role in future training programs, but no one should think that every quality course will be on the Internet for little or no money. The Internet does not have a chief training officer or the Systems Approach for Workforce Performance to ensure performance-based courses, job aids, or support systems for each critical job within every industry and organization.

On the other hand, the Intranet has all the advantages of the Internet with fewer disadvantages. An internal network can be managed for response time and quality performance. Security can be implemented. Some people predict that the Intranet will replace the need for CD-ROM on multimedia tutoring systems. It will be a central course library servicing low-cost tutoring systems. Time will tell if this prediction is correct, but it does highlight the need for a central training and performance department if an Intranet strategy is to be adopted. Probably the most important message concerning the Intranet is to get involved. A recent study by ASTD showed that under 30 percent of the Intranet projects had any involvement by the training and performance department, which should be the leaders in determining how to use the advanced technology strategies of their organizations for training.

Selecting a Delivery System

Delivery-system decisions are initially part of the curriculum design. As the curriculum is enhanced and modified over the years, decisions are made whenever there are major changes. Factors to consider are:

- Number of students for the life of the course.
- Number of locations in which the course will be offered.
- Estimate on the lessons' stability.
- Course-development time.
- Types of learning methods involved.
- Complexity of the lessons.
- Performance level required.

Most organizations have documented guidelines on how to select the various delivery systems. A few companies use "expert systems" to help with these decisions. However, much of the decision-making process comes down to judgment calls. There are no precise rules. Common sense is paramount, but the guidelines should exist to provide adequate information for these important decisions.

Delivery-System Strategies

As noted, the delivery-system strategy will significantly influence the cost and quality of training. The new interactive learning systems that can exist in a classroom, a learning center, or at a work site can provide mastery of learning. Using the old bell-shaped curve will place an organization at a competitive disadvantage, unable to achieve mastery of performance.

Educators should not worry about being unemployed when the new multimedia tutoring systems are implemented. Fewer lecturers will be in the classroom, but many more educators will be needed to create courses and performance systems. Training and performance will be a growth industry after senior executives start demanding mastery of learning and performance. Instructors who resist change will be in deep trouble, but trainers and performance consultants who embrace new delivery systems will have a prosperous future.

Why has technology moved so slowly through the education and training fields? Frankly, educators are focused more on "training as usual" than on how to move their organizations toward mastery of learning and performance.

The millions of younger employees between twenty and thirty-three years old, sometimes called Generation X, are bringing pressure to bear on organizations to use technology for delivery lessons and support. These people have used computers at home, in school, or in previous jobs. They like training that is focused on outcomes. Their generation accepts hard work as a way of life. One way to keep their attention is to keep training experiential and to use plenty of visuals. They appreciate just-in-time training and like to stop and start the process themselves.

The reality is that students want better courses and mastery of learning. Certainly, executives also want mastery of learning and performance. However, it will not happen until senior executives bring workplace performance into sharper focus. Not every line executive can be an expert on all the elements of a delivery-system strategy. A CTO does not have to be a technical expert, but he or she must know how to make decisions about technology and be the sponsor of a delivery system strategy.

Every intermediate and large organization will need a person who is familiar with technology issues, often called an education technologist. Large organizations often have a small department of education technologists who design the overall delivery system with input from the human resources and information systems departments. The chief information officer and the technical staff should be consulted frequently to ensure that the company's personal computers can be used to tutor employees at their work stations now and in the future.

The delivery-system strategy is an important part of the Systems Approach for Workforce Performance. No organization will achieve a breakthrough in workforce performance if it continues to support hit-and-miss training sessions centered around classrooms. Those courses worked twenty-five years ago, but they are the road to failure in the next century.

Chapter Ten

Develop On-the-Job Training Assignments

Most learning today takes place on the job. The American Society for Training and Development (ASTD) estimates that two to five times more time is allocated to on-the-job training than to structured training in classrooms or learning centers. In many companies, formal training accounts for only 10 to 20 percent of learning. The remaining knowledge and skills are learned on the job.

This is the case in most organizations because training is poorly planned and managed, but even if an organization has a superior management system for training, it needs to have outstanding on-the-job training assignments to maximize workforce performance.

In the December 1996 issue of *Training Magazine,* Bob Filipczar wrote an interesting article titled "Who Owns OJT?" He stated, "The short answer to that slightly accusatory question is: Probably no one. And that's a problem. If no one owns the on-the-job training process, can we be sure it's getting done, and getting done right? Truth be told, most OJT isn't done well at all. It's treated by training departments like a crazy aunt in the attic—out of sight, out of mind, and a little disreputable. It's a throw-together training strategy concocted on shop floors and in back offices by harried line managers who don't have the time, the resources or the know-how to construct a 'real' training program. The British call it 'sitting by Nellie,' and it's usually not much more complicated than that" (pp. 44–49).

In the Systems Approach for Workforce Performance, on-the-job training represents a major facet of the overall system. The training and performance department should be as involved in the design, development, delivery, and evaluation of on-the-job training events as it would be for a computer-based training course in a learning center.

Fortunately, two recent books can help a chief training officer and performance consultant focus on this important subject. In 1994, William J. Rothwell and H. C. Kazanas published *Improving On-the-Job Training*, which describes how to establish and operate a comprehensive OJT program. This text was followed by *Structured On-the-Job Training* (1995) by Ronald L. Jacobs and Michael J. Jones. Following are a few key messages from these books.

Problems with On-the-Job Training

All the authors and experts will admit that most OJT today is ineffective and costly. Most OJT assignments lack planning and structure. Fellow workers, with good intentions, try to help the more inexperienced employees, but they are not trained as tutors or instructors.

Like everything else in the workplace, there are best practices for OJT training. It must be designed, developed, delivered, and evaluated like any other training event, quite the opposite of a supervisor saying, "Stay close to John or Jean, and learn your job," which is what usually happens.

Why is this? *Most organizations have few systems that determine the cost of OJT training.* They view it as free because the two employees' salaries would be paid whether any training occurred or not. Quite often, OJT has little or no documentation. To make matters worse, no one evaluates the results of the training. It does not cost anything, but in most situations it is hardly worth anything.

The second major reason why OJT fails is the fact that *most people are not great teachers.* They provide long-winded and confusing answers to questions. They talk about a task, but they do not make it clear how to do the task. Then they criticize the puzzled employee when he or she does not perform the task correctly.

A third reason for ineffective OJT assignments is the *lack of time available to the supervisor or fellow worker who is supposed to do the training.* Too often, the OJT task is assumed to require no additional time, so nothing is formally scheduled, and it becomes secondary to meeting production schedules or deadlines.

A fourth reason is the *constant series of interruptions at work sites.* Learning is difficult if it is sandwiched between telephone calls and other daily interruptions that are quite normal for the work location.

A fifth reason for ineffective OJT is the *belief that one learns by leaping from crisis to crisis.* After all, the supervisor had to learn by the school of hard knocks, so why not the new employee? In such an environment, OJT turns into a Marine Corps boot camp. Veteran supervisors believe that tough basic training is good for the new employee, but it is a painful learning experience in the workplace that leads to low morale and high attrition rates. Remember, Marine Corps recruits cannot quit their jobs; most entry-level employees can.

A sixth reason is that *many executives and managers do not realize that OJT can be structured and planned.* They think it must always be haphazard. Too many trainers and training managers are not trained themselves on how to develop planned and structured on-the-job training assignments, so it continues to be done poorly.

The seventh reason is that *many employees do not want to help their fellow employees become outstanding performers.* Sometimes, the incentive system causes this unfortunate situation. Learning by osmosis is doomed to failure if the instructor wants to be a better performer than the learner. In Asian Pacific countries like Japan, OJT is much more successful because the instructor never worries about a new or younger employee taking his or her job. In the United States, this concern is real.

The final reason for ineffective OJT is that most new hires view on-the-job training as training in a sink-or-swim work environment. *New hires always have more confidence in a formal training situation* as a base for starting or changing careers.

Essential Components for On-the-Job Training

In the *design phase,* a company must build the following components into its OJT program:

- Intent of the assignment.
- Learning objectives.
- Needs and task analysis.

- Instructor responsibilities.
- Learner responsibilities.
- Learning prerequisites.
- Schedules for each assignment.
- Measurement system for determining success.
- Incentives or rewards
- Development and delivery budget.

In the *development phase,* the company needs to add the following components:

- Teaching guide for the instructor.
- Workbook for the students.
- Job aids for reinforcement.
- Demonstrative models.
- Exercises to ensure learning.
- Assessment exercises.

In the *delivery phase,* the company must introduce the following components:

- Instructor-training sessions.
- Time allocated for OJT training.
- Administration of assessment exercises.

In the *evaluation phase,* the company needs to improve and update its OJT program just like any other training event. Any tests administered at the end of the program must be performance-based.

Cost of OJT Assignments

The time and cost needed to develop effective OJT training is similar to the time and cost required for developing a self-study course.

The cost to deliver OJT is quite expensive because OJT is essentially a one-on-one tutoring system. For this reason, many large- and intermediate-size organizations have converted many OJT assignments to learning centers or classroom courses. In small organizations, OJT assignments are often the only practical way to train new employees because these companies hire only one or two people each month, quarter, or year to do a particular job.

Learning on the job usually takes longer because it is not a full-time effort. Mistakes are part of the process, so the company incurs cost to rework or fix problems.

On-the-job training may not be perfect, but it is still essential for almost every job because formal training events rarely provide all the knowledge and skill needed to do a job.

Process for On-the-Job Training Events

In World War I, Charles R. "Skipper" Allen developed a four-step approach to structured OJT for shipbuilders. In World War II, this process was expanded to seven steps:

1. Show learners how to perform the task.
2. Review key points.
3. Instructor performs the task a second time.
4. Allow learners to perform the simple part of the job.
5. Guide learners to perform the entire job.
6. Let learners perform the whole job, but closely monitor their performance.
7. Release learners from training to do productive work with normal supervision.

Some companies added a beginning step, which was to explain why the tasks need to be performed. With or without that step, the new employee listens, observes, practices, learns by trial and error, and occasionally receives tutoring from the instructor, usually a supervisor. Allen's learning method is not complex. In fact, it proves that almost every supervisor or instructor can teach effectively when OJT assignments are professionally developed and documented. Well planned one-on-one tutoring is the most successful way to teach learners on the job.

The performance consultant or curriculum manager must determine which knowledge and skills the students will learn through formal classroom courses, learning center courses, and in OJT assignments. Most job categories require all three to achieve optimum performance at the optimum cost.

The overall training program's administrative system should treat OJT assignments like any other course. It should maintain complete training records and ensure that adequate resources are available.

When to Use On-the-Job Training

Although there is no precise answer or formula for when to use OJT, the following are some examples of successful OJT applications.

Practice Lessons and Skills. In many sales-training programs, instructors teach the process of selling, structured sales calls, listening, questioning, presenting, demonstrating, and proposal writing in a classroom or in a learning center. Then the trainees spend weeks or months with an experienced salesperson applying the lessons to ensure that they are ready to assume their own sales territories. Thus, the experienced salesperson assumes the roles of on-the-job tutor and mentor.

Administrative Tasks. In numerous organizations, a new person in an administrative position works with an experienced person or supervisor to learn the job. Here, OJT substitutes for formal training courses.

Repetitive Manufacturing Tasks. On-the-job training began here because only one or two employees needed training on these tasks every month or quarter. Repetitive tasks lend themselves well to OJT.

Phased Training. In many restaurants, a new employee learns how to clear the tables, serve water and rolls, and pour coffee before he or she becomes a full waiter or waitress. In many jobs, a new employee must master each job phase before moving on to more complicated tasks.

Complex Training. Interns and residents in hospitals rely heavily on OJT. They practice on patients under the supervision of a qualified doctor. In poverty-stricken neighborhoods, the learning is often accelerated because the interns and residents are allowed to perform more complicated procedures on nonpaying patients.

Service Tasks. More and more training for equipment repair has moved to formal classroom and computer-based training courses because well-trained service representatives are far less costly than partially trained people who make mistakes that must be corrected by second and third service calls. On the other hand, all service job training cannot take place in a classroom or learning center. Some on-the-job training is needed to achieve mastery of learning and performance.

Meeting People. Meeting people and customers requires on-the-job training in positions such as delivery routes or outside sales. The same is true for financial services.

Low-Volume Positions. Small companies use on-the-job training assignments most frequently. Unfortunately, most of these assignments are unplanned and unstructured, which is a costly mistake. Insufficient and ineffective training leads to very high attrition rates in many small organizations. Structured OJT could solve this problem.

Supervision and Coaching

Supervisors need to reinforce lessons from on-the-job training as often as they would lessons from classroom courses. This should be a natural step because supervisors are usually involved in developing and delivering the OJT assignments.

Coaching should also be more effective with OJT because the supervisor is usually more involved with the assignments. Quite often, the supervisor holds that job because he or she performed the tasks covered in the OJT assignment at an above-average level.

Apprentice Programs

After World War II, business and government leaders came to the United States to learn how Americans had been so productive during the war years. In recent years, American executives found new ideas and programs from organizations overseas. For example, Japan gave lessons on quality, "first time right," just-in-time, and mastery of learning and performance. Germany has shown the world how to educate, train, and develop young people through its apprentice programs.

A few organizations in the United States are now trying apprentice programs. Siemens, a German company with a plant in North Carolina, takes high school graduates and associate degree students into its apprentice program because there is a shortage of qualified entry-level employees. Siemens' program involves three hundred thirty-seven people.

Vocational high schools could help to solve the challenge of developing well-qualified entry-level employees, but it is not happening yet in most cities. The schools do not have a working partnership with local companies or government agencies, they are underfunded, have outmoded equipment, and simply do not have up-to-date courses. State governments do fund a number of apprentice systems.

Advantages of On-the-Job Training

Some of the more obvious advantages of OJT are listed here:

1. The training is available almost every day, thus eliminating the problem of waiting for a scheduled class.
2. The people who are the subject-matter experts and sometimes the OJT assignment developers know the lessons based on actual job experience.
3. The instructor has up-to-date field operating experience.
4. Course materials and instruction are easy to update.
5. Training schedules can be flexible and the training takes place at the best times for both the instructor and the learner.

Remember, a company gains these advantages only when its on-the-job training is structured and planned. If training is unstructured, OJT will just be an accumulation of misinformation, bad habits, and inappropriate shortcuts that other employees practice. Unstructured training leads to more mistakes, greater costs, lower productivity, and unhappy employees. Fortunately, most employees somehow overcome ineffective OJT and learn to do their jobs at a minimum performance level, but today we ask employees to know more and to do more, so organizations must structure and plan their on-the-job training.

On-the-job training is one of five methods for employees to acquire knowledge and skills within a performance system. It is part of the fourth step in the Systems Approach for Workforce Performance and usually a major part of the performance system. In the next chapter, ways to reinforce the lessons learned will be described.

Chapter Eleven

Develop Support Systems for Key Jobs

Too often, an outstanding training program fails because the students never apply the lessons and skills they learn to their jobs. Most trainers do not accept this fact because they have student evaluations stating that their courses are outstanding, the course materials are excellent, and the instructors do a superior teaching job.

Various research has shown why students do not learn and apply what they are taught. The Research Institute of America found that thirty-three minutes after a lecture is completed, students usually retain only 58 percent. By the second day, only one-third of the information is retained. Another study (Peoples, 1992, p. 78) tells us that of all the information we know, 75 percent came to us visually, 13 percent through hearing, and 12 percent through smell, taste, and touch. This means that the instructor's "golden words" are almost forgotten unless there is some form of reinforcement.

Other studies (Peoples, 1992, p. 6) state that only 15 percent of knowledge is retained three weeks after a course is completed. In some cases, the students cannot remember the course's name, the instructor's name, and most of the lessons just a year later.

To achieve a breakthrough in workforce performance, employees and managers need more than a training event. They need coaching and supervision to reinforce lessons or they will return to "business as usual." Another and usually low-cost way to reinforce lessons is to develop basic "low-tech" support systems. (High-tech integrated electronic performance support systems will be covered in the next chapter.)

Support systems play an important role in the performance system within the Systems Approach for Workforce Performance. If support systems are not an integral part of a performance system, then the organization will have a very low return on its training investment no matter how entertaining the instructors are.

One-time events designed to help students apply their lessons are usually ineffective. For example, many courses provide the students with a wallet-size reminder card that incorporates the main ideas from the lesson. Most students' wallets or purses are already filled with credit and ATM cards. Furthermore, if an employee carried every reminder card around in a suit jacket, he or she would develop serious back problems. Besides, many employees no longer wear a suit jacket as the offices adopt casual dress.

Whatever support systems are developed need to be used frequently to reinforce the methods taught in a course. They must ensure that employees perform best practices and complete all procedures in their regular work routines.

Support systems can be classified into four major categories: Databases, job aids, procedure manuals, and periodic performance reviews. These are described below.

Databases and Knowledge Systems

Databases existed prior to the invention of computers, but were called by other names. For example, sales personnel used to carry brochures and proposals in the trunks of their cars. Many file cabinets served as databases. In some organizations, bookcases built around desks contained dozens of three-ring binders that stored valuable information.

The current workforce has the advantage of electronic databases. Employees can extract the best parts of superb proposals and use them to create a new proposal. Key parts of letters and reports can be duplicated as well. Today, employees must be provided with outstanding information to become top performers.

Some consulting firms store their service lines' entire backgrounds in a database that lists the following types of information:

- Overview of the service line.
- Experts within the firm.

- Presentations for clients.
- Methodologies of the service line.
- Deliverables of the service line.
- Differentiation of the firm.
- Suggested sections of a proposal.
- List of satisfied clients.
- Answers to the most common questions.
- Financial justification and cost estimates.
- Answers to the most common objections.
- Project-management information.

With this database, a consultant can become an expert in no time at all, able to sell more engagements and to manage engagements better to achieve a greater profit. With this type of sophisticated support system, firms can reinforce the lessons on how to sell and manage engagements.

In recent years, the term *knowledge system* has been used by some organizations rather than the term *database*. In fact, some organizations are investing thousands or millions of dollars to manage their knowledge assets. Knowledge management is defined as the process of creating, capturing, and using knowledge for organizational performance. Their goal is to capture, store, transfer, and apply knowledge that is required by the employees and customers. In some companies, there is a Chief Knowledge Officer, who sometimes is in charge of training.

Some people have asked the question: Is knowledge management just a passing fad? The answer is yes if the organization spends enormous sums of money to create databases of knowledge that only a few people use, which has happened in some large corporations and government agencies. The answer is no if the investment in knowledge databases is controlled by performance consultants who manage the expense by only asking for knowledge databases that are justified by performance systems within major job categories.

Financial services may combine several databases for a single customer, allowing an employee to know and do more after he or she receives proper training on job procedures. Sales organizations provide databases on best proposals, sample presentations, and customer references so that salespeople can sell more effectively after attending sales school.

Support systems can reinforce lessons by prompting an employee with questions such as, "Have you used customer references in your proposal?" The support system needs to be incorporated into the overall training design to achieve maximum performance.

With desktop and portable personal computers, companies can give their employees all the tools they need to achieve mastery of performance. Too many organizations provide the hardware and software and then hope that the employee knows how to use the equipment and information. In the same vein, they hope employees apply the lessons in their training program. Hoping for results is not good enough. Companies need to implement a management system, such as the Systems Approach for Workforce Performance, to ensure that employees and managers achieve optimum performance.

Job Aids

A job aid is a prompt or guide for doing a task, a low-cost approach to reinforcing course lessons because it can be printed on a card or document. This is a low-tech support system at its best. Almost every job needs one or more job aids to reinforce even the most outstanding training event, but trainers often ignore the need for job aids. For this reason, performance consultants are more likely to design and implement them. The Systems Approach forces people to think of job aids because they play such a major role in the overall performance system.

A to-do list is a job aid. A checklist in an airplane cockpit is a job aid. Some job aids consist of a one-page document with pictures and words that describe the overall process. Joe Harless said it best in 1980: "Inside every fat course, there is a thin job aid crying to get out."

Employees use job aids in complex job situations to remind them not to take shortcuts or miss an important step in the process. Job aids are also helpful in positions that have a number of infrequently used procedures. The job aid quickly reminds the employee which steps to take to complete the task.

The advantages of job aids include the following:

1. Employees do a complete job.
2. They make fewer mistakes.

3. They require less supervision.
4. They do the job in less time.
5. They perform the tasks as they were instructed in their courses.
6. Employees can do more jobs when they are crossed-trained on several jobs.
7. Management becomes convinced that the course lessons will be applied to the job.
8. Management appreciates the cost savings due to the elimination of remedial training.
9. Employees spend less time away from their jobs because training courses are shorter.
10. New procedures can often be implemented with a revised job aid rather than an expensive new training program.

Some companies abide by a simple rule: When you can, use job aids; when job aids will not do the job, use training plus job aids. It is a shame when companies misuse or seldom use this great inexpensive tool for achieving performance breakthroughs, especially when many employees want their employers to provide job aids so that they can avoid learning procedures on a hit-and-miss basis.

Job aids are simple to design. First, an instructional designer, performance consultant, or course developer performs a task several times. Then, in simple sentences, the person writes down all of the steps needed to complete the task. He or she creates some visuals, then designs the overall job aid. Finally, he or she tests and revises the job aid until the employees and managers are able to use it to achieve mastery of performance.

Every person involved in curriculum design, course development, and course assessment should attend a workshop on how to design, develop, and implement successful job aids, as well as read numerous books and articles on the subject. Allison Rossett and Jeannette Gautier-Downes have written a book (1997) on the subject of job aids.

Procedure Manuals and Guidelines

Many jobs require a procedure manual or guidelines to achieve mastery of performance. For example, publishers do not offer a training course for authors who sign a contract to write a book.

Instead, they send the author an Author's Guide. They expect the author to read the guidelines and to follow them as he or she writes. The editor makes corrections and refers the new author back to the guidelines if he or she has made a consistent series of errors.

During the investigation of a major employee grievance at one company, the investigator spent nearly three weeks determining all the facts and writing a final report. With no training and no guidelines for the investigator, the task took twice as long as it should have. In the end, most of the work had to be redone. This expensive process of investigating grievances ended only after job guidelines for the task were printed.

When students leave a course, they should carry out guidelines and procedure manuals on how to do the tasks that are essential to their positions. Too often, students are given only a beautiful notebook with copies of the visuals and exercises, plus miscellaneous notes. These notebooks usually rest on a shelf until one of their children needs a good-looking binder for a school project.

A student binder should serve two purposes: *An exercise manual for the class* and *a reference book for the job.* If job procedures are missing, students will not be able to apply what they have learned back on the job. In fact, it may take the students weeks or months before they can implement the course lessons. The course developer or instructional designer needs to provide two items: A reference manual for all the knowledge the students need over the next couple of years and an action planner that serves as a road map for implementing the course lessons. These materials also work well in management and executive-development courses.

Service organizations often produce outstanding reference manuals that their course graduates can use for several years. Of course, much of this information is now stored in electronic databases.

Periodic Performance Reviews

Numerous organizations conduct performance reviews after they complete major projects to remind everyone of how the process should have gone. For example, a major computer company conducted a win-loss review after each major selling opportunity, asking the following questions:

1. Did we understand the customer requirements?
2. Do we have a working partnership with the senior management team and line executives?
3. Do we have a working partnership with the chief information officer and all the key managers on his or her staff?
4. Did we make an outstanding presentation to create interest and differentiate our products and services?
5. Did we submit a superior proposal?
6. Did we handle the questions and objections in a satisfactory manner?
7. Did we reference the successful installations of our products?
8. Did we have the lowest-cost proposal?
9. Did we have an overpowering story on how to justify the additional expense?
10. Did we win or lose in this opportunity?

This fifteen- to sixty-minute meeting reinforces all the lessons taught in the sales curriculum and ensures that these lessons will be applied for upcoming projects.

A management-consulting firm had a similar system, but with different questions, after each major proposal for a professional engagement. They asked consultants whether they were working with an executive sponsor who could afford the study, who needed the study, and who had the authority to commission the study.

It is amazing how influential these periodic reviews can be on performance. They identify employees who are taking shortcuts or doing half the job. The manager can put these people on an improvement program, a remedy that works in most situations.

Service organizations often use checklists to determine if their employees are doing a complete job. A supervisor of hotel maids and a restaurant manager could also use these checklists. The automobile companies either call customers after their car has been serviced or ask them to fill out a survey to ensure that the dealer is doing a complete job.

It is really a waste of training resources not to follow up and ensure that jobs are being performed in accordance with the course lessons and support systems' guidelines. Performance evaluations are just another way to support your employees in achieving mastery of performance. These periodic reviews need to be viewed as positive because they allow employees to demonstrate how well they are doing their jobs.

In some organizations, trainees and employees receive a document that clearly outlines the personal-development tasks, on-the-job training assignments, training courses, and support systems that will help them master their jobs. As a result, the trainees and employees are highly motivated to achieve mastery of performance. After all, they know that mastering the job means more compensation, recognition, and job security. Employees who possess such a document are truly empowered people working within a learning organization.

Other organizations may utilize terms such as "empowered employees" and "learning organizations," but when one looks for the corresponding management system, one finds only a catalog of employee-development courses. Every organization needs the Systems Approach for Workforce Performance in order to build a workforce full of empowered employees working within a learning organization.

Support systems enable employees to know more and do more on their jobs. For this reason, they are an essential component of the performance system within the Systems Approach for Workforce Performance. In the next chapter, an entirely new level of support systems aimed at mastery of learning and performance will be described.

Chapter Twelve

Investigate Electronic Performance Support Systems

With advances in technology delivering so much more capability over the years, it was time for people to develop an entire new vision on how to train and supervise employees doing complicated tasks. The integrated electronic performance support system, invented by Gloria Gery and six others at AT&T in 1989, is a giant leap toward mastery of learning and performance.

Since then, authors have written many articles and a few books on the subject. Good resources are *Electronic Performance Support Systems* (1991) by Gloria Gery and *Future Work* (1994) by Andersen Consulting partners Charles D. Winslow and William L. Bramer. The American Society for Training and Development also has provided an outstanding *Info-Line* brochure. Today, there are at least three terms for this subject:

1. Electronic Performance Support System (EPSS),
2. Integrated Performance Support (IPS), and
3. Electronic Performance Support (EPS).

In this chapter, Electronic Performance Support System (EPSS) is used because it is feasible only through electronic computers and networks, and it truly is a system. The term Integrated Electronic Performance Support System is more accurate, but five words seems lengthy.

Definition of an Electronic Performance Support System

An EPSS has been defined as a computer-based system that provides on-demand access to learning procedures, coaching, databases, and tools to enable a user to perform a task quickly and accurately with a minimum of support from other people. Virtually every EPSS has the following components:

On-Line Databases. Rather than storing information in file cabinets, three-ring binders, procedure manuals, and books, EPSS stores information in computer databases that make retrieving data easy and accurate.

On-Line Help. The employee can ask the computer where information is and how to do certain procedures and tasks.

Integrated Training and Tutoring System. The training is just-in-time, with the employee learning at his or her work station rather than in classrooms or in a learning center. Usually, the employee receives the training in small modules, rather than over several days. The tutoring can be made available for rarely performed procedures and tasks. Training often includes simulations, tutorials, practice, and assessments.

Monitoring and Feedback System. If an employee makes a mistake, the computer quickly informs him or her that something is wrong or missing. This on-line supervision helps the employee achieve "first time right" performance.

Expert Knowledge System. The computer provides best practices based on exemplary performers, enabling the employee to become an A or B performer. An expert system is essentially an electronic job aid and support system.

Link to Other Applications. Although the goal of any EPSS is to enable an employee to complete basic business processes, sometimes it needs to work with the other applications in the organization.

Electronic Reference System. With EPSS, an employee can perform powerful on-line searches for the information needed to complete a task.

Some people are so enthusiastic about EPSS systems that they predict that all training in the future will be accomplished on such a system. This may be an overstatement because many jobs simply do not require the sophistication and cost of an EPSS system. An Electronic Performance Support System is one of five methods for acquiring knowledge and skills within the Systems Approach for Workforce Performance. It will be a major delivery system for high-volume jobs doing complicated tasks.

Recently, ASTD commissioned a study by SB Communications of Hingham, Massachusetts and received 639 replies. The study showed definite activity on EPSS projects within large organizations. Seventy-one percent of the respondents plan to take at least one EPSS development project past the proposal stage in 1997. Company areas most likely to use EPSS are customer service, support, operations, and sales, as well as complex administrative functions.

Benefits of EPSS

One benefit of EPSS is that it provides mastery of learning and performance, thus meeting the quality objectives of Total Quality Management (TQM). Almost every company that has invested in EPSS has been a leader in the quality movement.

A second benefit is that a well-designed EPSS should reduce operating expenses because it maximizes the performance of information systems, databases, and employee performance.

Third, and in most cases, an EPSS will increase customer satisfaction because the front-line workers know more and can do more for customers.

Fourth, an EPSS will reduce the cost of training, job aids, and support systems in many companies.

Fifth, an EPSS will increase employee morale and make workers feel more empowered to do a complete job. This higher job satisfaction usually reduces the attrition rate and cost of hiring entry-level employees.

Sixth, the EPSS has a built-in change-management system so that it can be improved continuously. Companies can continually update all of their procedures and training modules.

Seventh, an EPSS can be customized by a job's task requirements so that an employee will not have to accommodate the challenges of several information systems. An EPSS exemplifies a user-friendly system. As Gloria Gery (1991, p. 34) states, "The goal of an electronic performance support system is to provide whatever is necessary to generate performance and learning at the moment of need."

Essential Elements of an EPSS

An EPSS typically consists of multimedia personal computers, an enterprise computer, databases (including still images and videos), a wide-area network with workgroup server, a local area network with work stations, a user interface system, instructional design, application software, cognitive sciences (how people learn), help systems, an expert system (artificial intelligence based on knowledge-based systems), assessment systems, systems integration, and change-management systems.

An EPSS requires a strong working partnership between a company's training function and its information systems group. In some companies, the information systems group, working with line management, has taken the leadership role in designing, developing, and implementing EPSS projects. Integrating multiple systems to form a performance-support system is not a task for a beginner. Although many people can talk about an EPSS, only a few have actually designed one. Even fewer people have ever installed such a system.

Examples of Electronic Performance Support Systems

Intel, the leading manufacturer of chips for personal computers, developed an EPSS for the critical job of identifying chips with problems and determining how to fix them. The new system enabled operators to make immediate comparisons between the new chip and the standard ones stored in the computer. This new EPSS, which included audio coaching, drastically reduced operating expenses because it provided a productivity breakthrough in workforce performance.

A major defense contractor implemented an EPSS to assist maintenance technicians in the job of diagnosing and repairing jet engines. Previously, if a pilot detected a problem in flight, the maintenance technicians would take hours to discover the exact problem, locate parts, and make repairs. With the new EPSS system, they completed this task within thirty minutes.

A computer company developed an EPSS to enable its service personnel to diagnose and repair equipment problems. The company combined new diagnostic systems with new tutoring systems and databases to provide service employees with the "best thinking" concerning each potential problem. Here again, EPSS increased customer satisfaction and reduced operating expenses.

Andersen Windows, a leading manufacturer of windows and patio doors, developed an EPSS because its dealers and customers could no longer understand all the information available on its hundreds of products. Each product required a library of binders to explain its options and features. The new EPSS brought the retailers and contractors together in a dealer's office to determine which product best suited the customer. As a result, the company went from every fifth shipment having an error to almost zero shipping errors. Needless to say, this EPSS caused a breakthrough by lowering selling and distribution expenses and increasing customer satisfaction significantly.

An expanding hotel chain discovered that traditional training was not meeting its needs. Employees would go to a central education center for two weeks of training on basic reservation and billing systems. Too often, employees would leave the business within a few months. Their successors would be given unstructured on-the-job training that ultimately failed. With the new EPSS, training is available at each hotel when it is needed, which reduces the cost of training, cost of errors, cost of supervision, and cost of attrition.

Feasibility of an EPSS

Too often, an EPSS is compared to an outdated series of content-based courses. This comparison is usually invalid because it involves two extremes. The unstructured, nonmeasured, poorly managed training system will, of course, look bad compared with an Electronic Performance Support System. An EPSS should be compared with performance-based training courses, structured on-the-job training assignments, and outstanding basic support systems that include appropriate job aids. Then, the training and performance department can determine if a large investment of resources is justified to create a customized Electronic Performance Support System. In most organizations, only a few jobs justify an EPSS. These jobs have at least one of the following characteristics:

- Front-line workers who interface with customers on complex issues requiring an extensive knowledge base.
- Many employees working at remote locations such as branch offices, retail stores, manufacturing sites, and hospital chains.
- Information that needs to be updated frequently and be available to employees immediately.
- Jobs requiring mastery of learning and performance in a short time.
- Jobs that can help the organization achieve a strategic advantage, resulting in increased market share and earnings.
- Jobs for which an EPSS will reduce operating expenses.
- Jobs for which employees use numerous electronic databases and interface with information systems throughout the work day.

Barriers to Using EPSS

Deciding to use EPSS is much like deciding to reengineer: It represents a radical departure from, rather than an enhancement to, an existing training program and support system. Electronic Performance Support Systems aim for daily optimum performance and for a major breakthrough in workforce performance, not for incremental improvements. Of course, whenever there is a giant leap forward, barriers to change arise.

Some persons, including a few educators, continue to resist the use of technology. They believe that knowledge can be transferred only in a classroom setting with eye contact. Fortunately, the number of those resisting technology is decreasing rapidly due to the widespread use of personal computers, FAX machines, ATMs, and electronic mail. In fact, resistance to technology decreases every day and will not represent a serious barrier in the very near future.

A far more serious barrier is the basic education of potential employees. To operate an EPSS, an employee needs to have a solid high school education. Only 75 percent of today's high school graduates fall into that category. With 60 percent of high school graduates going on to institutions of higher learning, a shortage of employees qualified to operate an EPSS may develop soon.

In the United States, 9 percent of the population cannot read or write well enough to meet an entry-level job's basic requirements. This translates into twenty-seven million people who can do only the most simple jobs. Some retail establishments use cash registers that have pictures of the products on the keys, a feature that permits functionally illiterate people to operate them. An EPSS, however, does not use pictures on its keys.

Another problem is that seeing the big picture is difficult for many. An EPSS crosses functional and departmental lines, so there are organizational barriers that must be overcome to create an outstanding system.

Old habits are difficult to break. In one merchandising organization, the buyers implemented an outstanding EPSS system. Unfortunately, they insisted on printing out their outmoded reports because they wanted to order merchandise the way they did with their old ledger card system. Several months elapsed before the buyers adapted completely to the new system.

Systems design can also create barriers if the EPSS development team does not abide by the ease-of-use principle. It is very easy to build in so much complexity that the system is difficult to use.

Probably one of the greatest barriers to overcome is the magnitude of change. The more incompatible the design is with organizational structure, political groups, measurements, reward systems, and culture, the harder it is to sell an EPSS to a company or government agency. The first project is always the greatest challenge because people still view an EPSS solution as being high-risk. The "small thinkers" within an organization usually sit on the sidelines and let the "big thinkers" and "pioneers" make this decision. It takes a true organizational leader to approve the first EPSS project. Typically, the number-one concern is how to justify the cost to develop an electronic performance support system.

Justification for an EPSS

In feedback from the study by SB Communications, ASTD reported in the January 1997 issue of *Training and Development* magazine that only 10 percent of EPSS projects had been evaluated for improved job performance and only 5 percent for return on investment. Like many other types of training, the most commonly used evaluation method was participant feedback. This news was almost unbelievable! Given the expense of such systems and their potential impact on productivity, EPSS evaluations will need to become more sophisticated and meaningful.

Gloria Gery (1991, p. 179) states that the first step in selling an EPSS is to demonstrate business impact—to show how the proposed EPSS will help an organization achieve its operating and financial objectives.

Chapter Seventeen addresses the subject of justifying simple training systems as well as EPSS systems. The key to the latter is economic justification. The training organization must answer the following questions:

1. How long does it take at this time for an entry-level employee to achieve job mastery? What are the costs associated with this training period?
2. What are the current true costs to perform all the tasks an EPSS will cover?
3. What additional benefits will an EPSS provide?

After these questions are answered, an EPSS also needs an executive sponsor who has the need for the system and who can afford and approve it, usually a corporate officer or senior executive. It would be a rare situation for a middle manager to approve an electronic performance support system. Quite often, the senior executive needs to represent several line organizations or functions because the EPSS crosses organizational boundaries.

A company must practice the principles of change management when implementing an EPSS. For this reason, the project leader is typically a change agent from middle management. As stated earlier, a strong working partnership must exist between the training, information systems, and line organizations in order to design and install a successful EPSS.

The ASTD *Info-Line* has an EPSS Project Plan that outlines seventeen necessary steps for design and implementation. Several companies now specialize in the design and implementation of EPSS. The Princeton Center in Pennington, New Jersey, has designed off-the-shelf shells, called Hy Performance, that reduce EPSS development time and cost. In some cases, the Hy Performance shells satisfy 80 percent of a project's performance support needs at 20 percent of the cost.

Talent Needed for an EPSS

An EPSS project requires the following specialists:

- Producer or Project Manager (who handles schedules, budgets, and personnel; resolves conflicts among creative talent; and holds progress meetings).
- Subject Matter Experts (supplied by the line organization).
- Performance Consultant.
- Instructional Designer.
- Writer.
- Editor and Proofreader.
- Illustrator, Animator, or Graphics Specialist.
- Audio Technician.
- Video Technician.
- Systems Programmer (from the information systems department).
- Authoring System Personnel.
- Interface EPSS Designer.
- Tester, Evaluator, or Assessment Specialist.
- Implementation Specialist.

Although multimedia tools and authoring systems make it possible for one or two persons to handle all of these roles, few people have the training, technical, artistic, and management skills to perform all of these jobs at an optimum level. Therefore, an EPSS is developed best by a cooperative and talented team of experts.

Very few government agencies and corporations can afford a full-time staff for developing an EPSS. For this reason, companies often hire an outside firm. These firms may be large organizations such as Andersen Consulting or small businesses that specialize in EPSS projects. These companies have learned how to develop a cost-effective EPSS the hard way. Why reinvent the tools, processes, and control systems? It makes little sense to be a pioneer when professionals have already learned how to develop a successful and affordable EPSS.

How to Start

Every large- and intermediate-size organization has a potential need for an electronic performance support system, although most people do not believe it. They think that an EPSS is only for large, rich, and pioneering organizations.

This misunderstanding permeated the airline industry in the 1960s. A few creative people and a sponsoring executive from American Airlines had a brainstorming session that created what we now call an airline reservation system. With the limited technology of the 1960s (mainframes tied to typewriters), most people would not have considered the original airline reservation system to be the beginning of an EPSS, but that is exactly what it evolved to be.

American Airlines teamed with IBM to create the pioneering system. There were many mistakes and cost overruns, but American Airlines emerged with an industry-wide strategic advantage that lasted for decades. The first reaction from competitors was, "That reservation system is just a publicity stunt using technology that only a rich airline could afford." The competitors predicted that the typewriters would break down, resulting in long lines of unhappy customers. Instead, the airline reservation system gave American Airlines control over its inventory of seats, and customers preferred the system.

Eventually, a few other airlines tried to develop a smaller and less costly system. It turned out to be a second-class effort that was later scrapped for a first-class one. Today, almost every major airline has a reservation system. Many small- and intermediate-size airlines share a system.

Later, American Airlines tied its famous Frequent Flyer program to the reservation system to extend its strategic advantage. Over the years, advancing technology made the system more flexible and less costly, so the company added even more programs to it. Today, thousands of travel agents use the system, and passengers can access it from their home computers.

Federal Express built an EPSS for employees who pick up and deliver packages. Once again, the competition laughed it off as a promotional stunt. Federal Express gained market share and increased revenues by proving to its worldwide customers that the company knew where every parcel was every minute of the day. Now, competitors are building similar systems.

Executives in charge of training and performance should ask these five basic questions:

1. What application or business process would our competitors select to build their first EPSS?
2. What advantages would they achieve with an EPSS?
3. How long would it take our organization to duplicate their EPSS?
4. How much market share would our company lose before customers accepted our EPSS as being equal to or better than their system?
5. How much damage would our "progressive" reputation sustain if we put forth a great come-from-behind effort on EPSS?

A come-from-behind effort normally takes at least two years. Therefore, a chief training officer or director of training should determine which two or three critical jobs could achieve breakthroughs in workforce performance with an EPSS, then communicate this information to the CEO and other senior executives. The senior management team should understand thoroughly how an EPSS can achieve potential breakthroughs in workforce performance. They should also know the potential benefits as well as the costs to develop and implement. The line executives should also know the risks of *not* implementing an EPSS.

The senior executives will undoubtedly want to know which application area or process should be used for a pilot test. The CTO must be ready to make a recommendation, forecast costs and schedules, and know vendors who can help to develop and implement the EPSS. A pilot test should be completed before an EPSS is implemented throughout the organization. During the test, the CTO can demonstrate that he or she knows how to create and manage change. An EPSS should also be considered during every major reengineering effort.

Some people are wondering whether electronic performance support systems are just another flash in the educator's pan of tricks. The answer is clearly no. If employees (especially front-line employees) have databases, knowledge, training, and decision-making tools at their fingertips, they can achieve mastery of learning and performance and satisfy customers. They can also be more creative, more efficient at developing products, faster at delivering services, and more helpful at meeting higher customer expectations. The EPSS can lift a workforce's performance and professional reputation to a higher level.

Gloria Gery and other experts on this subject predict that many large- and intermediate-size organizations will develop EPSSs over the next twenty to twenty-five years. Small organizations will share an EPSS, just as several small airlines share complex reservation systems today.

Electronic performance support systems do not stand alone as the only program in workforce training; they are another essential component of a performance system within the Systems Approach for Workforce Performance. Fortunately, given their complexity and expense, only a few jobs within each organization demand the resources of an EPSS at this time. Most employees can achieve mastery of learning and performance with a combination of performance-based training programs, personal-development projects, on-the-job training assignments, and low-tech support systems.

Technology alone cannot make an employee smarter, but it can turn an average performer into a superior one by providing online sources of knowledge and expert systems. An EPSS supplements an employee's memory and opens up a new world for performance consultants and instructional designers.

Chapter Thirteen

Develop Reward and Recognition Programs

The workplace is changing. Executives have delegated more responsibility to managers, supervisors, and employees, who are required to complete tasks right the first time to achieve quality objectives. Executives expect them to be creative and to make decisions as empowered employees. As a result, traditional reward and recognition programs have become outdated.

In the past, rewards were linked to promotions. In the new flatter organizations, there are simply fewer promotions, so recognition and rewards must change. This situation is actually healthy, because too many employees and managers focused their activities on getting promoted rather than on increasing performance and achieving results.

The old saying goes, "Our most important assets walk in and out the door every day." Almost every annual report states, "Our most important asset is our employees," but few organizations have a sound reward and recognition strategy that is tied to business objectives and on-the-job performance. The Systems Approach for Workforce Performance is not complete until reward and recognition programs have been included. These programs motivate employees and managers to apply the knowledge and skills obtained in the performance system to achieve superior workforce performance. After all, if reward and recognition systems remain the same, employees will revert to business as usual. The Chief Training Officer must ensure that the performance consultants work closely with the HR specialist in charge of recognition programs to ensure that every performance system includes reward and recognition programs.

Reward and recognition systems help stimulate change. They enable employees and managers to feel a sense of responsibility and ownership in an organization's strategic directions and in its annual operating objectives. Two excellent books on the subject should be read by all managers: Bob Nelson's *1001 Ways to Reward Employees* (1994) and Thomas Wilson's *Innovative Reward Systems for the Changing Workplace* (1994).

As Ken Blanchard said, "If there's one thing I've learned in my life, it's the fact that everyone wants to be appreciated. This goes for managers as well as employees, parents as well as children, and coaches as well as players. We never outgrow this need. Although this might sound like common sense, so often I've found that common sense is not common practice in organizations today" (Nelson, 1994, p. ix).

Tie Reward and Recognition Programs to Objectives

It makes sense to tie reward and recognition programs to organizational objectives and job performance, which is why they are part of the management system. It may be near the end of the steps for the Systems Approach for Workforce Performance, but it represents one of the key factors in making the overall system a success.

The business objectives for which employees are rewarded may include things such as increasing shareholder value, meeting specific quality objectives, achieving production goals, reaching sales quotas, processing a stated number of documents, increasing customer satisfaction, achieving higher employee morale, reducing the cost of supervision, lowering operating expenses, building stronger partnerships with vendors, increasing the speed of a process, bringing products or services to market faster, increasing earnings, or increasing market share. Performance objectives are usually more specific, such as servicing all calls within one hour or having no complaints after a product has been serviced.

A reward and recognition program is any process or event within an organization that encourages, reinforces, or compensates an employee for achieving a high performance level. This reward may be a salary, bonus, informal award, formal award, cash award, or noncash gift. The program must motivate an employee to achieve results in order to earn the reward and recognition.

Avoid Negative Results

Sometimes reward and recognition systems do not function as intended. For example, in a large computer company, the sales vice president decided to pressure branch office managers on preparing trainees for sales school. He told the sales school managers to rank all graduates on their test scores, attitudes, presentations, demonstrations, and sales calls. The branch managers were later ranked within districts in a national field operations report.

It did not take long for the branch managers to react to this new ranking system. They sent only their star performers to sales school. The other trainees were assigned to sales territories without the benefit of training. Thus, the people who required the training the most were not sent to classes.

In other incentive programs, the best performers hide their secrets for achieving outstanding performance because they are paid more if the rest of their group performs at a lower level than they do.

In some organizations, employees cheat to achieve certain objectives. It is difficult for people to remain honest when objectives can be so easily faked. Cash, head count, sales, installations, or number of documents are firm objectives that can be recorded accurately. Giving awards for good attitude, on the other hand, opens the door to subjectivity and dishonesty.

In a few organizations, the sales personnel will sometimes book bad business to increase their numbers. The punishment for this must be decisive and swift.

Too often, incentives make superiors look good, but force employees to do some unnatural tasks to please their bosses. This reduces customer satisfaction. Wall Street is now experiencing this problem. To avoid negative results, all new reward and recognition programs should be tested to ensure that they help the organization achieve the desired result.

The classic example of a reward program that is out of control may be CEO compensation. Tying pay to performance is a great idea, but when the stock market goes over the top, the pay for

CEOs far exceeds what compensation committees had intended. It has turned into an embarrassment of riches that is difficult to explain.

Successful Elements of a Reward System

Due to misdirected and ineffective programs in the past, some organizations try to operate with a reward and recognition system consisting only of a monthly salary. This program might work in an organization in which everyone is highly motivated and aims for a high performance level. In most American organizations, however, this system rarely works because of the work environment's immense diversity and complexity.

The American workforce has a history of rewarding only heros and top performers, but now teams need to be rewarded as well, another reason why reward and recognition programs must change.

Some people believe that rewards reduce creativity and risk taking and cause only a temporary sense of accomplishment. They also claim that reward systems reduce cooperation between employees. For example, teachers' unions sometimes oppose special awards to teachers, saying that all teachers do an outstanding job, which is simply not the case.

Successful reward and recognition programs need to achieve the following:

1. Help employees achieve organizational objectives.
2. Have a positive impact on performance.
3. Enhance collaboration within the workplace.
4. Be viewed as fair by fellow employees.
5. Focus performance on serving the customer.
6. Be effective in good and poor years.

Base Pay as a Reward System

Base pay is the compensation that an employee or manager earns for coming to work and doing a job as required. Employees count on this money to pay their basic living expenses, to buy a house, to fund a child's college education, and to save for retirement. The vast majority of employees receive only base pay. They do not receive an incentive bonus. Occasionally, they may receive an informal noncash award. Base pay forms the foundation of the contract between the employee and the employer.

Base pay is often a point of discussion and contention; many employees feel underpaid. After all, everyone would like an above-average salary that keeps pace with inflation. Sometimes, unions and management struggle over what the rate of base pay should be. For this reason, companies often evaluate jobs by level of complexity, risk, and achievement to determine a fair base pay.

Base pay represents a fixed expense in most organizations. Increases to base pay become fixed increases in the cost of labor, which is why many management teams choose to downsize to reduce operating expenses. For example, a 5 percent annual increase becomes almost 28 percent more over five years. If productivity increases by more than 28 percent, this wage adjustment is affordable. If not, the organization must charge more for its products or services or show a reduction in profits. In the world of government agencies, higher taxes result when agencies fail to achieve productivity gains.

The purpose of base pay is to attract and retain very good employees by providing a basic standard of living for their work efforts. The pay scale is often based on what is fair in the industry. A few organizations have a stated policy to pay above-average wages in order to obtain top performers and to achieve lower attrition rates. Employees want a fair system, as does management. Compensation companies can help to create this equity with salary studies and advice to corporations and government agencies.

Paying for Knowledge

The revolutionary idea of paying for knowledge turned up a few years ago in manufacturing companies. Now, numerous service organizations have adopted the concept, including Federal Express.

Sometimes called pay for learning or skill-based pay, the intent is to link employee skills to compensation. Of course, most training managers support this new reward system because it creates an incentive for employees to attend more courses and learn additional skills. The employer benefits by having a well-trained workforce that is cross-trained on several jobs. Customers are pleased because more employees understand many steps in the overall operating process.

Some companies reject the idea because it forces the organization to pay for knowledge and skills not used by an employee in a particular job. Too often, knowledge and skills are lost over time when they are not used frequently and are not there when needed.

Pay for knowledge has been used for years in the fields of education, law enforcement, firefighting, and military organizations. About 8 percent of manufacturing companies use it; only 2 percent of service organizations use it.

One of the most satisfied companies using pay for knowledge is Shenandoah Life Insurance Company in Roanoke, Virginia. They believe that they are doing more work with fewer employees, while simultaneously increasing customer satisfaction. They have had so many visitors to their facilities that they now charge a fee for each visit.

Pay for Performance

Mike Hammer, one of the authors of *Reengineering the Corporation* (1993), wrote an article for the September 1996 issue of *Chief Financial Officer* magazine. He said it was time to slaughter the most sacred of corporate cows, the compensation system. He recommended a new five-part system designed to focus on performance:

1. Base pay (determined by HR department).
2. Bonus for process results (determined by the executive who owns the process).
3. Personal contribution to process results (determined by the teammates or manager).
4. Company results (determined by the CFO).
5. Personal development (determined by the employee's manager).

This, of course, means that no single individual determines what an employee earns. This type of pay system would definitely require more effort and energy to manage, but it clearly focuses on employee performance.

Bonus as a Reward

More and more organizations are looking at other pay-for-performance systems to replace their base-pay systems. These systems may include the following elements:

- A bonus for achieving productivity goals.
- An annual bonus for executives, based on various measurements such as earnings, revenues, shareholder value, market share, and customer satisfaction.
- An annual bonus for first-line supervisors and middle managers based on business objectives.
- Sales-incentive plans based on quotas.
- Team incentives based on group accomplishments.
- Piece-rate incentives based on individual performance.
- Profit-sharing plans.

The basic reasons why companies are shifting to these incentive plans are that: (1) They want their employees and managers to be more involved in overall operating goals; (2) They want to recognize outstanding performers; (3) They want the annual expense of compensation to be more variable; (4) They want to avoid annual fixed salary increases; and (5) They want the focus to be on performance rather than on pay.

Incentive plans require a great deal of effort to administer. In too many situations, the bonus becomes an annual fixed cost because employees expect and are paid a basic bonus. Incentives are also not easy to establish. If they are wrong, they generate negative reactions and require many meetings to fix.

On the other hand, anyone who has ever been on an incentive system knows that it does motivate an individual to perform better. Team incentives pose a greater challenge, but they still motivate many teams to higher performance levels.

However, in many systems, managers unintentionally shortchange their star performers and overpay their sluggards. Steven Kerr, the chief learning officer at General Electric, made this observation after studying the compensation and reward systems of seventy-five companies. He concluded that to truly motivate people, the incentive pay or award must be at least 10 to 12 percent above base salary. He believes that compensation must be linked to job performance rather than to promotions. His aim now is to increase the variable pay at GE from 7 percent to 12 percent.

Informal Awards and Recognition

Informal awards can be given with only one or two approvals and can be done in a relatively short period of time. In fact, the recognition works best when it appears to be spontaneous. To achieve maximum impact, the recognition should be given in the following manner:

1. The manager should have a private meeting with the outstanding performer to say how pleased management is with his or her performance.
2. The manager calls a meeting to recognize the individual in front of his or her peers.
3. The manager and middle manager send a personal note of appreciation.

Napoleon Bonaparte knew the value of a military decoration. He once remarked, "A soldier will fight long and hard for a bit of colored ribbon." The same is true for a salesperson, who wants to wear a special badge or ribbon for belonging in a top sales group. Informal awards should be recorded in the personnel files as recognition for superior performance.

These awards are often inexpensive, but they make a great impact on the workforce. Here are some examples:

- Employee of the week or month (picture on the wall, special parking place).
- Day off with some spending money.
- Night on the town with spouse or friend.
- Dinner and tickets to the theater.
- Tickets to an athletic event.
- Trip to headquarters and lunch with senior executives.
- A check of up to $500.
- Name on a special plaque or trophy.
- A special gift such as a piece of Steuben glass.
- Picture on a Hall of Fame wall.

- Catalog of gifts for outstanding performers.
- Lunch with a corporate officer.
- Team dinner or team outing.
- Blazer jacket.
- Individual home computer or desk set.
- Limousine ride.
- Gift certificate.

It is wonderful for an employee to come home to his or her family with good news about an individual or team recognition. Remember, recognition programs are even more important today because they often substitute for pay raises and promotions.

Thank You Awards and Service Awards

Thank you awards or service awards represent recognition for doing a job over an extended period of time. Examples of such awards include flowers, a note of thanks, doughnuts and coffee, a luncheon, or just some praise.

With so much downsizing and reduced job security, many people believe that service awards should be eliminated. On the other hand, long-term dedicated employees are always the backbone of any workforce. Many progressive companies reward these people with such things as:

- A new service pin for every five years.
- Special recognition at the twenty-five-year mark.
- A luncheon every five years.
- A note of appreciation from a senior executive.
- Additional vacation days.

Formal Awards

Formal awards usually involve a significant amount of money with a series of sign-offs to be certain that the awards are given consistently. These awards are given to recognize employees and managers who make a special contribution to the organization.

The person may be the inventor or creator of a product or service that has done well in the marketplace, someone who creates a special training program that increases workforce performance, or someone who breaks a performance record. The award should be given only for performance that is above and beyond the call of duty.

Senior executives should approve these awards and present them. There should be no doubt that the individual or team deserves the award. The reaction of their peers should be positive. The recipient(s) should receive major publicity throughout the organization (a photo session with the senior executives, a write-up in the company newspaper, a formal announcement of the award).

Mary Kay Cosmetics awards pink Cadillacs, mink coats, and diamond rings to its top performers. IBM had a corporate awards event that lasted three days. To be invited, each person had received a $10,000 Outstanding Contribution Award. Then, on the final night, the CEO handed out more awards that ranged from $10,000 to $100,000. In addition, several employees were designated as IBM Fellows and received five years' worth of research money for their new projects. This may seem like an enormous amount of money, but remember, it was individuals and team performers who helped IBM become a $70 billion company. The awards were more then earned.

Remember, the CTO, curriculum managers, and performance consultants do not have to be the experts on reward and recognition systems, but they need to have a continuous working partnership with the people in HR who are.

Companies should have a reward and recognition program for every major job category, an essential element of the Systems Approach for Workforce Performance. Very few organizations integrate recognition and reward programs with training and support systems. Therefore, most organizations do not receive a full payback for their performance systems.

Chapter Fourteen

Evaluate Job Performance

Most organizations do not have a systematic method for improving workforce performance. They use traditional performance-management systems that are based on generalized objectives and appraise workers annually on the famous bell-shaped curve.

Problems with Performance-Management Systems

In May 1996, Chris Lee wrote an article on this subject in *Training Magazine* ("Performance Appraisal," pp. 44–59). Her subheadline was right on target: "The annual performance appraisal may be the most universally hated ritual in corporate life." She added, "Call them appraisals, evaluations, or reviews, the ugly truth is that most employees dread receiving them almost as much as managers hate giving them." How could this situation exist after thousands of companies have invested so much time and so many resources improving their performance-management systems?

Most managers or supervisors are weak at establishing good objectives, and most dislike telling employees how to improve. On the flip side, most employees dread annual appraisals, because they resent what they believe is petty criticism when they are working hard. Because many organizations tie their appraisal systems to annual salary increases, managers are forced to have the proper balance of A, B, C, and D performers to stay within the budget for salary increases. As a result, many employees believe that they receive inaccurate appraisals for budgetary reasons. Unfortunately, they are often correct.

Obviously, employees resent C and D ratings, especially if they were A and B students in school. Most employees start out as C or

D performers after being promoted to a new job, but it is still a painful experience to receive the rating. Employees also know that companies can use their appraisal ratings to terminate them if the company suddenly downsizes for financial reasons, even if they are satisfactory performers. Although most performance-management systems are started with good intentions, they often become a negative motivator.

For C and D performers, the performance appraisal represents the most negative event in the entire work year; this is also true for B performers who believe they are A performers, so their self-esteem is lowered during the appraisal.

Most large companies and government agencies have revised their performance-appraisal forms dozens of times and spent millions of dollars to train managers and supervisors on improving the system. This time and money has not been well-spent. In addition, the wording used to describe an A, B, C, D, or Failure on most appraisal forms is amusing to read and terribly ineffective at differentiating levels of performance. Of course, the Equal Opportunity Employment commission (EEOC) lawsuits have not helped matters either.

Research by the Hay group (Weiss and Hartle, 1996) tells us that employees want to know the following information about their performance:

1. What am I expected to achieve in my job and how will success be judged? They want statements that define mastery of learning and performance for each major job category.
2. How am I doing? How close am I to the standards for the job?
3. Have I achieved mastery, and if not, where should I improve?
4. Where am I going in the organization?

Since 1988, according to Tracey Weiss and Frank Hartle (1996) of the Hay Group, writing in *Reengineering Performance Management,* the percentage of employees—from hourly employees to top managers—who say they understand how their performance is judged has hovered around 50 percent. Even worse, more than half say poor performance is tolerated in their company. Even a larger percentage agree with the following statement: "In my area, some people do most of the work, while others do just enough to get by."

Reengineer the Performance-Management System

Scores of documents illustrate the problems with performance-management systems, but few people have developed break-through ideas on how to fix them. Dr. W. E. Deming, the quality expert, probably gave the most direct advice: "Remove barriers that rob people in management and in engineering of their right to pride of workmanship. This means *inter alia,* abolishment of the annual or merit rating and of management by objectives, management by the numbers" (Walton, 1986, p. 35). In most seminars, Dr. Deming was quite clear: "Throw out the bell-shaped curve" (point 12 of Deming's famous 14 points). This viewpoint shocked the HR and personnel community.

Dr. Deming believed that 95 percent of quality problems are built into an organization's systems by bad managerial decisions. He also believed that it is management's responsibility to improve the performance of an organization's basic business processes. He insisted that organizations adopt "first time right" as their goal so they could aim for employee mastery of learning and performance. *All* employees should be A or B performers. If an employee cannot reach that level, he or she should be reassigned to a job in which he or she can achieve that level or be gently terminated. Dr. Deming stated that organizations must think differently.

Unfortunately, few organizations have changed their traditional bell-shaped grading systems and their bell-shaped performance-management systems. Not making this change represents one of the major reasons why most organizations have not implemented a successful quality system or successful reengineering project.

For the training department, the following simple grading system will help motivate students.

Pass with Honors. This grade goes to the top-performing students within each class, those who demonstrate superior skills in case studies, role plays, sales calls, classroom exercises, and presentations. The number of students achieving this grade can range from 10 percent to 35 percent of the class. (Remember that this grade is not used in learning-center courses.)

Pass. This grade should be obtained by virtually all students in a learning-center course and the majority of students in a classroom course. It indicates that the student has mastered the lessons and acquired the skills taught in the course.

Fail. If a company has a satisfactory system of recruiting new employees, this grade will be given to under 1 percent of employees. In most cases, it is used only when a student has a serious personal or attitude problem. If at least 99 percent of the students cannot pass the course, then the course content and delivery system should be reviewed to determine how the course can be enhanced to reach the goal of mastery of learning. Students rarely lack the intelligence to pass a well-designed course. If there is a higher level of failure with entry-level courses, it is probably due to bad hiring decisions.

A similar system can be used for a performance-management system if an organization is willing to take a giant leap forward to mastery of learning and performance. The ratings could be as follows:

Outstanding Performance. This rating applies to those few employees (5 to 10 percent) who not only master their jobs, but who also contribute ideas on how to improve the job. They display leadership qualities that enable the organization to ask them to take on special assignments. In many situations, these people appear on the high-potential list for promotion. There are always a few exemplary employees within every major job category who deserve a special performance rating and additional compensation and/or recognition. The organization does not want to lose them, so they must be recognized and rewarded.

Very Good Performance. Most employees fall into this category. They learn how to master their jobs, and they are the solid day-to-day performers. Every organization needs many very good performers.

Needs to Improve Performance. This temporary rating stays with the employee until he or she masters the job, which should be as soon as possible. If employees cannot master their jobs within a reasonable length of time, they should know that they will be reassigned to a job that they can master or the organization will terminate them. The goal is simple: Only A and B performers will be kept by an organization that aims for mastery of learning and performance. The old solid C and D performers will have to find work elsewhere.

The Systems Approach for Workforce Performance is essential for organizations that aim for mastery of learning and performance. It represents a simple contract between the employer and the employee. The employer commits to establishing an outstanding performance system for each major job category. The employee commits to achieving mastery of learning and performance objectives. It is a win-win situation. When properly implemented, the system supplies the organization with the lowest cost of people and the highest productivity and earnings possible.

Unfortunately, Deming and other quality instructors never designed the complete management system to achieve the "first time right" goal, but using the Systems Approach for Workforce Performance forces management to articulate clearly what the employees must know and be able to do within every job category. A good performance-management system with individual appraisal sessions that motivate employees to work harder is the next step.

To determine the individual ratings, an organization can use either a 360-degree feedback process or a traditional manager-employee meeting. The organization may also use either a performance-based compensation plan or a salary scale. With a performance-based system, it is easier to reward top performers with larger increases that minimize the attrition rate. When an organization shifts from measuring performance on the bell-shaped curve to mastery of learning and performance, executives, managers, and employees exhibit a more positive attitude. Achieving mastery of learning and performance represents a giant step forward in meeting an organization's quality and operating objectives. Every employee wants to be a successful performer, which creates a very positive work environment.

Watching C and D performers leave an organization actually increases morale because the employees know that management is serious about mastery of learning and performance. For too many years, top-performing employees have watched C and D performers hide behind the bell-shaped curve and weak managers who could not handle terminating a poor performer. No one likes to do the work for a poor performer. This new system forces the supervisors and managers to do their jobs.

A study by Hunter (1990), published in the October 1995 *Harvard Business Review,* showed the productivity differences between top performers, average performers, and low performers. In *low-complexity jobs,* top performers achieved 300 percent more productivity than low performers. Average performers did 50 percent better than low performers. In *medium-complexity jobs,* top performers were 1,200 percent better than low performers, and average performers were 85 percent better than low performers. In *high-complexity jobs,* top performers went off the chart (were unmeasurable) compared with low performers, and the chart already showed that they were immeasurably better. Average performers were 125 percent better than low performers. This study documented what many people have believed for years: If you retain only A and B performers and provide good training, your organization will achieve a competitive workforce that knows more and does more than any other company within your industry.

The Systems Approach for Workforce Performance can be implemented without changing a performance-management system, but it is better to aim for a dramatic breakthrough in workforce performance by implementing the management system described in Chapter Three and changing the performance-management system as well.

Coaching and Developing Employees

Employee development should be one of the major job responsibilities for all supervisors, managers, and executives. Every employee should have a personal-development plan that his or her supervisor reviews at least once a year. It can be as simple as a one-page plan that outlines which training events should be scheduled, if any, during the next year, which personal-development activities should be completed, and which on-the-job training assignments should be tackled. The plan could also include special assignments such as being on a task force.

The manager or supervisor must continually help the employee master his or her job and tell subordinates why courses are so important to their careers. After they complete a course, the manager or supervisor should reinforce the lessons to ensure that the employees apply their new knowledge and skills to their jobs.

Many companies have implemented mentoring systems for career development, especially in equal-opportunity programs. Mentoring has been especially helpful to many women and minorities as they move into management ranks. A good mentoring system should be treated like a good coaching system. Supervisors, managers, and executives need to coach their subordinates frequently to ensure that they are achieving mastery of performance. They can also apply Situational Leadership ™ lessons so that a new person in a job receives much more coaching than an experienced person.

Managers must also remind employees that they are responsible for their own performance and mastery of job responsibilities, but a coach can help employees improve their performance and achieve greater satisfaction from their jobs. A coach usually has more experience and knowledge about a job, which can be a big help to those who work for the coach. The coach can also ensure that new people do not "drown" by taking on high-risk assignments with a high potential for failure.

Coaching is a two-way partnership. The new employee must ask for help, be willing to learn new tasks, and be eager to improve; defensiveness is not helpful. The coach, in turn, must maintain a positive and helpful outlook, rather than criticize. Organizations using the Systems Approach for Workforce Performance are better able to supervise and coach because job responsibilities and performance standards are so well defined.

Evaluating Team Performance

In the past, supervisors and managers used their "people-management" skills to work with individuals to increase performance. Now, many organizations have turned to using small work teams as a breakthrough strategy for reengineering their basic processes and gaining commitment to operating objectives. Most of these small groups have succeeded at generating innovative ideas and high-quality solutions to problems, capitalizing on the creativity and skills of the employees who are closest to the actual job. Some of these teams, with an emphasis on improvement, are referred to as "quality circles."

There are several types of teams. One type is referred to as the *baseball team* because each member has an assigned responsibility. Surgical teams are often organized this way, as are sales teams in complex high-technology markets and automobile-design teams. Essentially, the employees play different roles for the team, each with specific responsibilities. Employees on these teams receive evaluations that are very similar to individual performance reviews. The evaluations can single out individuals who are great performers, even if the overall team fails to meet key objectives.

The second type of team is more like a *football team.* Each employee has a specific job to do, but all members of the team must perform at a high level of achievement in order to meet the current objectives. A symphony orchestra exemplifies this type of team, and Japanese auto designers use this model to produce outstanding cars and trucks. For the football team, there must be evaluations of both individual and team performance. This type of team requires a strong leader.

The third type of team described by Sonnenfeld is a *tennis doubles team* on which employees have the same responsibilities, but change positions frequently. Employees are supposed to cover for fellow team members if they fail to complete a task. Here, the emphasis is on team performance, rather than individual performance.

Unfortunately, too many teams have been created as a substitute for well-defined performance requirements for major job categories. Companies believe that teams will figure out what to do to achieve organizational objectives. The result is the old bell-shaped curve, rather than mastery of learning and performance.

Teams are being discontinued by some companies, for a variety of reasons. Florida Power & Light employees complained that team meetings and problem-solving assignments were interfering with the "real work" of achieving monthly objectives. The Saturn division of General Motors has been replacing teams with individual performance in order to reach profit objectives. On the other hand, Motorola and other organizations have had tremendous success with teams.

If an organization does use teams, the Systems Approach for Workforce Performance needs to be implemented for both individual and team performance. Training and support systems are essential to successful teams, just as they are to individuals. An untrained team will not be any more successful than an untrained employee. Letting the better team members make up for the poor performing members does not work. This is just like the old unstructured on-the-job training system that rarely works.

The following elements are needed for a team to be successful:

Clear Performance Objectives. These should be created both for individual team members and for the team.

Outstanding Talent. All members should be high performing, as poor team performers can be very disruptive and can drag down team morale.

Clearly Defined Roles. Split responsibility within a team means no responsibility for results.

Documented Procedures and Methods. Team members must learn every procedure and learn how to make decisions, solve problems, share information, and avoid conflicts.

Effective Coaching and Reinforcement. Members must be coached in all procedures and reinforced in the lessons they learn, usually by other team members and supervisors.

On-the-Job Training Assignments. These must be given so that everyone learns and produces at a high level.

Support Systems. These ensure that the team achieves maximum results.

Training on Interpersonal Relationships. People who are trained on how to relate to each other well will be more productive.

Change Management System. This is necessary to keep the team working through times of constant change.

With all of these elements, teams often succeed at achieving breakthroughs in workforce performance.

When evaluating individuals or work teams, managers should remember the words of Dr. Deming: "Most performance problems are built into the system." When performance is lower than expected, the first place to look is at the system. Individuals do not create system problems and cannot solve them by themselves. In many cases, revising the business processes creates new training and support-system requirements. Teams can recommend changes, but cannot enforce them organization-wide.

Executive and Line-Management Participation

A stronger focus on job performance requires a new level of leadership from managers, who must clearly state what employees should know and be able to do. They must empower employees by articulating clear directions and goals.

Too many executives and managers just set broad objectives and let their "empowered" employees figure out how to achieve the goals. Empowerment is often used as an excuse for weak leadership. Millions of "empowered" employees are trying to figure out what their executives want them to do. Even if the employees can put the puzzle together, they rarely have adequate training and support systems to achieve organizational breakthroughs. For this reason, most organizations have just a workforce with some training rather than a competitive workforce.

The Systems Approach for Workforce Performance is empowering for a workforce because the tasks that employees must accomplish to achieve the organization's goals are clearly stated. The tasks stem from best practices used by subject-matter experts and exemplary employees. Performance evaluations administered by supervisors, acting as coaches, provide key information about what needs to be done and how performance will be measured, which will be discussed in the next chapter.

Chapter Fifteen

Implement Measurements and Benchmarking

For decades, educators and trainers have avoided measurements because they want to be evaluated on hard work and good intentions, rather than on the number of students who learn and apply their lessons. They believe that teaching is their only responsibility and that the students are responsible for learning the lessons. This short-sighted attitude has cost teachers significantly in compensation, recognition, and professional status.

The situation is comparable to a salesperson who does a great job of selling, but customers never buy the product. Selling, like many other professions, is based on achieving results. The customers must buy in order for the salesperson to be recognized as a top performer who earns an above-average income.

Measurements must be implemented in order for executives to accept education and training programs as "must do" activities. Improved job levels, compensation plans, and recognition programs for training personnel depend entirely on the training organization accepting the fact that students must learn their lessons, acquire skills, apply the lessons or skills, and achieve operating objectives. This applies to commercial companies, government agencies, and not-for-profit organizations.

Costs of the Training Function

For years, senior executives asked few questions about training. In most organizations, the training was decentralized and considered a minor expense because no one ever tallied the overall cost.

Accounting methods were inconsistent. For example, a sales meeting could be considered a training event, even if little or no training took place. Staff travel for training was frequently not separated from other travel.

All this is rapidly changing as tight expense control has become a part of almost every organization. With corporations and government agencies spending approximately $60 billion on training and another $60 billion for student salaries, they need to accurately account for the money. Evidence also exists that the $120 billion may even be understated. Virtually every organization that guesses at its total training expense understates it by 25 to 50 percent, according to a number of cost studies being performed by consultants. Probably less than 50 percent of all large- and intermediate-size organizations have conducted firm-wide cost studies of training cost, such as:

People in the Training Function. These include executives, managers and supervisors, performance consultants, instructors and course coordinators, course developers and instructional designers, education specialists (assessment, graphics, or other specialties), computer support personnel, general administrative personnel, class administrative personnel, and part-time personnel (converted to full-time equivalent).

Operating Costs. These include salaries of full-time training personnel, salaries of part-time training personnel, fees paid to external instructors, course-development expenses for internal or external projects, staff travel and living expenses, student travel and living expenses, course materials, administrative support, computer and technology support, rent and depreciation of facilities such as education or learning centers, furniture and fixtures, utilities, office equipment and information systems, and general overhead.

Student Payroll and Benefit Costs. These expenses must be counted for the time when employees leave their jobs to attend courses at either education centers or learning centers.

Every organization should know its overall training costs, although a special cost study may be required because traditional accounting systems rarely capture this information consistently.

Typical cost studies for very large organizations can be completed within sixty days.

Quantity Measurements

There are two major areas to measure for all training organizations, *quantity* and *quality*. Almost every training organization has quantity measurements, including:

- Number of executives, managers, and employees who require training.
- Number of completions per course number and description.
- Number of student hours or days planned versus time actually spent in training.
- Average training hours or days per employee.
- Cost of training for each course.
- Average cost of training per employee.
- Total hours of class time put in by instructors.
- Total hours of course development put in by instructors and course developers.
- Total hours of class-management time.
- Total hours of learning-center courses.
- Total number of courses completed in learning centers.
- Total number of hours or student days by each major type of delivery system.
- Total utilization of education centers and learning centers.
- Number of late cancellations and no-shows.
- Number of students on waiting lists for each course.
- Budget figures compared to actual figures.
- Average class size.
- Average cost per hour of training.

These quantitative measurements show that the training function is using its assets and resources in a cost-effective manner. Training personnel must always focus on cost containment. The following suggestions should be used to eliminate excess expenses:

- Courses with no firm business requirements should be eliminated.

- The wrong people attending the wrong classes is a waste of resources.
- Small classes should be combined.
- Duplicate or overlapping classes often are a major waste of money; these exist frequently in large organizations.
- Many courses are too long because they are developed by instructors who measure themselves on how much content is included, not on what lessons need to be learned.
- In large organizations, students are sometimes studying similar lessons every few years that are part of new course topics and new course names. This happens because the students did not learn or apply the lessons from previous courses.
- When lessons are not reinforced on the job, the training is usually a waste of time and resources.
- Most organizations that do not have an optimum delivery-system strategy use a more expensive delivery-system strategy.
- Many organizations develop and maintain several enrollment or administrative systems for their various training departments, compared to having one firm-wide system. In addition to being costly, these systems confuse managers and employees who must interface with them.
- Many organizations allow each training department to buy the same or similar courses from course-development companies without obtaining a quantity discount.
- In some organizations, there are simply too many courses.

In many cases, cost-containment measures as just described enable the company or government agency to reduce its overall training expenses by 10 to 20 percent. Maintaining a focus on cost containment must be a constant responsibility of the managers in charge of the training and performance organization.

It is important to remember that an employee must have an "embraceable responsibility." Too often, an organization continues to add more and more responsibility to a job until reaching the point at which it is impossible for one employee to do a complete job. In some situations, it is better to create two or three additional jobs and reduce the number of courses to a reasonable level. Overtraining can be quite costly.

Quality Measurements

Professor Donald L. Kirkpatrick from the University of Wisconsin invented the most widely used model for evaluating the quality of training in the 1950s. Although this model is forty years old, few companies have been able to implement it. The training function could have been a leader in the quality movement, but it lagged behind instead because most training departments failed to use quality measurements unless senior management insisted on it. The Kirkpatrick model proposes four levels of evaluation.

Level I: Evaluating Reaction

Kirkpatrick said that evaluating reaction is analogous to measuring customer satisfaction. Information about the student's satisfaction with the course is collected on some type of form, often called "happiness" or "smile" sheets. On the sheets, companies need to ask the following questions:

- Did the course meet your training requirements?
- How effective were the instructors?
- How do the education center's operations rate?
- How could the course be improved?

This valuable feedback enables the instructors and course developers to enhance the course as needed. The feedback should be compared with a standard of performance. Level I evaluations should always be utilized by the CTO and the management team.

Based on years of experience with Level I forms, the author recommends that the form be one page, no more than two. Tired students do not want to fill out a thirty- to sixty-minute feedback form unless it is for a pilot class. Most forms use a scale of five or ten ratings. The author found that a three-rating scale is best, because the students can distinguish easily between outstanding, good, and needs to improve. Many have a difficult time distinguishing between excellent and very good or poor and fair.

A consistent form and rating scale should be used throughout the organization for purposes of comparison. Most experienced instructors are masters at obtaining good ratings. (One instructor even had a wine and cheese party at his house the evening before he handed out the rating forms.) The one drawback to feedback forms is that companies tend to drop subjects that do not receive high scores and to include subjects that consistently score high, even if they are out-of-date. Because the entertainment factor plays a large role in the ratings, it is important to review course content periodically to ensure that the lessons are meeting the true course requirements.

Level II: Evaluating Learning

A training course should provide new knowledge and skills. In some courses, the lessons can also help change students' attitudes about a subject. It is important to measure if the students really learned the lessons, acquired the skills, or changed their attitudes. If learning does not take place, there is no hope for a change in performance.

The most common method for evaluating learning is to give a test. Especially for a pilot class, the students should take a pretest to measure what they know coming into the class. Then, at the completion of the course, they take a post-test to show how much more they have learned and what skills they have acquired. In many courses, only a post-test is used to be certain that the students have mastered the lessons and acquired the skills.

Another measurement method requires the students to develop plans of action for what they will do when they return to their jobs. This method works best in management-development courses.

Two important factors determine a test's worth: Reliability and validity. *Reliability* refers to the need for measurements to be consistent each time they are used and to produce consistent results. *Validity* refers to an instrument's ability to measure what it is intended to measure (such as ensuring that a test of knowledge actually covers all the important course content). Writing good measurement tests requires training on assessment methods.

More and more software manufacturers are requiring certification. Rather than taking the word of job applicants, chief information officers want to hire only systems programmers and application specialists who are certified on subjects such as networking, database management, and computer operations. This new emphasis creates a win-win situation for the employee and employer. The employer knows what talents a new hire will bring, and the employee is often paid more because he or she has certified knowledge and skills. Employers now pay for most certification-related training, which consists of the initial training required to be certified and the training required to maintain the certified status. Certification has been widely accepted for years in the fields of medicine, law, accounting, and insurance.

Novell, a large supplier of network software, has trained over 75,000 Certified Novell Engineers and over 60,000 Certified Novell Administrators. To receive a Novell certificate, a student must pass a series of challenging tests. At a cost of $5,000 per employee, these tests and courses represent a major investment in training. Here again, companies and government agencies are willing to pay for "must do" training that increases performance in key jobs. Although some trainers feel nervous about certification because it means that students must learn their lessons, the demand for training will expand at an enormous rate if this trend toward certification continues.

If the course features skill building, such as giving effective presentations, the students should demonstrate that they have acquired the skill. Training on presentations, sales calls, business writing, or many other topics requires the students to demonstrate that they have mastered the skills. Many organizations use before-and-after videotapes to show how much a student has improved.

Level III: Application of Lessons and Skills to the Job

Kirkpatrick calls this level "evaluating behavior," but the term sounds more like psychiatry than training to some executives, who are uncomfortable with the idea of changing or evaluating behavior.

Very few organizations do a good job measuring the application of lessons to the job because they try to do it one course at a time. The number-one reason why organizations have a difficult time with these measurements is their lack of focus on job performance. For example, it is almost impossible to apply Level III measurements to an awareness course on quality. Most course catalogs are merely a listing of courses by subject area; no curriculum of courses by major job categories exists. After an organization changes its focus to job performance and lists necessary courses by major job category, Level III measurements become quite simple.

Early in the performance system planning phase, an organization should identify what the employees within each major job category should know and be able to do. Then the training and performance organization works with subject-matter experts and line executives on task and needs analysis. At that stage, they ask line executives to determine what will be measured to show application of learning to the job, rather than trying to decide how to measure it after the courses are created and delivered.

Performance-based training leads directly to Level III performance-based measurements. The measurements can be made during interviews with supervisors and/or with program graduates. Usually, a sample of the course graduates is necessary. Sometimes, work observations are required. Operating records often provide Level III measurements, such as the number of proposals written or lines of code developed or internal audits completed.

Because it is important to allow time for the program graduates to implement their new knowledge and skills, Level III measurements are often made three to six months after a curriculum has been completed and the performance system is fully implemented.

Line executives want to know whether the employees who work for them are properly trained and whether they apply the lessons to their jobs. They seldom want to know the details of every course in the curriculum. Thus, Level III measurements applied to the entire curriculum and the overall performance system, rather than to each course, are more practical and cost-effective.

Level III measurements will usually result in changing or even eliminating some courses because lessons are not being implemented on the job. Some years ago, IBM had what many people viewed as a leading-edge ten-week Software Engineering Institute. It was a great honor to be invited to the Institute. Level I and II measurements showed that the students liked the course and learned their lessons. The faculty, which included external experts in the field of software engineering, believed it was the finest course in the country. When Level III measurements were applied to the overall curriculum for software engineers, it was a great surprise to find how few lessons were being applied to jobs. Accordingly, the Institute was completely redesigned, based on input from line executives who were in charge of software. The Institute's new design reduced its length to six weeks. As a result, IBM realized significant savings and improved performance.

In many situations, students return to their jobs and find substantial barriers to application of the lessons they have just learned. Sometimes, Level III measurements highlight problems within job procedures and methods that should be fixed. If that is the case, the performance consultant should focus on Step 2 of the Systems Approach for Workplace Performance.

A control group is often used to show the differences between trained and untrained employees. One automobile rental company had fifty new employees try to write rental agreements without training, then compared them to a group that had been trained. The comparison clearly showed what the executives wanted to know: Trained workers do more work, make fewer errors, and require less supervision. In this case, a one-time Level III evaluation justified training for future years.

Companies often use surveys to do Level III measurements. Of course, some students will say that they implemented the lessons even if they continue to work in the old manner. Therefore, telephone calls to supervisors in order to verify answers are usually a worthwhile investment.

In some situations, there is no reward or recognition for applying the lessons of the performance system. To fix this problem, the performance consultant should work on Step 5 of the Systems Approach for Workforce Performance.

If there are problems with the performance system after Level III measurements are implemented, the performance consultant should also review the effectiveness of coaching in Step 6 of the Systems Approach for Workplace Performance.

Level IV: Evaluating Results

Everyone agrees that Level IV is the most difficult and least performed measurement. Very few organizations really do a good job of evaluating results. Once again, the factor that hinders Level IV measurement the most is that the training consists of a patchwork of courses rather than a curriculum of courses and a complete performance system for each major job category.

The line executives should determine Level IV measurements while performing the needs and task analysis early in the performance system design phase. After all, they are conducting the training to improve the organization's overall performance. Trained employees will have a positive impact on many of the following measurements:

- Revenues or market share.
- Operating expenses.
- Cost of rework.
- Productivity.
- Product quality.
- Costs of supervision.
- Morale and job satisfaction.
- Attrition and cost of employment.
- Customer satisfaction.
- New strategic directions.
- Implementation of tactical decisions.
- Earnings.
- Communications.

Level IV measurements are much like Level III measurements in that the focus must be on the results of an entire curriculum and the entire performance system rather than on results from individual courses.

Because numerous factors can contribute to breakthroughs in operating and financial performance, trainers sometimes hesitate to say that training is a significant factor. Trainers should use measurements to take whatever credit is due them. For example, after a new product is announced, trainers should compare the sales records for trained and untrained sales personnel. A new product rarely sells by itself.

Arthur Andersen & Company used Level III and IV measurements to show that a trained group of tax professionals significantly outperformed a group of untrained tax specialists when they entered new markets for state and local taxes. It was clear that, even though all these tax professionals were successful in the federal tax market, they still required extensive training to achieve the firm's revenue objectives in state and local markets. Once again, performance evaluations proved the need for performance-based training within a major job category. The resulting five weeks of training (two weeks of self-study and three weeks in the classroom) were easily justified by the eventual revenue growth.

Level IV does not mean 100 percent proof that training is responsible for improved performance. Executives are simply looking for evidence that training and the performance system have had a positive impact on operating and financial objectives. Kirkpatrick used a great quote at the 1997 ASTD conference—"Be satisfied with evidence if proof is not possible." Too many trainers seem to think that they must have a precise mathematical system carried out to the fourth decimal point, when in most cases evidence beyond a reasonable doubt will suffice.

Kirkpatrick used a saying attributed to Mark Twain to describe the reality of measurements: "Everybody talks about it, but nobody does anything about it." Well, not exactly. In a recent *Training Magazine* survey ("Who Is Learning What?," 1996, p. 63) the respondents stated that 86 percent used Level I (reactions) on 85 percent of their courses. That is a believable figure because most training departments want feedback from their students. The respondents also stated that 71 percent do Level II measurements on 51 percent of their courses. This represents a big step forward from a few years ago when very few organizations used Level II measurements. However, it still is not adequate, as executives want proof that students learn the lessons and acquire the skills in all courses that they take, not just 51 percent of them.

Level III and IV feedback rates from the survey are almost unbelievable, based on the author's own work with over twenty-five clients. Even *Training Magazine* said the numbers seemed mendaciously high to many observers and could reflect the respondents' guilt rather than their actual practice. The respondents reported that 65 percent of them applied Level III measurements to 50 percent of their courses. They also claimed 49 percent of them used Level IV measurements on 44 percent of their courses. If these figures are even half true, a real breakthrough in measurement usage has occurred in recent years.

The American Society for Training and Development published the results of their "Benchmarking Forum Comparative Report" in the November 1996 issue of *Training and Development* magazine. They said 95 percent of the courses use Level I feedback measurements and only 34 percent measure Level II to be certain that the students learn the lessons. Only 13 percent of the courses had Level III measurements, which would tell the trainers if their lessons were being applied to the job. Only 4 percent use Level IV measurements, which tells us that very few organizations evaluate training results. These numbers are quite consistent with what the author has experienced during the past eight years with corporations that have large training departments. This set of facts tells us that even the best training organizations continue to struggle with how to implement the simple four-level Kirkpatrick model that has existed for forty years.

If senior executives understood the four levels of quality measurements, they would insist on applying all of them to every curriculum of courses and to the performance systems of their major job categories. As a former chief training officer and line executive, the author would not fund courses that did not fit into a curriculum for major job categories unless all four measurement levels were implemented. A few employee-development and management-development courses would be an exception to that rule. Almost every organization can improve on its quality measurements. Having worked with many of the ASTD Best Corporate Training Programs companies, the author knows even leading-edge corporations have a long road ahead of them before they reach the point at which all four quality measurement levels are implemented.

ROI and Other Measurements

Some people want a fifth level of measurement: Return on investment or ROI. Kirkpatrick said that he laughs when he hears people say that training professionals should be able to show benefits in terms of return on investment. On the other hand, more people are trying to achieve an ROI measurement. Some are forced into ROI by their financial executives because they have failed to implement the four levels of quality measurements and financial people need something to use. If a well-constructed Level IV measurement is developed for a curriculum by major job category, an ROI measurement is usually feasible. However, it would be a mistake to try to be too precise or to use too many assumptions. Senior executives are famous for poking holes in ROI justifications that are based solely on assumptions.

Numerous articles and books are available on measurement, such as *Evaluating Training Programs* (1996) by Donald L. Kirkpatrick. Jack J. Phillips published *Measuring Return on Investment* in 1994. This important book contains many fine articles on effective measurements.

Benchmarking Job Performance

A benchmarking forum that involved the leading training organizations and ASTD was discussed in Chapter Two. The forum resulted in the development of industry-wide benchmarks on such items as organizational structure, basic financial information and costs, facilities and equipment, administrative systems, and measurements.

Missing in most benchmarking studies is a focus on job performance within major job categories. Very few organizations compare their application programmers against other leading information systems users. Key finance jobs are not studied, even when a process such as accounts payable is benchmarked. The only job that is benchmarked consistently is sales.

In the future, when everyone is using good measurement systems, benchmarking will be utilized to determine how major job categories compare with their counterparts in similar organizations. Of course, companies must be willing to share information with benchmarking partners. Robert Camp, the benchmarking specialist from Xerox, has a ten-step process for this huge task:

1. Determine what to benchmark.
2. Identify the best organizations in those areas.
3. Collect data to measure your own and your benchmarking partners' performance.

4. Determine the current performance gap.
5. Project future performance levels, which become the new benchmark to achieve.
6. Communicate benchmark findings and gain acceptance.
7. Establish functional goals.
8. Develop action plans.
9. Implement specific actions and monitor progress.
10. Recalibrate benchmarks.

Other information on this subject is in Camp's book *Benchmarking* (1989) and in Michael J. Spendolini's *The Benchmarking Book* (1992).

Skills Inventory

Numerous companies and government agencies have attempted to maintain a skills inventory on their employees. The main purpose is to determine how many employees are fully trained in a particular job category and how many are partially trained. A number of skills-inventory systems have failed because they maintain too much information on each employee. To avoid such a failure a company must develop a list of critical (key) jobs, as described in Chapter Five. Next, the company must have a management system such as the Systems Approach for Workforce Performance.

Skills inventories serve another purpose: determining the true training requirements for the annual budget. They help trainers decide how many employees must be trained to reach the competence level required to meet the next year's operating objectives. A skills inventory also enables companies to redeploy employees to other jobs, for example, if there is a shortage of chemical engineers, some mechanical engineers may become chemical engineers with the proper training.

Sometimes a skills inventory categorizes employees based on their abilities within a service line or product area, for example, a skills inventory for a sales position could read as follows:

Level 1: Provide awareness information.
Level 2: Develop and write a proposal.

Level 3: Perform the entire selling process.

Level 4: Supervise the installation process.

Finally, a skills inventory enables a company to prioritize who will be enrolled first in courses that are overbooked. A first-come-first-served enrollment system may not be the most effective option in an organization that is experiencing explosive growth.

Additional Information on Measurements

At least three companies have established separate assessment and evaluation staffs. Arthur Andersen & Company is the leader. Sound auditing practices state that instructors and course developers should not perform their own evaluations, rather like having the cashiers audit a petty-cash fund. Andersen has an evaluation department staffed by assessment specialists. Motorola and AT&T have also established separate staffs for assessment and evaluation, and several other companies are in the process of creating such departments.

Quality evaluations build credibility with line and senior executives. As a result, training moves from a "nice to do" activity to a "must do" program that is as important as finance, manufacturing, marketing, and service. As Kirkpatrick said in his book, "When you are accepted, trusted, respected, and needed, lots and lots of wonderful things happen." For example:

- Your budget requests are granted.
- You keep your job and sometimes you are promoted.
- Your staff keeps their jobs.
- You are given more responsibility.
- You are consulted on all key decisions.

Do not just do it for the line and senior executives. Implement quality measurements for your own career and job satisfaction.

Line and senior executives love to hear any of these statements:

- The students will like their training.
- The students will learn their lessons and acquire the proper skills.

- The students will apply the new knowledge and skills to their jobs.
- The training will have a positive impact on operating and financial objectives.

Training departments need to be viewed as cost-effective leaders and as major contributors to organizational objectives. Few training and performance departments have reached this credibility level, which is why training budgets are reduced and downsized in too many organizations. To reach this credibility level, a chief training officer must establish measurements as one of the top priorities in his or her plan of action.

Part Four

How to Justify a Competitive Workforce

In almost every organization, resources must be transferred from other departments and projects to properly staff the training and performance functions. This is called *trade-off* planning. The cost and time to reach mastery performance in major job categories must be calculated, and justification must be given for why investing funds and resources in new performance systems is more important than investing in traditional projects and programs.

Chapter Sixteen

Determine Cost of Poor Performance

A common saying heard at education and training meetings is, "If you think education (training) is expensive, try ignorance (poor performance)." People laugh and shake their heads in agreement. Unfortunately, only a very few organizations measure the cost of ignorance or poor performance. If you doubt such a statement, ask a chief financial officer or line executive, "What is your cost for poor performance?" In almost every organization, they will give you a blank stare.

The good news is that *the cost of poor performance can be measured.* In fact, poor performance should be measured to justify developing the necessary training, job aids, support systems, and on-the-job training assignments to support high performance. When an organization has untrained or incompetent employees, the following are evident:

- Higher operating costs.
- More people doing the same job.
- Lower customer satisfaction.
- Lower employee satisfaction.
- Higher attrition rates.
- Greater costs for new hires.
- Higher supervision costs.
- Greater rework costs.

All of the above are measurable. Line organizations tend to become nervous when the training and performance department starts to measure poor performance, but they are most willing to cooperate when the training department wants to improve the performance of their critical jobs. If they want an improved performance system or an EPSS or additional resources, line managers will gladly support this new measurement.

Numerous terms have come to stand for levels of performance. For years, performance *competence* was measured as part of the bell-shaped curve. Today, the more competitive organizations want their employees to achieve *mastery*, which means being able to do the job completely and accurately every time. Mastery achieves the "first time right" concept that Dr. Deming and the TQM programs set as their main objective. In order to be competitive, organizations will have to achieve mastery for all jobs in the 21st century.

Cost of Hiring

Hiring is not the responsibility of the chief training officer or the training and performance department, but they should be involved in the process nonetheless. Finding outstanding or better-than-average personnel is vital. If an organization hires from the bottom of the class or from the bottom of employees available, the time and cost to achieve mastery will increase significantly.

Although many organizations recognize that their workforce is really a case study in successful mediocrity, they have learned how to get the most out of ordinary folks, while other organizations are trying to hire only highly intelligent people who are proven performers. Microsoft is a classic example. They receive 120,000 resumes each year. Only the top performers receive an interview.

Microsoft is not the only organization focused on hiring above-average entry-level employees. One grocery store chain makes a real effort to hire the best part-time students from local high schools, aiming to hire honor students and school activity leaders. The store management realizes that most of these part-time workers will only be with them for a few years while they complete their educations, but they are superior performers during those years. For full-time employees, they hire the best of those who do not go on to higher education. They also hire many adults who need part-time employment and senior citizens who want full-time work. In all categories, they aim for above-average employees. The result is clear—better revenues than other grocery store chains and greater earnings.

In most organizations, a job requisition or job description form lists education and experience required to do each job. The hiring decision is often based on assumptions about what someone can do based on credentials, resume, and interviews. Unfortunately, many new hires do not live up to their impressive credentials.

Many companies are now looking beyond resumes and interviews because they have found that applicants pad their resumes and claim that they can perform far better than they actually can. To combat this, more and more companies are starting to use various assessment methods to raise the percentage of successful hires. These methods include paper-and-pencil tests, exercises on personal computers, role-playing exercises, and decision-making simulations. Some organizations put candidates through a long series of interviews with psychologists or trained interviewers, who rate them on questions such as:

- Can they do the job?
- Are they creative?
- Do they have entrepreneurial skills?
- Can they lead and coach?
- Are they team players?
- Are they capable of learning new tasks?
- Can they function well under pressure?
- Will they fit into the organization's culture?
- Do they have a sense of urgency?
- Do they have a passion for their work?
- Can they be trusted?

These tests, interviews, and exercises can take from half a day to several days. Japanese companies that have set up manufacturing plants in the United States are leaders in how to select outstanding employees and managers. They invest several days testing for even low-level jobs. In Tuscaloosa, Alabama, more than

40,000 people applied for 650 well-paid jobs when Mercedes-Benz built a new manufacturing plant. Thousands of applications were processed through as many as eighty hours of intensive measurement.

Carol Hacker (1996) addresses the cost of hiring the wrong people in her new book, *The Costs of Bad Hiring Decisions & How to Avoid Them*. Listed below are some of these costs:

- Poor performance until the person leaves.
- Counseling person to improve performance.
- Classified advertising.
- Recruitment agency fees.
- Travel expenses.
- Interviewer's salary and benefits.
- Cost to replace lost customers.
- Training a replacement and resulting lower productivity due to inefficiency while replacement learns job.
- Severance package.
- Possible unemployment compensation claim.
- Potential lawsuit.

The U.S. Department of Labor estimates that the average cost of a bad hiring decision has climbed to 30 percent of the first year's earnings.

The cost to employ new hires using some form of assessment system ranges from $1,000 for low-level jobs to over six figures for executive positions. This may seem expensive, but it is worth the investment to avoid making costly wrong decisions. When line managers hire people they like rather than outstanding performers, 10 to 30 percent of new hires stay with a firm for less than a year. Attrition is extremely expensive.

Time and Cost to Achieve Mastery

Customers, fellow employees, and managers expect all new employees to attain mastery of their jobs rapidly and to sustain that level of mastery. Gone are the days when employees were not expected to be great performers during the trainee phase.

Yet only a few organizations measure the time and cost of reaching mastery of tasks within each major job category. This situation exists, once again, because most organizations simply do not have a formal system for identifying the requirements of key jobs (Chapter Seven). Therefore, they continue to have long training periods that include a few classroom courses, no structured on-the-job training assignments, and inadequate support systems. Most new employees must learn on a trial-and-error basis.

The chief training officer should assign the performance consultants to determine the time and cost required for entry-level employees to reach mastery for each of the organization's major job categories. In many cases, the performance consultants will have to make assumptions and estimates because perfect data rarely exists. This task can be accomplished within a few days or weeks for each job.

When the time and cost to achieve mastery is reviewed, the typical reaction is that it takes too long to train entry-level employees. Usually, these training programs can be improved significantly, lowering their costs, by looking at these potential problems:

- *Not Complete.* The training program is not complete, which creates a great many errors, rework, and low morale within the employee ranks.
- *Too Much Training.* By the time the trainee uses the lessons, he or she has forgotten how to do the task.
- *Insufficient Application.* Lessons are not applied to the job, so the knowledge needed to do the task is forgotten. The program probably also needs more job aids and support systems.
- *Lack of Learning Outside of Class.* There are no personal-development and on-the-job training assignments for the students.
- *No Attention to Self-Esteem.* The program does not build self-esteem and confidence. In fact, some training programs reduce confidence and create high attrition rates.
- *Insufficient Mentoring or Coaching.* If there is no mentoring or coaching, it means that lessons are not being reinforced. In many operating units, the trainee is ignored.
- *No Attention to Performance.* The training may be seen as a series of events to be completed, rather than as a way to attain a high level of performance.

- *Out-of-Date.* Many entry-level training programs are out-of-date because no one has the formal responsibility for ensuring that course content is kept current.
- *Feelings of Isolation.* Trainees may feel ignored rather than welcomed into the organization. The manager or executive who hired them walks by without saying hello or asking how the training is progressing.
- *Excessive Costs.* The cost of training exceeds budget.

Everyone has heard the horror stories. Sometimes a company will spend thousands or millions of dollars to recruit a new class of trainees. Within two years, 50 percent of them have left the organization; five years later, they are all gone. It is an incredible waste of resources, not to mention the fact that former employees quite often wind up working for the competition.

Once, the author observed a couple at the next table in a New York restaurant. Within minutes, the woman told her date what a terrible job she had as a reservations clerk at one of the leading New York City hotels. She told her friend that they had received only a few hours of unstructured training before meeting their first customers. They knew how to register a customer into a room, but they could not answer any questions pertaining to the hotel or to the city's attractions. The customers, who were paying nearly $500 a night for their rooms, believed that the person behind the desk should be able to provide information about New York City. Many customers became quite hostile, and most employees left within three or four months.

In this situation, no trainee achieved job mastery because the job's performance requirements were not well defined and the training program was inadequate. These deficiencies resulted in higher operating costs, low employee morale, poor customer satisfaction, high cost of hiring replacements, and reduced revenues. As this example demonstrates, poor performance and ignorance are very expensive.

Avis has a world-wide reservation center in Tulsa, Oklahoma, in which over one thousand agents answer millions of telephone calls annually. They must be outstanding performers at the job, which entails responding to customers in a friendly manner. The job goal is simple: Make sure the customers rent the type of automobile they want at a price they can afford.

Previously, trainees received three and one-half weeks of training before they handled their first productive calls. Even with this training, they did not become proficient for another twelve to twenty-four months because of the job's complexity. High employee turnover resulted during the first two years, which meant a lot of problems for the company in terms of customer dissatisfaction.

With a new electronic performance support system (EPSS), Avis trainees now achieve job mastery in six months. The personal computer acts as the coach with databases and up-to-date procedures. Avis is now experiencing a dramatic decrease in training cost and time and a giant leap forward in customer satisfaction. In short, this new performance support system provides the necessary information, knowledge, and methods for doing work "first time right." The fact that an electronic performance support system enables a new hire to achieve mastery in the shortest possible time is one of its major justifications.

It is not uncommon for large organizations to save millions of dollars and reduce training time 50 percent by applying a management system, such as the Systems Approach for Workforce Performance, to their critical job categories. A few organizations have carried this application to one more level of detail. They show their management team the following information:

- Time and cost for training with little or no formal training, no job aids, no on-the-job training assignments, and no support systems. Included in the presentation are how few transactions are completed and how high the error rate is as the result of an untrained workforce.
- The same information is provided for an ideal training and support system, like one achieved by the Systems Approach for Workforce Performance, that creates a competitive workforce that achieves mastery of learning and performance.

Figure 16.1 shows how entry-level employees with a performance system can achieve mastery in half the time and at half the cost. Of course, each job category is different for both time and cost. The senior executives should see a chart like this for every key job.

Figure 16.1. Cost and Time for Mastery Performance.

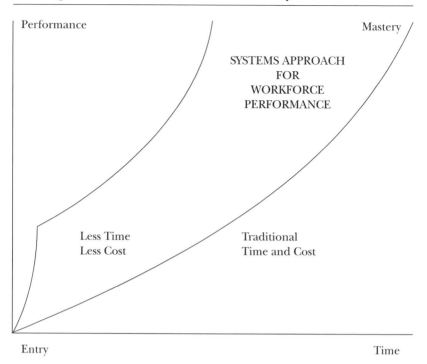

Attrition Rates

It is amazing how few organizations can tell a performance consultant what their attrition rate is for each major job category. In most companies and government agencies, one attrition rate is tracked for the entire organization, but it needs to be broken down by department and job if an organization is going to solve its attrition problems.

Attrition is not always bad. In law firms, advertising agencies, auditing firms, and management-consulting companies, attrition exists because only the very top performers become partners. Other employees leave the firm, most of them moving to organizations that are potential clients, so the termination process is handled in a positive way. The number-one reason why these people join this type of a firm to begin with is to gain more training and on-the-job experiences during their early years of professional employment.

For most organizations, high attrition rates are not good. They usually create low employee job satisfaction and increase employment and training costs. We have all been to retail stores, banks, grocery stores, gas stations, restaurants, and drug stores in which we never see the same employee twice. Employees in these places can rarely answer a customer's question and can barely complete a sale; the customer has to tell the employees what to do. It does not take long before the customer seeks out an organization in which there is more employee stability.

In summary, the training and performance department should work with the line organization to determine three key figures for every major job category:

1. What is the cost of hiring?
2. What is the time and cost to achieve mastery?
3. What is the attrition rate?

This information will help the training department develop an outstanding document that justifies a performance system for each major job category, which is the subject of the next chapter.

Chapter Seventeen

Use New Justification Methods

Today, organizations review their training budgets more frequently to determine if more work can be accomplished with fewer resources. At the same time, several forces in the marketplace are mandating the need for additional training, job aids, and support systems. The forces of change include intense domestic competition, global competition, advancing technology, and the ever-increasing organization changes affecting every organization, even those that have downsized. As a result, the pressure to determine the financial value of training and support systems has reached an all-time high. Senior executives, struggling to make their organizations lean and competitive, are demanding accountability from every department.

At the end of 1996, ASTD published the *Training Data Book* (Bassi, Gallagher, & Schroer) to provide more and better statistics for the industry. This document provided the following information:

- At least 70 percent, possibly more, of U.S. firms provide some type of formal training for their employees.
- This figure is close to 100 percent within large corporations and government agencies.
- Training expenditures average $569 per employee in the private sector, which includes $295 for indirect costs such as salaries during training.
- Private employers spent 0.9 percent of their payroll on training.

- Only 16 percent of the civilian workforce, approximately twenty million workers, received formal training from their employers.

All of these statistics suggest that training is inadequate in the vast majority of government agencies and corporations.

Accountability and budget cuts create problems for 99 percent of training organizations because they are already inadequately funded. Only 1 percent of training departments have the adequate resources to turn their employees into a competitive workforce, because most training departments focus on justifying a course or a training event rather than on measuring how well the employees perform after taking the course. Only a few companies have a formal process for justifying their training expenses based on performance systems.

In the past, training managers would take last year's budget, add a few percentage points to cover growth and inflation, and submit these revised figures as the next year's budget. If the organization had a good year, training would receive a growth budget. If not, training would receive a flat budget or a 10 percent reduction. There was little investigation by companies to determine what went into creating their total training budgets.

Today, more training managers have to justify every line item within their budgets. Accordingly, they need a formal justification process that reveals their exciting accomplishments. The training department also needs support and endorsement from line executives.

Justifying training and support systems starts with a management system, such as the Systems Approach for Workforce Performance. Justification also requires a working partnership with line executives (Chapter Five). Most important, the training department must focus on job performance (Chapter Seven). An organization must also identify its major job categories in order to have an optimum system for justification.

Assume that a management system has been implemented, a working partnership with line management has been established, and the major job categories have been identified. Now it is time to justify the costs of training workers to achieve mastery of performance.

Life-Cycle Costing

When a course, curriculum, on-the-job training assignment, or support system is being developed, the costs should be spread over the project's entire life cycle. For example, if a company wants to insert an advanced sales training course into its sales training curriculum and they plan to use the course for five years, the forecasted costs of a classroom course would include:

- Costs of a needs and task analysis
- Costs of course design
- Course development, including a student workbook, student handouts, instructor guide, and audio or video materials
- Pilot tests and validation
- Course delivery
- Measurements of effectiveness
- Projected enhancements to the course over five years

If the costs were not spread over the life of the course, they would be prohibitive and give an unrealistic cost picture. Assume that front-end costs would total $50,000 and that the estimated number of students is one thousand, two hundred per year. The cost to do the analysis and course development is $50 per student over the five-year life of the course. If the developmental costs were not spread out, they would total $250 per student for the first year.

If the cost of delivery is $500 per day per student and the course is three days long, the delivery costs would total $1.5 million for one thousand students over five years. If calculated over the life of the course, the cost for delivery per student over five years would be $1,550. If only the first year is used, cost per student in the first year would be $1,750 because all development costs are charged to the first year.

If the course were delivered at a learning center and the three-day course could be accomplished in two days at a delivery cost of $200 per student, the delivery costs would total $200,000 for one thousand students over five years. Assume that the development costs are $200,000. If two hundred students attend the course in the first year, and all development costs are charged to the first year, the cost would be $1,200 per student. If life cycle costing over five years were used, the cost would be $400 per student. This example shows that the delivery system decision is the number-one factor in determining the total costs for a course. The learning center approach ($400,000) is less than one-third of the classroom ($1,550,000) approach.

Many organizations expense all of their training and support systems so the impact on the first year must be budgeted. Even if an organization uses this accounting method, it is important for the CTO to be able to show financial executives what the costs are when amortized over the entire life of the course.

Levels III and IV Quality Measurements

The importance of measurements was discussed in Chapter Fifteen. Senior and line executives want to know whether the students will apply the lessons to their jobs (Level III) and whether their improved performance will have a positive impact on the organization's operating and financial results (Level IV). If these measurements are positive, then justifying the training is usually easy. Remember, it is more effective to use Level III and IV measurements at the curriculum level or performance system than at the course level.

Level IV measurements include such things as increased market share, additional revenues, lower operating expenses, greater productivity, acceleration of change, strategic advantages within the marketplace, higher customer satisfaction, lower attrition rates, increased employee satisfaction, reduced employment costs, lower supervision costs, fewer management levels, faster development of new products or services, successful reengineering projects, and higher quality levels.

The cost of people (total payroll, benefits, and cost of support such as office space, utilities, computers, FAX machines, copiers, telephones, or office equipment) will decrease with a competitive workforce that knows more and does more. The automobile industry is an example. In the 1970s, the Big Three automobile manufacturers were shocked to learn that the Japanese automakers' labor costs were substantially lower than theirs. Had the dollar not fallen from over 250 yen to under 100 yen, the Japanese companies would have taken even more market share. After twenty years, the Big Three still have greater labor costs than the Japanese, even though the latter's wages per hour are greater.

Xerox learned a similar lesson in the copier business. If the cost of labor goes out of control, it takes years for a company to regain a competitive position. The Systems Approach for Workforce Performance aims to maintain optimum levels for labor costs. For this reason alone, the organization's CEO, chief financial officer, and senior management will be interested in implementing the lessons in this book.

Total Cost Approach

If a company has focused on performance in each major job category, it will have the ability to justify training costs by using the Total Cost Approach. Companies should always relate the cost of their training and support systems to the total cost of the process and to the output from the process. This enables them to justify costs by concentrating on productivity and performance.

To illustrate this approach, assume that a company has $500 million in sales and five hundred sales personnel. Each sales representative sells $1 million worth of products and services. The company has not achieved its sales quota for two years so the sales vice president has fired the advertising agency and replaced one-third of the district managers who, in turn, replaced 25 percent of the sales force. Needless to say, within the organization there is a lot of tension.

Last year, the former sales vice president convinced the CEO to have a national sales rally, which cost several million dollars. Everyone left the rally feeling good, but there were no breakthroughs in sales. The new vice president of sales has been meeting with the new chief training officer and sales training manager. The new CTO has asked for two things: A detailed needs and task analysis for sales jobs and the total costs for selling products, which follow:

Cost of salaries and benefits	$50,000,000 ($100,000 average times 500 people)
Selling expenses (cars, meetings, brochures, entertainment, mementoes)	$12,500,000 ($25,000 average times 500 people)

Sales management	$5,000,000
(one to twelve ratio)	
Advertising	$20,000,000
Product announcements	$5,000,000
Marketing headquarters staff	$1,500,000
Training	$1,000,000
Basic support (Office space,	$5,000
utilities, FAX machines,	
copiers, computers,	
telephones, networks)	
Total marketing and selling costs	$100,000,000

Total marketing and selling costs are 20 percent of revenues. Training expenses equaled 1 percent of marketing and selling costs, and they equaled 2 percent of payroll. Various ratios between costs indicated no "red flags."

When the needs and task analysis was completed, though, a red flag appeared. The sales personnel had various courses on basic selling skills, effective presentations, proposal writing, and negotiation techniques, all by different vendors, which meant no integration for the selling process. Every salesperson did the job differently, using common sense, hard work, and good intentions; the company had no standard selling process, no job aids, and almost no support systems.

The performance consultant recommended the development of a selling process that would include five phases:

Phase 1: Gain attention and differentiate the products.

Phase 2: Conduct a survey for basic information.

Phase 3: Determine explicit needs and recommendations.

Phase 4: Develop and present a proposal.

Phase 5: Obtain an order for products or services.

In this sales organization, direct face-to-face contact with customer executives and personnel secured additional business. The sales were complex, taking weeks and sometimes months to complete. The company needed a significant increase in its sales performance in order to improve its results, which were below quota.

The new selling process would permit district managers to work closely with sales personnel, helping them determine which prospects warranted the time and cost of a full proposal. The cost to prepare a proposal was from $5,000 to $15,000. Only 30 percent of the sales proposals resulted in sales. With coaching and a win-loss review after each proposal, the sales force decided to aim for a 60 percent success rate.

A job aid for the selling process was created to reinforce the lessons taught in the three-day advanced sales training course. The company hoped that this job aid and coaching would help transfer the lessons to the workplace. The district managers and the headquarters marketing staff also developed a basic support system, featuring an on-line database that contained the following information:

- Potential client objections and appropriate responses.
- Potential client questions and appropriate answers.
- Proposal paragraphs.
- Presentation scripts and visuals.
- Best reference stories.
- Justification methods.

The company emphasized adapting the best practices used by top performers. The sales personnel were also instructed to study business subjects and industry publications so that they would know the latest trends. All of these programs would cost an additional $1 million in the current training budget, doubling it to 4 percent of payroll.

The chief training officer and sales training manager gave a joint presentation to the management team. The vice president of sales had helped them develop the presentation, so he played the role of inside mentor at this meeting. The presentation started with a list of performance problems in the sales force, then progressed to the proposal that $1 million be transferred from the advertising budget. The sales vice president already supported this method of funding the expanded sales-training program and the new performance-support system. Thus, the executives used trade-off planning methods to fund the new programs.

The CEO learned quickly that the previous year's multimedia sales rally was a quick-fix, feel-good solution, whereas the presentation for a new support system, job aids, and an advanced sales training course represented a viable solution to the performance problems. The CEO was sold on having a performance system for each sales personnel. For this reason, he agreed to transfer funds to the training and performance department.

Years ago, it was feasible to ask for incremental funding because most corporate officers reserved monies for unexpected situations. Today, tight budgets have soaked up these extra funds. Now it takes trade-off planning. Using the Total Cost Approach, all funds are on the table to help solve a performance problem. In most situations, the training budget is a small portion of total expenditures as it was in this situation.

In this short case study, it is clear that the chief training officer is offering a new performance system for the sales department, rather than selling a course. This is the product that the new type of training and performance department sells to management. It designs, develops, and implements performance systems for a major job category, rather than propose one course at a time. Justification must be focused on the performance system and what it will do to reduce operating expenses and create additional revenues.

The chief training officer must be bold when asking for more resources. He or she must show how the Systems Approach for Workforce Performance will lead to major performance breakthroughs and that it is in senior management's best interest to devote more funds to the training and performance department.

The CTO and the management team of training and performance can identify which resources they need so that they can implement the Systems Approach. The CTO should not ask for any extra "nice to do" project money, but must aggressively pursue the resources the organization will need to progress from a workforce with some training to a competitive workforce.

Return on Investment (ROI)

Some financial departments insist that all major investments be subjected to an analysis of return on investment. In other words, the program benefits identified by Level IV measurements must be converted into dollars. For example, if a company's attrition rate has dropped from 25 percent to 15 percent, that information must be converted to a monetary value. If the cost of employment and cost of training entry-level employees decreases by $90,000 and the new training program now costs $30,000, then the ROI will equal 200 percent. The ROI is calculated by subtracting the program cost from the program benefits (equaling net program benefits), which is $60,000 in this case. The $60,000 is then divided by the $30,000 program cost. The resulting number is then multiplied by 100 percent to obtain a 200 percent ROI.

Benefit-to-Cost Ratio

Using the same numbers, assume that the company's total benefits from the training program equaled $90,000. Dividing that figure by the $30,000 program costs yields a three to one benefit-to-cost ratio. For every dollar invested, $3 worth of benefits are returned.

It is easy to calculate financial ratios after benefits have been determined through a Level IV evaluation. These ratios help companies focus on performance within each major job category.

Numerous situations require assumptions and estimates. For example, if returns of merchandise decrease by 10 percent, the company may need to estimate the resulting benefits because accounting systems usually do not provide a precise number for the cost of processing returned merchandise.

If the customer-satisfaction survey goes up by 10 percent and revenues increase by 5 percent, the company will need to estimate the portion of the revenue increase that was generated by improved customer satisfaction. This estimate can be expressed as a percentage of sales. No matter how these assumptions and estimates are determined, the senior executives must believe in them.

Barriers to Justification

Lack of Focus on Performance. The primary barrier to justification of costs is the lack of focus on job performance. It is difficult to justify stand-alone courses and training events. The Systems Approach can help a company clear this barrier.

False Beliefs. Another common barrier to taking the time and effort to justify costs is the belief that senior and financial executives do not require evaluation and justification. Those few who still believe this are living on borrowed time; eventually, all executives will ask for evaluation and justification. A proactive chief training officer will implement measurements and justification before being asked for them.

Too Expensive. Another barrier is many trainers' belief that evaluations, measurements, and justification are too expensive to attempt. In fact, the true cost can be less than 1 percent of the total cost of the training and support system if a company implements the Systems Approach for Workforce Performance.

Insufficient Information. Lack of information can be another barrier. Even though most information does not flow neatly from traditional accounting systems, it can still be obtained, or estimates and assumptions may be used to overcome this barrier.

Too Many Variables. Thinking that there are too many variables affecting employee performance for training to take credit for positive change represents another barrier to measurement of performance. The training department should be aggressive and take as much credit as possible. Line executives can help by signing off on the final figures. Unfortunately, too many trainers do not have a working partnership with line executives, which makes the justification process even more difficult.

Do Not Believe in Justification. Some trainers simply believe that training cannot be justified by numbers and that senior and line executives should buy their programs solely on good faith. This belief is dangerous because as soon as someone states that an area cannot be justified, that area could be eliminated.

Justifying a Performance System

Whoever is responsible (curriculum coordinators, curriculum manager, performance consultant, instructional designer, course developer) for a major job category's performance should also have the *continuous* responsibility for justifying the performance system, which consists of the curriculum, personal-development tasks, on-the-job assignments, and support systems to achieve the desired performance requirements.

This assignment of responsibility is missing in most training organizations. Justification is looked on as a one-time event or something to be concerned about only when there is a need for more head count or dollars. The chief training officer should insist on updated and documented justifications for each major job category. In addition, the CTO should have a justification presentation ready for any future meeting, containing the following information:

- Job category name.
- Line executive sponsor.
- Number of employees in the job category.
- Cost of people in the job category (total payroll, benefits, and support).
- Attrition rate (actual versus objective).
- Basic tasks to be performed (job complexity).
- Past performance problems.
- Need for a performance system.
- Performance-based training courses.
- Personal-development tasks.
- On-the-job training assignments.
- Support systems.
- Design and development costs (budget).
- Time and cost to achieve mastery of performance.
- Four quality-measurement levels.
- Impact on operating and financial results.
- Training delivery costs (budget).
- Justification of performance system.
- Recent enhancements within performance system.
- Alternatives (more people and more costs).
- Rewards and recognition.
- Candidate for electronic performance support system.

Trainers always want to know how to obtain adequate resources. The answer is simple: *One major job category at a time.* Few senior executives have ever received such a presentation, but it is exactly what every line and senior executive should receive from the chief training officer. This presentation reminds senior executives that the company has a management system for performance systems, which will have a major impact on operating and financial measurements.

The Systems Approach for Workforce Performance

Some jobs require only a personal-development task and a simple support system. For example, employees may need to read only one or two books and then follow a procedure manual in order to do their jobs. Sometimes they need just some guidelines and some coaching based on the guidelines or procedure manual. This approach is low-cost and low-tech, but it is an effective system for achieving a higher performance level.

However, most jobs require training. Years ago, secretaries could be hired directly from business schools or high schools. They had already learned typing, shorthand, filing, mail handling, and answering telephones. A few guidelines and job aids were all they needed to do the assigned work. Today, secretaries need personal computer courses so that they can handle word processing, graphics, spreadsheets, databases, electronic mail, sophisticated telephone systems, FAX machines, copiers, and other high-tech office applications. They often need a combination of classroom courses, learning-center classes, personal computer courses, job aids, on-the-job training assignments, and basic support systems.

New secretaries should be given enough training to begin, but should not be overtrained so that they learn more than they can possibly use. Remember, if lessons are not used on the job, the employee quickly forgets them. More will be learned from job aids and on-the-job training assignments. Courses also should be based on what the employee needs to know, rather than having everyone go to every class. For example, someone may know Windows 95, but not Word Perfect, because they used Microsoft Word for word processing at their previous job. Other secretaries, however, will need all the courses. Individualized training and development programs are essential in order to minimize training expenses.

The most cost-effective training and development elements must be selected that still allow the employee to achieve mastery in the shortest time. Thus, the performance consultant should focus on these key issues:

1. How do we improve the quality of training?
2. How do we minimize the cost of training?

3. How do we fully utilize personal-development tasks, job aids, basic support systems, and on-the-job training assignments to reduce the number of formal training events?

4. How do we ensure that the lessons and skills are applied to the job?

5. How do we achieve mastery and maintain a level of mastery of performance in the shortest time and for the lowest cost?

6. How do we keep the courses, personal-development tasks, on-the-job training assignments, and support systems up-to-date so that they reflect the latest tactical and strategic decisions?

Sample Programs

The U.S. Office of Personnel Management (OPM) has one of the world's largest training systems, training millions of government employees with a budget that exceeds $1 billion. It uses instructional-design processes to increase quality in government training. The Office of Personnel Management assigns a team to develop courses, all of which must meet the four levels of measurement (Chapter Fifteen). As a result, OPM is shifting from a workforce with some training to a workforce that knows more and can do more.

An insurance company, with the help of a consulting firm, developed a training program for underwriters that progressed from satisfying only Level I and II measurements to satisfying all four measurement levels. Now this program consists of a revised twenty-three-week program that includes eight weeks of self-study reading, five weeks of classroom lessons and demonstrations, four weeks of individual case practice, and six weeks of on-the-job practice. The new hires achieve mastery of their jobs within six months, a process that used to take one to two years. In addition, by training supervisors on what points of performance to reinforce, they too have achieved mastery of learning and performance. This new performance system has also reduced expenses by using new cost-effective course delivery systems.

A manufacturing company's supervisors were concerned with performance problems. At first, they thought the employees might be suffering from a motivational problem or a lack of technical knowledge. Many employees were immigrants from Asia and Latin

America whose reading scores ranged from the second- to the fourth-grade level. Their math scores ranged from the third- to sixth-grade level. Some Americans who had lived in the United States their entire lives had some of the lowest scores, despite the fact that they had graduated from high school.

At first, the company tried to make literacy training voluntary, which was a big mistake. If an organization wants to achieve mastery of learning and performance, training must be mandatory. The supervisors eventually added formal job training to the literacy program, which reduced operating expenses, increased job satisfaction, and raised productivity. The return on investment was impressive. The monthly reduction in scrap and rework paid for the program.

The company learned one other lesson: Literacy programs should be held entirely on company time to obtain 100 percent participation and to prevent employees from believing that they are being punished for low reading scores. Although there are many volunteer literacy programs available, a company or government agency needs to implement a formal literacy program for selected employees if it wants to achieve superior workforce performance.

One computer company implemented account marketing teams with a systems engineer responsible for every major application within a customer's organization. Another group of systems engineers was responsible for every major systems software area. The account executive was responsible for executive-level contacts within the customer's organization and served as the master planner of innovative systems for organizational processes. The systems engineering manager and one or two other senior systems engineers were responsible for overall systems design. With an outstanding training program and its strong support systems, the computer company doubled revenues within five years. Advancing technology helped out, but it was the company's performance system that propelled its employees to A and B performance levels.

In the May 1997 issue of *Training Magazine* (pp. 58–67), an interesting article by John Murphy appears entitled "Results First." John is the former manager of management development at GTE. He started his article by describing a gentlemen's agreement that existed in many organizations:

One has to wonder how we have gotten away with such feeble impact for so long. My theory is that we have been protected for years by a kind of gentlemen's agreement. We all know how it works: Management agrees to fund courses and facilities, and even pays for us to bring in the occasional big-name speaker. In return, we agree not to pester management about understanding exactly what we're teaching, why we're teaching it, how well people are learning it, or whether it pays off in business terms.

He then states, "Management training's reputation for failing to impact business results stems from the simple fact that it isn't aimed at results." John believes all management training can be measured on how much it impacts the business by having a results-first method that is used in a model like the Systems Approach for Workforce Performance.

A health-care organization is currently developing an electronic support system to improve customer satisfaction and reduce operating expenses. The company hopes that this system will increase revenues and expand its market share. The system's intent is to provide one-stop shopping for patients who need to see specialists and who must take numerous prescriptions. One customer service representative ensures that all the administrative tasks are handled at the lowest possible cost.

Numerous studies have shown that a well-trained competitive workforce provides many benefits. Mark Huselid (1995) of Rutgers University recently surveyed more than 3,400 firms. His results showed that investments in training and other high-performance work practices lead to lower employee turnover, greater productivity, and better financial performance. Another study showed that companies with no training programs had lower stock market values.

Organizations will improve their operating and financial measurements if they implement the lessons from the Systems Approach for Workforce Performance. Part Five in this book deals with the implementation process.

Part Five

Required Leadership from Senior Executives

The transformation from a *workforce with some training* to a well-trained *competitive workforce* will not happen unless senior executives become involved. A few hours of executive leadership are required to achieve breakthroughs such as lowered operating expenses, increased revenues, plus the strategic advantage of workforce performance for customer satisfaction.

The final chapter in this book is an executive summary for busy senior executives who want to focus on workforce performance without reading all the chapters on how to make it happen.

Chapter Eighteen

Optimize the Organization and Staff Programs

Organizations' excuses are often used to maintain the status quo within the training department, but in this chapter every excuse will be refuted. Within many organizations, some training functions are centralized and others are decentralized. However, the Systems Approach for Workforce Performance works in all cases, in every industry, in large, intermediate, and small organizations. The system also works in commercial companies, government agencies, and not-for-profit organizations.

One major advantage to this management system is that it operates independently of organizational changes. When training and support systems are designed for major jobs, the job categories rarely change, even though the performance requirements within a job change frequently. The training and performance function is able to respond quickly to organizational change because the basic jobs requiring training and performance systems remain the same.

Now that the CTO and the management team have a Systems Approach for Workforce Performance, it's time to optimize the organizational structure to achieve maximum effectiveness with their systems performance.

Identification of Tasks

The first step in making proper organizational decisions is to identify the major tasks to be performed and whether they should be done by staff or line people. Here is an example:

Headquarters Staff Tasks

- Develop an organization-wide mission statement for performance.
- Develop a management system.
- Develop key strategic directions.
- Determine best practices within the organization.
- Document guidelines for best practices.
- Transfer best practices to operating units.
- Establish an organization-wide measurement system.
- Develop an overall budget and accounting system.
- Conduct an annual review for executive management.
- Represent the organization at external meetings:
  Universities
  American Society for Training and Development (ASTD)
  Society for Applied Learning Technology (SALT)
  International Society for Performance Improvement (ISPI)
  Government agencies
  School-reform meetings

This set of staff (headquarters) tasks requires two to four professionals in large organizations and one or two people in intermediate-size organizations. Remember, the headquarters staff is not responsible for developing or delivering any courses, nor for designing performance support systems. This is the responsibility of the line organization.

Line Tasks for Training and Performance

Following is a list of responsibilities of the line organization:

- Establish a working partnership with line executives.
- Identify major key job categories.
- Develop performance systems for each major job category.
- Determine personal-development assignments.
- Develop a curriculum for each major job category based on needs analysis for organizational requirements.
- Develop, buy, or modify outstanding courses.
- Design a delivery-system strategy.
- Document on-the-job training assignments.
- Design and develop support systems.

- Establish a requirements process (true volume of enrollments by course).
- Implement both quantity and quality measurements.
- Develop recognition programs with HR.
- Implement an enrollment and administrative system.
- Recruit outstanding people into training.
- Deliver courses in education and learning centers.
- Maintain tight financial control.
- Manage the education and learning centers.
- Enroll the right person in the right program at the right time.

The actual development and delivery of courses take place in the operating units, supervised by a manager or director of training.

In some organizations, there are several headquarter's departments working in various areas of performance but not taking full responsibility for the performance of the workforce. These departments are often titled *training, performance improvement, human resources,* and *organization development.* This is a lot of expensive overhead for split responsibility.

The Systems Approach for Workforce Performance minimizes the cost of staff work and has one department—training and performance—partnered with the line organization that shares full responsibility with the senior line executives to achieve maximum performance from the workforce at the lowest possible costs. The performance consultants architect the performance systems. The instructional designers develop new course requirements, and the instructors deliver the courses. The quality measurements are in place to be certain there are results for this investment in workforce performance. Thus, a simple, straightforward, and cost-effective training and performance department exists, no matter how the organization is structured.

Centralized Organization

In a centralized organization, all the personnel and resources for training and performance report to one executive: the chief training officer. Both the staff responsibilities and line responsibilities are on a direct solid line to the CTO. The big advantage to this organizational structure is the complete focus of responsibility.

There are no excuses for not performing. Decisions can be made quickly, and program implementations have fewer barriers when everyone in training and performance is working in one organization. Of course, one organization can have many locations. In most centralized organizations, the CTO appoints a director of training for every major functional or operating area within the organization.

Arthur Andersen and Andersen Consulting represent centralized systems within large organizations. All training decisions are made at their facility in St. Charles, Illinois. Courses can be delivered at learning centers, in any of their many offices, or in a few overseas education centers. A managing partner of professional development serves as chief training officer for each business unit in St. Charles. The company believes that its centralized organization helps them achieve a standard of practice throughout the world that is a strategic advantage within the auditing, tax, and consulting professions.

McDonald's operates a similar system with Hamburger University in the Chicago area. They also aim for strict performance standards on a world-wide basis. As these two companies demonstrate, a centralized organization can work well in either high-tech or low-tech companies.

In a centralized system, the CTO must continually work with line executives to assure them that training is responsive to their requirements. A rapport is established by having a training director attend staff meetings and allowing line executives to have a voice in the selection of the training director.

Many government agencies also have centralized training systems, and this organizational structure is common in intermediate-size organizations and, of course, if the organization only has one location.

Decentralized Organizations

Numerous large corporations have totally separate training departments within each major functional or operating unit. This setup works well if the senior executives are willing to have some duplicate efforts and programs. Each group has a tendency to reinvent every new approach for training and performance, a costly process;

it is not uncommon to see several incompatible networks and computer-based training (CBT) systems.

However, the one big advantage to a decentralized organizational structure is that line executives have control over their own training programs, performance systems, and budgets. If the training and performance department reports to the line executive, he or she believes that training will be immediately responsive to the line's strategic and tactical decisions.

Some large companies have found that with a CTO and a few professionals from headquarters performing staff responsibilities the amount of duplicate effort and costs can be minimized by instituting corporate-wide guidelines and best practices. In the early 1980s, IBM used this organizational style successfully.

When a company is fundamentally decentralized, such as Hewlett Packard, a decentralized training system makes sense. It can be organized around functions such as engineering, manufacturing, finance, marketing, or service, or it can be organized around operating units.

Combination of Centralized and Decentralized

Many large organizations use a combination of the two methods. They usually have a strong chief training officer at headquarters who is in charge of the corporate-education center and the corporate headquarters training staff. The corporate-education center often hosts executive education, management development, financial training, personnel training, and other courses that headquarters wants selected audiences to attend. The training centers for engineers and manufacturing personnel who report to the site general manager are at the manufacturing plants.

General Electric and Motorola use this type of organizational structure. Both companies have strong CTOs who are also corporate officers, but they do not have line authority over every member of the training organization nor over all training expenses.

Responsibilities Within an Organizational Structure

The supervisor or manager has the following responsibilities with either a centralized or decentralized organization:

- Help plan training programs for employees.
- Schedule training.
- Schedule on-the-job training events.
- Coach and reinforce lessons.
- Counsel on career plans.
- And evaluate performance.

The employee responsibilities include: help plan their training programs; meet all training prerequisites; be successful at training sessions; and achieve mastery on the job.

The training and performance department is responsible for the following: Determine personal-development programs; offer on-the-job training sessions; offer a curriculum of courses for each major job category at education and learning centers; provide support systems; implement measurements; provide guidance to line management; and establish a company-wide management system for training and support.

Reporting Structure for the CTO

Great debate has taken place on the subject of who should manage the CTO. A similar controversy raged for years over the report structure for the chief information officer (CIO). In some organizations, the chief financial officer (CFO) did not want the responsibilities of computers and communication networks, so the CIO reported to the chief operating officer (COO) or the chief of corporate staff. As the years passed, more and more chief financial officers realized that all of their transactions were going through information systems, so most CIOs eventually reported to the CFO, unless they reported directly to the CEO.

In the HR community today, numerous line executives and training directors believe that HR executives are excellent on compensation issues, career plans, industrial relations problems, benefits, and morale surveys, but that they are weak leaders in terms of training and performance. Some HR executives even believe that training and performance responsibilities belong to line executives.

The American Management Association conducted a survey in 1995 of senior HR executives and received 519 responses. Only 47 percent listed training among their top three choices for ways to implement specific changes. In organizations in which HR avoids training and performance responsibilities, the CTO often reports to either the chief operating officer or the chief of corporate staff services.

At the same time, a number of HR vice presidents have been promoted to executive or senior vice president in recent years. They clearly view HR as being responsible for enhancing workforce training and performance and insist that the chief training officer report to the senior vice president of HR. These enlightened HR executives also realize that they need a strong, creative executive in the CTO position.

Too many companies spend too much time reorganizing the training function every two or three years with the hope that they will somehow achieve a breakthrough in workforce performance. In reality, breakthroughs are created by the management system and the director of training. Being centralized or decentralized is not a big issue. Every type of organization should focus on the leader first, the management system second, and the organization third.

Every line executive is not going to be an expert on a management system for workforce performance, instructional-design systems, delivery-system strategies, measurement systems, recognition programs, support systems, on-the-job training programs, and integrated performance support systems. For this reason, every large- and intermediate-size organization needs a chief training officer reporting to a senior executive, both focused on training and performance.

In the January 15, 1996, issue of *Fortune*, Thomas A. Stewart argues in his article, "Taking on the Last Bureaucracy," for the abolishment of the HR department. Stewart recommends outsourcing all HR responsibilities. As for training, he said, "Will every reader who has taken a training course sponsored by his HR department and found it valuable, please raise your hand?" He believes training should emanate from line functions. Many people disagree with him, but this article shows that HR needs to take on heavier management responsibilities. Training and performance is one area in which HR should take a leadership position. If not, more people will recommend outsourcing all of their responsibilities.

Staff Development

One of the major responsibilities of the chief training officer is to recruit, retain, and develop outstanding people for the organization's training and performance function.

People continue to debate the issue of whether training is really a profession. Ron Zemke wrote an article ("Is Training a Profession?," *Training Magazine*, 1996, p. 8) in which he emphasized that a profession must meet five criteria:

1. An organized body of knowledge.
2. Client recognition of the profession.
3. Community approval of the profession.
4. A code of ethics.
5. A professional culture, supported and advanced by academic and association activities.

Zemke concluded that training satisfies these criteria, although he would be willing to agree that training and performance can greatly improve their professional image. Using this book, in conjunction with a management system of best practices, will hopefully enhance the professionalism of training and performance personnel as well as consultants.

In the past, too many people thought that anyone could be an instructor, course developer, or education-center manager. The education profession has done a poor job of explaining that there is a science to developing courses and teaching, inferring instead that the ability is a gift given to only a select few. Unfortunately, there are some real charlatans who pose as trainers. They are mostly big on personality and entertainment.

If a training department is using only Level I measurements (happiness sheets), chances are that the organization is paying for a lot of "nice to do" courses. When an organization implements all four measurement levels, training becomes a must-do activity requiring well-trained educators to make it all happen.

A professional training organization needs job descriptions, career paths, compensation levels, recognition programs, training classes, and all other fundamental HR programs. Training cannot be viewed as a small department that does not need the basics. A chief training officer cannot attract or retain outstanding personnel if the department has inadequate job descriptions, no career paths, and low-level compensation rates. If training is as important as finance, marketing, manufacturing, merchandising, service, operations, and other mainstream activities, then the training and performance department deserves the full services of the HR organization.

Staffing Requirements

Listed next are the jobs that may exist within a training and performance department:

- Chief Training Officer
- Director of Training
- Education-Center Manager
- Instructor
- Class Coordinator
- Instruction Manager
- Performance Consultant
- Course Developer
- Instructional Designer
- Assessment Specialist
- Education Technologist
- General Staff Administrator
- Class Secretaries
- Computer and Communications Support Personnel
- Receptionist
- Logistics Coordinator
- Education Center Accountant or Administrator

In most residential education centers, the cooks, waiters or waitresses, and cleaning personnel are outsourced, but someone still has to coordinate their work with the outsourcing company.

The American Society for Training and Development has developed competency models for training and performance professionals. This information is most helpful when writing job descriptions.

Instructors come from several areas. Some professional instructors are former school teachers with outstanding teaching and presentation skills, but they may lack field knowledge and experience.

This can be corrected quickly by assigning them to a branch office, manufacturing site, retail store, or warehouse for one or two years.

Many organizations hire successful field personnel for two to three years. A formal rotational program worked well at IBM. The successful manager, programmer, salesperson, or service representative was given a pay raise to become an instructor. The location they came from had to agree that they could come back in two years with a pay raise and a promotion if they performed well as instructors. Except for positions as administrative assistants for executives, moving to the education center was viewed as a great career opportunity. In fact, most marketing and service executives had been instructors for two years at some point in their careers.

Not every area of the company took advantage of this formal rotational system. In some areas, training became a dumping ground for poor performers. If this situation is allowed to exist, it is not easy to place these people, so training in those areas soon acquired the reputation for employing the "has beens" of the workforce.

Some organizations, such as Arthur Andersen and Company, use successful personnel from the line organization to teach for a few weeks. Using part-time instructors is a high risk if the course is not professionally designed and developed. For this reason, Andersen employs a large instructional design and course-development group.

Required Training

All instructors need training. They can spend several days with a multimedia computer course to learn the basics and then move on to a one-week workshop to practice teaching skills. Performance consultants need several weeks of training on business fundamentals, as well as the organization and industry. They need to know how to do front-end assessments, reengineering studies, and needs and task analysis, plus have above-average communication skills. A really good performance consultant will also need a basic knowledge of instructional design and cost-effective delivery systems.

For course developers, the ideal training is instructional design, a one- to two-year graduate program offered at nearly a dozen universities. All colleges of education should offer a degree for instructional design, but only a few hundred of these degrees are conferred each year. At least there should be multidiscipline degrees on workplace learning. Many successful instructors and former schoolteachers who receive ten to twelve weeks of training on instructional design improve their course-development skills tremendously.

Most educational technologists have master's degrees or doctorates for this important job. They will soon be in greater demand as more organizations convert to performance-based training and integrated performance support systems.

As the training and performance field becomes more complex, more and more universities will offer degrees in instructional and performance technology, which will be far superior to two- and three-day workshops. The profession will receive more attention from universities once management systems and best practices are documented. In the meantime, conflict will arise between those with degrees and those without them. This was the case in the law and accounting professions, but degrees became mandatory as the professions matured.

Professional training and performance societies should work closely with universities to define what should be taught in degree programs. The Big Six accounting firms and corporate accounting departments have done an outstanding job of providing realistic course requirements in their profession. The computer industry, on the other hand, let the computer science degree mean almost anything, a situation that has hurt the profession.

Organization Development Personnel

Organization development (OD) and training personnel are often confused because their duties may overlap. Some companies and government agencies have had OD personnel for years. Allison Rossett ("Separated at Birth?," *Training Magazine,* 1996, pp. 53–59) of San Diego State University believes that OD and training should have a close working partnership.

Organization development has a very broad definition. It involves attention to diagnostic studies, strategies, roles, systems, processes, and measurements that enable organizations and people to achieve their goals. Many vague terms and good intentions characterize this profession, but not a management system that achieves breakthroughs in workforce performance.

Rossett has documented the similarities between OD and training personnel:

- Both traffic in change.
- Both are driven by clients' needs for improved performance.
- Both acknowledge responsibility for customer education and business partnership.
- Both are committed to assessment and measurement.
- Both are committed to systematic approaches.

There is a perception by some that OD specialists work with executives and trainers work with managers and employees, but this attitude is changing. The Systems Approach for Workforce Performance encourages trainers to work directly with senior and line executives. Performance consultants are doing more work that sounds like organization development. Training and OD should work cooperatively in the future, because a turf battle will only confuse line executives.

In the past, OD personnel, performance technologists, HR personnel, trainers, and line managers have all said that they were responsible for improving workforce performance. Each group carved out a niche of responsibility. Except in a very few organizations, these split responsibilities and overlapped efforts have not succeeded, so most employees continue to do business as usual. The Systems Approach for Workforce Performance is designed to take the best of these separate efforts and achieve a breakthrough in workforce performance. It takes a coordinated team effort by specialists and a management system to provide breakthroughs in performance. The focus must be on continuous improvement of job performance and not on a training event or a performance intervention.

Charge-Out Systems

The traditional way that educators and performance consultants charge students is tuition plus travel and living expenses. Many people believe that charging tuition forces line management to wonder whether the training is worthwhile. Frankly, it does not work that way in most cases. What happens is that, in the fourth quarter, line management stops all training to meet annual budgets. The education centers and trainers sit idle as training money is spent on other activities. The decentralized training funds are often spent on other activities throughout the year, which is often a source of conflict between training managers and line executives. Unfortunately, tuition is about the only system that can be used when an organization has a workforce with some training because the line executives are never sure if the training is necessary so tuition continues to be the most common method for charging out the training department's expenses.

When an organization is using a management system such as the Systems Approach, the training department should control all the resources, including travel and living expenses, so that they can provide programs for less. All remote locations are charged the same amount of travel and living expense per student. This system is fair because the location farthest away should not pay a penalty for training, nor should the local site have an advantage. The training and performance managers can police who is going to attend the training so that fewer seats are used for rest and recognition. With this system, wasted effort and negative meetings with line management about how to spend the training budget are eliminated. The CTO keeps a strong focus on continuous improvement and cost containment. When line executives are convinced that all the training is "must do," they quickly agree that the CTO should control the training and performance resources. Of course, if the training and performance organization is decentralized, the budget will be decentralized within the various training departments.

Outsourcing Training and Performance

A few companies are trying the strategy of outsourcing their training, on the basis that training is not a core competency of their business so it can be outsourced, as has happened with information systems in many cases.

Companies that are willing to outsource training usually have an ineffective and high-cost program. At best, they have a workforce with some training. In many cases, they just want to reduce expenses, which usually can be achieved with outsourcing.

If they do decide to outsource, a corporation or government agency should ask the outsourcing companies to design a training system that will enable their company to evolve from a workforce with some training into a competitive workforce. The outsourcing company should be capable of implementing a management system such as the Systems Approach for Workforce Performance. In fact, a company should not consider outsourcing its training to a training company that does not have a similar management system for workforce performance. The outsourcing company must be given access to senior executives, line executives, strategic decisions, tactical plans, and operating plans. Without this access, the outsourcing company simply cannot develop a competitive workforce that will give the organization a strategic advantage.

An alternative to outsourcing all training is to have performance consultants who work for the company oversee the performance systems that are designed, developed, and delivered by the outsourcing organization.

Outsourcing will probably evolve into a serious alternative for in-house training departments because many corporations and government agencies do not accept the responsibility for creating first-class training and performance organizations. Many small- and intermediate-size organizations will outsource their training and performance requirements. Outsourcing has advantages. These organizations have professional knowledge and experience to manage training and performance. They have talented people who can create performance systems at minimum costs. The client benefits from all their years of learning while working for other companies.

International Training Organizations

In 1995 ASTD's study ("The Rising Time of Global Training," *Training Magazine*, 1995) on international training organizations received seventy-nine responses. Most of the companies surveyed had not tried to form an international training organization; others, such as Arthur Andersen, have a global training organization that is both successful and cost-effective.

Although organizations in other countries tend to emphasize their differences, IBM found that when discussion is based on learning objectives and key lessons, the training is about 80 percent the same. Allowances must be made for local customs and unique country methods, but it is a waste of money to have every country reinventing every course and delivery system. A global training program with performance systems can achieve breakthroughs in workforce performance and save major resources. Training is much like manufacturing: The differences are usually minor, so a global plan is often feasible.

Chapter Nineteen

Decisions for Creating a Competitive Workforce

Senior and line executives are becoming increasingly interested in the training department for many reasons:

1. Employee costs (payroll, benefits, and basic support) average $25,000 to $60,000 annually per employee, with technology firms at the high end.
2. They now realize that employee performance is as important as computer performance to the success of the organization.
3. Jobs are more complex, so employees are expected to do and know more.
4. Workers are no longer just competing with other Americans for their jobs. The workforce is global, and many countries have school systems that prepare students better for joining the corporate workforce.
5. There is and will continue to be a shortage of qualified entry-level workers in the United States.
6. Public-school reforms are not achieving learning break-throughs, so company training programs are becoming "schools of last resort" and are teaching remedial courses in basic knowledge and skills.

In spite of this new interest, too many CEOs, COOs, CFOs, and line executives have not focused on workforce training or performance systems, even though they have the most to gain.

The primary beneficiaries of the Systems Approach for Work-force Performance will be the senior and line executives in most companies and government agencies. After all, they are measured on the overall workforce performance that significantly influences their organizations' operating and financial results. Senior and line executives should not accept a workforce with some training. They should demand a well-trained, low-cost competitive workforce instead. Hopefully, there will be many senior and line executives reading this book because it requires both the executive team and the training manager to implement the Systems Approach for Workforce Performance.

What Executives Should Hear

Senior and line executives are well-trained and comfortable at managing other mainstream functions such as finance, human resource, manufacturing, service, product development, marketing, merchandising, credit, and operations. In fact, most executives moved up from one of these organizational areas. Unfortunately, they have usually not received training on how to manage training and employee development. This subject was not covered in the old personnel administration courses, nor is it covered in graduate schools of business. With a few exceptions, the subject is missing from the many executive-development seminars that are presented at major corporations and leading universities.

Because there is no pressure from executives to increase workplace performance, most training departments continue to measure themselves on the size of the course catalog, number of seats filled, high marks on "happiness sheets," and ability to stay within budget. The focus is on training events, rather than on workforce performance.

Rarely does the manager or director of training make a presentation to a CEO and his or her management team with this type of information:

1. Here are the business and financial reasons for investing in training and performance systems.
2. Here is the management system that ensures that all courses are "must do" rather than "nice to do" and that all courses are tied to organizational objectives and goals.

3. Here is a detailed status report ensuring that the performance systems for each major job category focuses on the right issues.
4. Here is the delivery-system strategy that will increase quality and reduce costs.
5. Here is how we plan to implement the four levels of quality measurements.
6. Here is how the training and performance department is using job aids, personal-development tasks, on-the-job training assignments, and basic support systems that will lower training costs and help employees apply the lessons they learn to the workplace.
7. Here are the jobs that may require an integrated performance support system, and here is a recommendation for a pilot test.
8. Here is how the reward and recognition systems support the performance systems.
9. Here is how the training and performance organization has established a formal working partnership with line management.
10. Here is how the employees will outperform the competition.

Penetrating Questions from Senior Executives

If the senior and line executives have not received this type of presentation in the last year, it is time for them to ask some penetrating questions. They must demand answers to these questions:

1. Does the training department have a mission statement that clearly states that it must develop a performance system for the organization's critical jobs?
2. Have we identified all the major job categories, and do line executives concur with this list?
3. Do we have a management system such as the Systems Approach for Workforce Performance? Why is our management system better than our competitors' systems? If not, what do we need to do to enhance our management system?
4. Has the training and performance department established a formal working partnership with line management to design and develop a performance system for each major job category?

5. Have we established detailed performance requirements for each major job category, and do line executives concur with these requirements?
6. Do we have a professional group that knows how to buy, modify, or develop the required courses, design on-the-job training assignments, develop basic support systems, and assign personal-development tasks to achieve low-cost and successful performance systems?
7. Do we have a delivery-system strategy that ensures that our organization uses the most cost-effective methods?
8. Are we using all four levels of quality-control measurements for all curricula and performance systems?
9. Does our performance-management system aim for mastery of learning and performance, rather than the obsolete bell-shaped curve?
10. Is there a formal change-management system that continuously updates our courses, on-the-job training assignments, and support systems?
11. Do we need an integrated electronic performance support system within any of our major job categories?
12. Are we on target with our reward and recognition programs?

Training managers or directors must anticipate and be prepared to answer all of these questions because executives are learning more about education. The CTO must educate senior and line executives on the performance system's potential. It is an easy meeting to arrange: Chief executive officers and senior executives will always listen to specific suggestions on how to restructure training so that it focuses on workforce performance.

Executives may think that restructuring will just increase the training department's budget. If the Systems Approach for Workforce Performance is implemented, the training budget will increase only when other operating expenses decrease or when revenues increase.

The senior executives should insist on a shared vision for obtaining optimum performance. The vision should be a one-page, realistic summary that reflects the ideal for mastery of learning and performance and how it can be achieved. All of these people should share this vision: the CEO and senior executives, line executives and their staffs, middle management, first-line supervisors, employees, and training and performance personnel. The vision must be powerful and motivational, something that everyone can rally around. The Systems Approach for Workforce Performance is an example of an effective vision. Executives can hold people accountable to the vision until it is realized.

Implementing the Vision

Change usually comes from the top down. Accordingly, the CEO and senior executives must launch the implementation of a new vision. A clear signal is given to the entire company if a senior executive is designated to head a task force that will review the existing training programs and compare them with what programs and support systems should exist. This person is known as the "sponsoring executive" of the study and task force.

A second clear signal would be to put someone in charge of the company's training and performance functions, if the position does not already exist. This person can hold a corporate staff position with a very small staff or a line position with authority over the various training departments. A proven leader must occupy this position in order for the company to achieve results.

There is a proven methodology for restructuring the training department focus on workforce performance. This process begins with the appointment of a study group or task force. Appointing a chief training officer sends a strong message to the entire organization. In some organizations, the task force represents all of the company's major functional areas except training. Needless to say, trainers become quite upset when they are not represented. A more balanced approach is to select half the task-force members from the training department and half from the major functional or operating departments that utilize training and support programs.

The task-force members should all be outstanding performers and future organizational leaders. Because these people tend to be overly busy, being on the task force should not be a full-time job. When a full-time commitment to a task force is requested, only the "available" people will be assigned; in too many cases, available means the low performers. Because the executives' first impressions of a task force stem from the reputation of its members, it is important to have the right people on the task force when the final presentation to the executive team is made. Committing 25 percent of their time over a sixty-day period usually works for outstanding performers.

The kick-off meeting should take place thirty days after the company makes the initial decision to form a task force. This will give the task-force executive sponsor enough time to invite the right people to join. Written invitations following a telephone conversation are always a nice touch.

At the first meeting, the executive sponsor usually tells the members why the organization wants to restructure its training with a focus on workforce performance. He or she always thanks everyone for taking time out of their busy schedules to serve on this important task force. Then the executive outlines six meetings, indicating that the group will be a highly structured and productive task force. The balance of the meeting is spent on developing a work plan and discussing the next meeting's work assignments, which will involve finding out what is currently happening in the training department. The following questions will need to be answered:

1. What is the department's current mission statement and management system?
2. What line executives are involved, and what do they do?
3. What existing procedures determine when new courses are required?
4. How do the training departments estimate the number of students for each course in the annual planning cycle?
5. Who develops courses? Are instructional-design methods used?
6. Is there a delivery-system strategy? What percentage of student days is devoted to each major delivery system?
7. How does the department measure the quality of its training?
8. How does the department measure the quantity of its training?
9. Are there any pilot systems for integrated electronic performance support systems?
10. How does the department recruit instructors and course developers? What HR programs exist within the training department?

11. Does the department integrate personal-development guidelines, performance-based training courses, job aids, on-the-job training assignments, and basic support systems into a performance system for every major job category?
12. Does the department work with HR and the line organization on hiring practices and policies?
13. Does the department work with HR and the line organization on reward and recognition programs?
14. What are the attrition rates within job categories?
15. What is the current budget for all training, including head count and expenses?
16. What business goals and objectives do the courses support. When were the courses last updated?
17. Have any competitive benchmark studies been completed?
18. Has the department documented and determined the costs of its existing administrative and enrollment systems?
19. How are expenses charged to user departments?
20. What are the most serious problems with the existing courses, job aids, on-the-job training programs, and personal-development tasks?

Gathering all of this data will ensure that the task-force members understand all of the existing courses and programs.

At the second task-force meeting, all of this information is presented. Every task-force member will soon realize that the organization has a "workforce with some training." The attitude of the task-force members will shift from apathy to "Let's get these training programs restructured!" It is important, however, for them not to blame the current training conditions on any one person or department. At some point, *all* organizations have had unstructured and nonmeasured training departments.

The third meeting is more exciting because the members hear about and discuss new types of training and support systems. This educational session features presentations on instructional design, delivery systems, integrated electronic performance support systems, measurements, organizational structure, HR programs, and management systems.

The fourth meeting is devoted to developing the mission statement and management system. This is when the Systems Approach for Workforce Performance evolves. This decision-making meeting will not succeed until everyone understands the existing programs (meeting two) and the potential new programs (meeting three).

During the fifth meeting, the task force develops its report and presentation to the CEO and senior executives. Usually staff members will have prepared these two documents between the fourth and fifth meetings. The task force then rewrites and fine-tunes the report and final presentation.

At the sixth meeting, the chief training officer or the task force chairperson makes a presentation to the sponsoring executive who launched the study eight to ten weeks ago. This is an education session for the sponsoring executive, who will usually make a number of positive suggestions for both the report and the executive presentation. This meeting concludes when the executive sponsor thanks all the task-force members for their creativity and hard work.

The next meeting is with the CEO, alone or with the senior management team. Often the new chief training officer gives the presentation; in other cases, the sponsoring executive does this task. In a few situations, the entire task force is present. However, there is one risk with having all the task-force members in the board room: Some of them may not be accustomed to being in senior executive meetings and may make inappropriate comments that create tension among the executives. The meeting will undoubtedly be positive because the presentation is the overpowering story of why it is important to reengineer the training function to focus on workforce performance.

Principles of Change Management

This entire reengineering process for the training function must adhere to the generally accepted principles of change management outlined below:

Phase One: Develop an Overpowering Case for Change. Chief executive officers and senior executives will make a major investment in reengineering an organizational area only if they are convinced that they will receive a large return for their efforts, risk, and money. The main reason for restructuring a training department is to achieve workforce performance breakthroughs and to reduce operating expenses, so the executive presentation must build a strong case for instituting change.

Phase Two: Create an Exciting Vision. The vision must be easily explained and no longer than one page. The Systems Approach for Workforce Performance exemplifies an exciting vision.

Phase Three: Develop an Implementation Plan. The executives will want a quick overview of how the vision will be achieved. They will need to hear about the strategies and action programs that will be necessary for the organization to evolve from the current training methods to the Systems Approach for Workforce Performance. Significant costs must be discussed in this phase, as well as potential obstacles that could be encountered and a solution for each.

Phase Four: Pilot Test or Proof of Concept. Senior executives have no interest in a risky, unproven proposal that "bets the company assets." They want to know how the concept can be demonstrated and proven in the near future.

Phase Five: Institutionalize Change. Once they see "proof of concept," the executives will want to know the time and costs needed to implement the new approach throughout the organization. They will also want to know how the system will prevent the company from reverting to "training as usual."

Many successful executive presentations are made using this five-phase format to create and manage change. At the close of the presentation, the decisions necessary to launch a pilot test must be outlined.

Numerous articles have been written on why executives and managers resist change. These reasons include: needing more time to study proposals; the need to develop a detailed business case; wanting to be the last department to implement the change; and concern for the employees' well-being. All of these are actually excuses for not moving forward. If these excuses are used to halt the restructuring process, then the task force must demonstrate conclusively that the need for change is overpowering. If the task force has done its work well and the executive presentation is outstanding, senior executives quickly approve a pilot test.

Employees and managers welcome the changes for the following reasons: A well-trained employee has greater job satisfaction and higher morale; the changes often create more job security; the old system's problems start to disappear; operating and financial measurements indicate positive results; minorities and women view the Systems Approach as another step toward equal opportunity; and all employees and managers are pleased that senior executives are investing in workforce performance, which probably supports a statement in the annual report that reads: "Our employees are our most important asset."

After a decade of downsizing, most senior executives are looking for breakthrough strategies that will enable their organizations to grow and be more profitable. Implementing the Systems Approach for Workforce Performance will do just that.

Some leaders in the performance technology and consulting fields want to change the training department's name, adding "performance" with no mention of training. If an organization implements the Systems Approach for Workforce Performance, the department name should not become an obstacle. A compromise might work best, something like "the training and performance department."

Leading Change

John P. Kotter's latest book, *Leading Change,* was published in 1996 by the Harvard Business School Press. This well-known Harvard professor provides the lessons of experience in a nonacademic, practical guide for executives who must lead major change projects within their organizations. His first message is clear: "Only leadership can motivate the actions needed to alter behavior in any significant way. Only leadership can get change to stick by anchoring it in the very culture of an organization. Only leadership [not managing] can blast through the many sources of corporate inertia" (pp. 67–68). He outlines the eight most common errors that leaders commit in the name of change and how to avoid them.

Allowing Too Much Complacency. It is important to establish a sense of urgency by setting challenging goals for each major phase of implementation.

Failing to Create a Sufficiently Powerful Coalition. The Systems Approach for Workforce Performance develops a working coalition between senior executives, line executives, and employees through performance systems that exist for every major job category.

Underestimating the Power of Vision. The Systems Approach is a powerful vision that can be quickly understood by senior executives, line executives, middle management, first-line supervisors, and the training and performance organization. It creates a shared vision throughout the organization.

Undercommunicating the Vision by a Factor of Ten. The CTO must continually sell and communicate the vision throughout the organization. Early successes must also be communicated.

Permitting Obstacles to Block the New Vision. The CTO must quickly recognize potential barriers and take the appropriate actions to eliminate potential problems.

Failing to Create Short-Term Wins. The initial performance systems must be successful, and the success stories must be communicated throughout the organization.

Declaring Victory Too Soon. Kotter urges the executives to celebrate small victories, but not to imply that the task is almost over. The complete implementation plan must be communicated to everyone.

Neglecting to Anchor Changes Firmly in the Corporate Culture. The Systems Approach for Workforce Performance can be firmly institutionalized into the corporate culture by using an annual review by the senior executives.

Executive Time Required

In organizations in which the training department has been reengineered, the CEO typically has appointed a senior vice president or vice president to conduct a study on how to restructure the training organization to achieve workforce performance breakthroughs—the executive sponsor. The CEO takes this action originally because he or she learned about it while serving on an education-reform task force or while reading articles or books on how other companies have reengineered their training departments. In some situations, the CEO is disgusted with the performance results turned in by some of the organization's key functions and employees.

The sponsoring executive may be a chief operating officer, a chief of corporate staff, a corporate services senior vice president, an HR vice president, or a line executive. He or she will probably spend three days selecting a new chief training officer (if one does not already exist), appointing a task force, and attending the initial task force meeting. The executive sponsor will also invest one day reviewing the executive presentation and meeting with senior executives.

The total executive time required to start amounts to about five days. Time is not the issue; the issue is for the organization's senior executives to make an executive decision for a quantum leap toward managing workforce performance. Rather than approving one course at a time, senior executives should demand a performance system for every major job category. They should insist on a library of employee-development courses in the learning center, including basic-skills courses. They should also approve a series of courses for management development. It is not more complicated than making these three basic decisions.

If the existing chief training officer decides to educate the senior executive team on why the training department should adopt a new mission statement and a new management system such as the Systems Approach for Workforce Performance, then the executive presentation will take two or three weeks to develop. Most of this time will involve discussions among the training staff on what to say to the executives. Once again, time is not the critical issue: Leadership is. The management team in the training and performance organization must have the courage and confidence to make this presentation.

Appointing the Chief Training Officer

The chief training officer usually reports to the reengineering study's executive sponsor. In many situations, the executive sponsor does not fully understand how many changes must be implemented until he or she receives the executive presentation at the sixth task-force meeting. Consequently, he or she may have selected the wrong person to serve as chief training officer.

The executive sponsor should reread Chapter Four and may also want to ask an outside consultant what characteristics are needed to be a successful chief training officer. It is helpful to appoint the chief training officer prior to the start of the reengineering study. This way, the CTO becomes the study's chairperson as well as the primary change agent within the study.

The CTO appointment represents a major decision. The CTO must be a proven leader of change. At the beginning of this decade, Harvard Business School Professor John Kotter (1990, p. 10) said: "Most U.S. Corporations are over-managed and under-led." The same is true for most training departments. The CTO must sell a vision and a management system. The CTO must generate goals to stretch a training department that, until now, has been conducting "business as usual." The Systems Approach can be used to enable line executives and training directors to stretch themselves to achieve new levels of workforce performance.

Many organizations try to copy their competitors. Imitation may be the sincerest form of flattery, but it rarely helps a company achieve a strategic advantage within an industry. Why play catch-up when you can leapfrog your competition with a new break-through strategy? The CTO must sell this philosophy as he or she leads the training and performance department into a partnership with line executives that will ultimately create workforce performance breakthroughs.

Unfortunately, trainers are just like other employees. They resist change for the following reasons:

- Insufficient communication.
- Too many unknowns.
- Unrealistic schedules.
- Fear of having no work to do.
- Fear of having unreasonable work loads.
- Concerns about not being capable of change.
- Failure of past changes.
- Early implementation problems.
- Undefined personal roles.

The CTO must help employees cope with these and other concerns that arise during a major transition period. The CTO must communicate effectively and assure employees that they have positive roles to play. Leadership motivates employees by satisfying their basic human needs. Leaders must involve their employees in the transition from a workforce with some training to a well-trained competitive workforce. Being involved in the process gives the trainers a sense of participation and control.

Although the position is new, the CTO will become one of the most important members of the management team during the next decade. After all, the CTO influences the performance of the entire workforce. With the cost of people being most companies' number-one expense, CTO leadership will significantly influence organizational revenues, market share, customer satisfaction, employee morale, attrition rates, operating expenses, and earnings.

The top-performing chief training officers will gain notoriety, just as the superior performers within the CFO and CIO ranks have. It is a surprise to most people that the compensation for CFOs increased nearly 25 percent between 1992 and 1996, compared with 18 percent for CEOs and 13 percent for COOs. Julia Homer, editor of *CFO Magazine,* said the message is clear: "Financial executives are being paid for performance, not for keeping score." Eleven companies pay their CFOs over a million dollars in total compensation. Another group of twenty-five CFOs earn in excess of $500,000, but not yet over a million. These figures were unheard of fifteen years ago when CFOs played the role of scorekeeper.

When chief training officers are viewed as members of the executive team who can influence revenues, operational expenses, and earnings, they will be rewarded appropriately. At some time in the future, a chief training officer will earn in excess of a million dollars. To do that, the focus must be on workforce performance, not on training events.

To achieve that level of income, the CTO must implement a management system such as the Systems Approach for Workforce Performance and enable the organization to become a leader within its industry through outstanding employee, manager, and executive performance. He or she must be viewed as a creator and accelerator of change. In the future, successful companies will need outstanding performers in four executive positions:

- CEO, to provide outstanding strategic leadership.
- CFO, to control assets, expenses, and financial performance.
- CIO, to provide strategic advantages through leading-edge information systems.
- CTO, to provide superior workforce performance at a minimum expense level.

Of course, organizations always need outstanding functional and line executives to complete a top-performing management team.

Institutionalizing Change

After the pilot test provides proof of concept for one or two critical jobs, the training and performance department can accelerate the implementation process: Five jobs in the next year, ten jobs in the following years. Most organizations try to phase in the implementation over that period of time, although it is possible to do all jobs in under three years if the department has sufficient talent. If the changes come too fast, employees will fear them. On the other hand, if the conversion schedule drags on for years, people lose interest as key people receive promotions or retire.

Large organizations have a big advantage because the cost to develop a curriculum of performance-based courses and support systems can be divided by thousands of employees, keeping the cost per employee small while the benefits of increased performance can soar into the millions. For this reason, large organizations usually move at an accelerated pace. Intermediate-size companies purchase most courses and support systems, which eliminates development time.

The senior executives of more progressive organizations formally review the major areas of their businesses annually. In the same way, the training and performance department should be reviewed annually by senior executives. In fact, the chief training officer should volunteer to be reviewed, even if the executives fail to ask for the meeting.

The review meeting lasts about one hour, forty minutes for a presentation and twenty minutes for questions and answers. The CTO should start with a review of the mission statement and the management system being implemented, as it may have been months since the senior executives looked at it.

This should be followed by a quick briefing on every major strategy being implemented to achieve the department's ultimate goal: mastery of learning and performance. These strategies would include:

- Identification of Key Jobs.
- Establishment of a Working Partnership with Line Management.
- Development of a Performance System for Each Key Job.
- Development of a Performance-Based Curriculum.
- Development of Support Systems.
- Implementation of Quality Measurements.
- Implementation of Rewards and Recognition.
- Pilot Test for the Electronic Performance Support System.

Senior executives want to hear good news about the resources they have invested in the Systems Approach for Workforce Performance. They want to know if any areas are behind schedule, and what they can do to correct this. Senior executives want to work with the CTO to achieve breakthroughs in workforce performance.

The CTO should not use the meeting to ask for more staff or funding. The meeting should be used strictly to review how well the training and performance department is operating. Of course, the impression the CTO makes at this meeting will have a great impact on the senior executives when they approve or adjust future budgets. Having an annual meeting drives home the message that training is not a one-time event, but a continuous process designed to enhance workforce performance. The annual review is a way of life for all other organizational operating units and it should be for training as well.

The annual review keeps trainers from regressing to the world of course catalogs and "happiness sheet" measurements. Executives do not want to regress once they have heard the benefits that can be realized from the Systems Approach for Workforce Performance. Employees also do not want to regress back to content-based courses and a workforce with some training, because they now take great pride in their mastery of learning and performance.

Performance Systems in Corporate Scorecards

A new measurement tool called a corporate scorecard is being developed by some executive teams to help them be more successful. A corporate scorecard is a sophisticated business model that helps a company understand what is really driving its success. The scorecard can keep track of many organizational areas such as customer satisfaction and workforce performance. Motorola, for example, is measuring "key drivers" for its business. Scorecards must go beyond financial measurements, which tell a company where it has been, and focus on how to manage in the future. One company has fifteen nonfinancial measures on its corporate scorecard.

In the past, the training organization could not be included on a corporate scorecard because of lack of standards and measurements, but that will change with the implementation of the Systems Approach, which allows the number of fully trained and partially trained employees and the length and time to achieve mastery within each major job category to be measured. Benchmarking studies could also be included.

John Kay, director of Oxford University's new School of Management Studies, recently said, "You can't run a successful company if you don't care about customers and employees, or if you are systematically unpleasant to suppliers" (*Fortune*, 1997, pp. 133–134). Clearly, there are some areas that require measurement. Focusing exclusively on increasing shareholder wealth may preclude an executive team from doing things that would actually be in the long-term interest of shareholders. Improving workforce performance certainly is one of those.

The entire subject of measuring and reporting on integrated assets is being reviewed by the Financial Accounting Standards Board (FASB), the standard-setting body for U.S. accountants. So far, they have not made a formal study.

The Big Six auditing firms could offer their clients a program review of workforce performance in addition to a regular financial audit. The auditors could highlight areas that need to be improved as well as recognize which organizational areas have outstanding programs. Once again, standards of best practices and a generally accepted management system are needed to conduct such a review. Paying for a professional opinion about the number-one area of expense is certainly a worthwhile investment. Chief financial officers will be reviewing this subject in much greater detail when they realize how much money is invested in workforce performance.

Executive Participation in School Reform

In 1983, President Reagan's Secretary of Education Terrel H. Bell published the famous "A Nation at Risk" report. It sent a strong message: American public schools were in serious trouble. On average, 50 percent of students were not receiving a solid high school education. After spending ten to twelve years in the school system, thousands of students had only the equivalent of a fourth-grade education.

Since 1983, this subject has been reviewed by more than a thousand task forces and hundreds of reports. The annual public school operating costs have more than doubled since 1983 to over $300 billion. Unfortunately, the students' performance has increased only slightly.

School reform has been led by our country's governors and senior business leaders. In late 1995, forty-nine CEOs and forty governors discussed the public school challenge with President Clinton at a corporate education center. Their greatest concern was that the United States is splitting into a nation of the educated and uneducated. Something must be done to stop the continuous flow of unemployables from our schools that feeds the welfare and prison systems. In addition, top students should perform at higher levels than 13th- or 14th-place finishes they have achieved at international competitions.

Governors, mayors, state legislators, city council members, and business executives have been disappointed in school reform progress since 1983. After spending billions of incremental dollars, student performance is still not acceptable. A former New Jersey governor, Thomas H. Kean once said, "We have become masters at measuring poor performance." Presidents Bush and Clinton have both tried to be "the education president." The reform movement has not suffered from a lack of executive leadership, commitment, or resources.

Why has it been such a failure? Chief executive officers and business leaders did not take the time to fully understand the learning process. They looked for quick-fix and feel-good solutions such as longer school days, longer school years, parent involvement, more technology, increasing teacher pay, uniforms, and adopt-a-school programs.

They did not see that the problem lies in the classroom. Students start to fall behind, get lost, and give up. This is especially true of inner-city school children, who already have low self-esteem. The solution is to aim for mastery of learning and performance by implementing learning systems that include multimedia tutoring.

Most senior executives are afraid to confront school administrators and teachers with the fact that the root problem is in the classroom. The administrators and teachers, of course, say that the problem is the high incidence of poverty and broken families in our society. Nonetheless, school reform will not progress until everyone agrees to aim for mastery of learning and performance.

During the next several years, CEOs and senior executives should focus more on workforce training than on school reform. By adopting mastery of learning and performance in the workplace, senior executives will learn how this goal can be achieved within their own organizations. They will learn the difference between performance-based and content-based courses. The executives will learn more about integrated electronic performance support systems and computer-based training. They will see the power of combining multimedia tutoring systems with teaching.

After CEOs and senior executives have learned these fundamentals of education, they will be in a better position to advise school boards, superintendents, governors, and presidents on how to reengineer the American public schools. For now, they need to concentrate on reforming their own training departments.

A number of senior executives have been very helpful to the reform movement. Business executives have every right to participate in school reform. After all, their organizations receive public school graduates as new entry-level employees. It is a disgrace that corporations and government agencies have to provide basic reading, writing, arithmetic, statistics, and personal-computer application courses. People should acquire basic skills in the public schools.

The business community should not support massive tax increases for schools until school boards adopt mastery of learning and performance as a goal. All students who do not have a physical or mental handicap can be A or B performers through high school. The business executives should demand this performance level from both the public school system and their own training departments. If this performance level is mandated, the American workforce will once again be the envy of the world.

Senior executives should give the subject of workforce performance the same emphasis that they have given quality and reengineering, because it has the same potential to improve their organizations' overall financial performance.

Chapter Twenty

Essential Messages for Executive Management

This chapter is an overview of the key messages in this book, designed for senior executives who may not have time to read all the implementation information in previous chapters.

Number-One Expense

In almost every organization, the number-one expense is the cost of people, including payroll, benefits (including retirement), and support (buildings, utilities, office furniture, workplace fixtures, tools, telephones, FAX machines, personal computers, and copiers) for both full-time and part-time employees. On average, the annual cost of a full-time employee varies between $25,000 to $60,000, with high-tech companies being at the upper limits. No employee, manager, or executive is inexpensive.

Every organization should calculate its true cost of people, which takes only a few hours or days, depending on the complexity of the organization. This is the first step toward focusing on workforce performance, an attention to which will greatly influence the operating and financial results of an organization.

Number-One Crisis in Education

The number-one crisis in U.S. education, from an economic viewpoint, is not the performance of the public school system, but the inadequate training programs available to most of the workforce. Millions of employees, managers, and executives go to work every day untrained or only partially trained to do their jobs. America has a workforce at risk.

The Conference Board (Csoka, 1994) recently issued a report titled "Closing the Human Performance Gap," which said, "Despite major investments in technology, downsizing, restructuring, and reengineering to cut costs and to improve their competitive advantage, 98 percent of companies responding reported a need to gain more productivity and higher performance from their workforce." The report further stated, "The competitive advantage is people. Consequently, the quality of workforce performance has become a key business issue."

Two Worlds of Performance

Some American executives are finding the missing link that leads to growth and increased profits. They have discovered that a competitive, well-trained workforce remains as one of the last organizational strategies for distinguishing companies from their competitors.

Motorola, Federal Express, GE, the FBI, GAO, Arthur Andersen, Andersen Consulting, Xerox, Ford, Nordstrom, Southwest Airlines, Delta Airlines, GTE, McDonald's, The Southern Company, and a few leading-edge financial-service companies have invested adequate resources into performance-based training and integrated performance support systems in order to train and develop their workforces. These organizations have demonstrated that American companies can still have workforces that are the envy of the world.

It is not just resources, however, that have made these companies so successful. They have *management systems* that enable their training and support systems to continuously adjust to business objectives and the implementation of new strategic directions and tactical decisions. These organizations know that a well-trained workforce does more work, creates fewer errors, requires less supervision, and produces more output than a workforce with some training. They want a well-trained, low-cost *competitive workforce* that knows more and does more than other companies in their industry. Unfortunately, only a few organizations have an effective management system for their training and performance function.

Most organizations have just a *workforce with some training*. The training department offers generalized employee and management-development courses that have little impact on financial performance. Senior and line executives have not defined what they want their employees to know and be able to do within each major job category. Course curriculum and support systems for each major job simply do not exist. Few, if any, quality measurements exist on whether lessons are being learned or being applied to the job on a daily basis. Everyone comes to work with good intentions, but their inadequate training renders them second- or third-class performers. Employees make too many errors, requiring multiple layers of managers to audit their performance. Worse yet, senior executives view them as a variable expense and seek to reduce costs by eliminating employees or transferring jobs to lower-wage environments. Under such conditions morale is low and attrition high, leading to soaring recruiting and training costs. All of this increases the number of employees required to do necessary tasks. A *workforce with some training* usually has excessive costs due to poor performance.

Why This Situation Exists

Unfortunately, senior executives are not educated or trained on how to develop a well-trained, low-cost, competitive workforce. The subject is not covered in graduate schools of business nor in most executive-development programs. Not only are senior and line executives untrained, but individuals in charge of training are not trained to develop a competitive workforce. Therefore, they measure themselves on having classroom seats filled, receiving good student-satisfaction ratings, and staying within budget.

Because of this situation, 99 percent of all companies, government agencies, and not-for-profit organizations have a *workforce with some training* rather than a *well-trained, competitive,* and *low-cost workforce*. In fact, fifteen years ago, almost all organizations had a workforce with some training because the knowledge and management system for a competitive workforce did not exist.

Another major reason for excessive costs in the area of workforce performance is the traditional performance-management system. For decades, the bell-shaped curve has been accepted as the basic measurement system for performance. This situation led Dr. W. Edwards Deming (1986) to state, "The greatest waste in America is failure to use the abilities of people." With the new systems outlined in this book, employees can achieve mastery of learning and performance. In other words, all long-term employees can be A and B performers. The bell-shaped curve moves to the right, as in Figure 20.1, which reduces the cost of people because top performers do more work, require less supervision, and make fewer errors.

To achieve mastery, a performance system must be developed for each major job category within the organization. Performance systems are new. They consist of some combination of personal-development assignments, on-the-job training sessions, performance-based training courses, and support systems. The performance system must be customized to an organization's requirements based on the business or government agency objectives, established annually. The challenge is to minimize the cost and time it takes to achieve mastery of learning and performance within each major job category, as shown in Figure 20.2. Sometimes, both the time and cost can be reduced by up to 50 percent.

Intent of the Book

This book was written for the *training organization* and the *executive team,* both essential for achieving a *well-trained, competitive, and low-cost workforce.* Recently, a major insurance company's CEO stated, "We have been looking at learning as an outcome, when learning is only a by-product. Performance is what we want. As business managers facing a tough and unknown future, we cannot afford the luxury of learning when it's not accompanied by performance." This attitude needs to permeate all executive offices.

This book lists best practices from a dozen successful organizations that have achieved a *well-trained, competitive, and low-cost workforce,* which should be transferred to thousands of organizations that have only a *workforce with some training.* No one single organization has a complete and perfect system. However, the

Figure 20.1. The Great Transition.

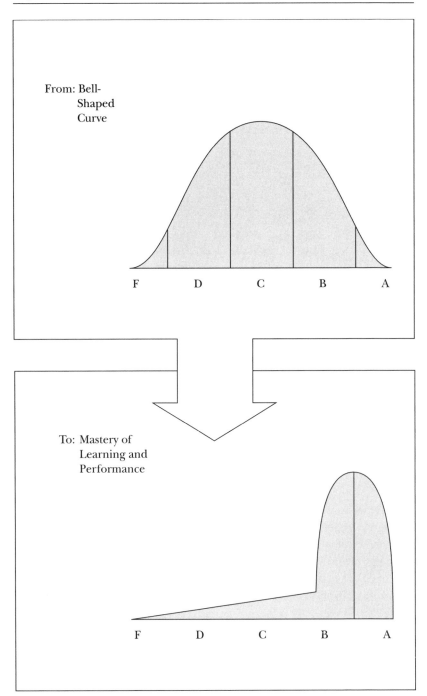

Figure 20.2. Cost and Time for Mastery Performance.

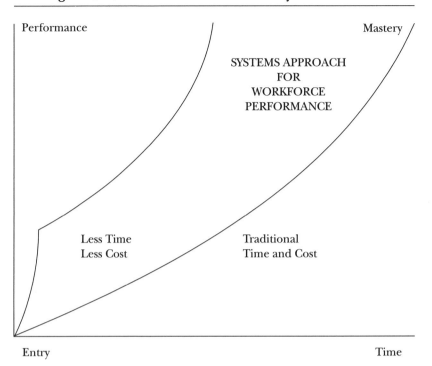

top-performing organizations all have some form of *management system* for training and performance that achieves many of the following results:

- Increased productivity.
- Reduced cost of people.
- Lower supervision costs.
- Reduced cost for rework.
- Increased revenues.
- Greater market share.
- Faster implementation of strategic directions and tactical decisions.
- Higher employee morale.
- Lower attrition rate.
- Reduced recruitment and employment costs.
- Increased job security.
- Increased job enrichment.
- Enhanced cross-training of jobs.

- Improved job performance.
- Full use of advancing technology.
- A strategic competitive advantage within the industry.

In addition, if an organization is really serious about total quality management (TQM) and reengineering basic processes, a new management system for achieving breakthroughs in workforce performance is absolutely necessary.

To achieve these significant advantages there must be a formal working partnership between senior executives and the management team responsible for training the workforce. There is no reason for an organization to learn by trial and error. We know what works and what programs are disappointing failures. Why reinvent successful best practices at great costs? Why not benefit from those organizations that have already achieved breakthroughs in workforce performance.

Restructuring a training department that now concentrates on training events into a training and performance organization that is focused on workforce performance is a major task, requiring many steps to achieve breakthroughs.

Start with a Mission Statement

Most training departments today have mission statements, but too many of them consist of generalized statements of good intentions. Here is an example of a more meaningful mission statement:

> Based upon business and performance requirements identified by line and staff management, our mission is to assess, develop, deliver, and evaluate effective training and support systems. These performance systems must empower our entire workforce to rise above the competition with a performance level that will contribute significantly to our leadership position within the industry.

Each organization should develop its own customized mission statement. In this example, the head of training is definitely moving his or her department into the organization's mainstream. The mission statement focuses on workforce performance instead of training events, mentioning support systems as well as courses of instruction. It clearly places the responsibility for determining business objectives where it belongs, on line and staff management shoulders. To accomplish a mission like this requires a comprehensive management system.

Overview of a Management System

Figure 20.3 illustrates a new management system for training and performance that represents the best practices of organizations that have achieved breakthroughs in workforce performance. This system has been developed over a ten-year period, with many organizations and individuals contributing to the vision. The Systems Approach for Workforce Performance is a systematic approach for achieving superior workforce performance. Each element links together to manage performance to achieve organizational objectives.

In most organizations, senior executives develop annual objectives, shown as Step 1 in Figure 20.3. In this example, business or government objectives are based on inputs from five sources:

- Customer requirements.
- Regulatory requirements.
- Strategic visions.
- Competitive requirements.
- Union contracts.

In Step 2 the organization's basic processes are *enhanced* or *reengineered* based on objectives established and decisions made by the executive team in Step 1. Too often, methods and procedures of the organization are not updated when new strategic directions and tactical decisions are decided by senior executives. It is shocking to see how many training programs and support systems are out-of-date because the basic processes have not been enhanced or reengineered for years.

Next, the training organization must work with line management to convert objectives (Step 1) and revised procedures (Step 2) into performance requirements (Step 3). Line executives must determine what they want employees *within each major job category* to know and be able to do. Most organizations never address this question. Too often, they talk about empowering employees or speak generalizations such as "work smarter, not harder." To

Figure 20.3. Systems Approach for Workforce Performance.

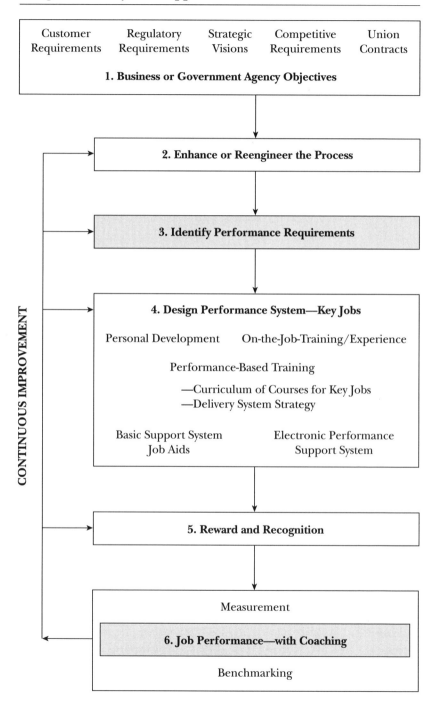

become a world-class workforce, employees must know what training they need and what tasks they must be able to do.

Defining jobs and performance requirements is hard work, requiring strong leadership on the part of line management. Equally important, the training organization must lead line executives through this process with methodologies such as front-end analysis or needs and task analysis.

Once line executives and the training department have documented these performance requirements, they must determine how their employees will gain the knowledge and skills of an A or B performer, using a performance system that is developed for each major job category. There are five ways to develop employee knowledge and skills, a process referred to as a performance system in Step 4.

Personal-Development Assignments. These can be a reading assignment, an employee-development course, a meeting, or a special assignment. These are all low-cost methods for improving performance.

On-the-Job Training and Experience. This is an essential part of the Systems Approach, but it must be highly structured and quite different from the hit-and-miss methods used in most organizations.

Performance-Based Training. This new instructional method enables employees to achieve mastery of learning and performance on the job. Almost every major job category requires a curriculum of courses so that employees can achieve maximum performance. The delivery-system decisions greatly influence both quality and instruction costs.

Support Systems. Support systems provide databases, guidelines, job aids, procedure manuals, knowledge systems, and periodic performance reviews to be certain that the course lessons are transferred to the job.

Electronic Performance Support Systems. This is a new paradigm for enhancing workforce performance using multimedia tutoring systems tied to networks. Employees learn with just-in-time lessons and perform tasks with electronic supervision, eventually achieving mastery of learning and performance.

The job of the *performance consultant* is to design a performance system for every major job category that minimizes cost and time away from the job. Just like a manufacturing system, the performance system must be designed to achieve business objectives, but at the lowest possible cost. To achieve this requires a team effort by the project manager, performance consultant, instructional designers, programmers, graphic experts, assessment specialists, and instructors.

The Systems Approach for Workforce Performance is built on a formal partnership between the line organization and the restructured training and performance organization, who work together to produce a superior performance system for every major job category.

In Step 5 of the Systems Approach, all HR programs that influence performance should be reviewed. That includes job descriptions, job levels, compensation programs, and reward and recognition systems. The workplace is changing. Executives are delegating more responsibility to managers, supervisors, and employees. These people must complete their tasks right the first time to achieve quality objectives. Rewards and recognition programs greatly influence workforce performance.

Finally, in Step 6, employees' and managers' performances are evaluated to determine if they are achieving the objectives that were established in Step 3. If not, either the basic process (Step 2) or the performance system (Step 4) or the reward and recognition systems (Step 5) must be enhanced. Of course, if the problem is individual performance, that situation must be addressed by the manager.

The goal is to move the bell-shaped curve to the right by achieving mastery of learning and performance within all major job categories, as in Figure 20.1. Recent research has proven that A and B performers are far more productive and valuable to the organization than C and D performers. The organization needs to identify C and D performers through a performance system and reassign them to a job in which they can achieve A or B performance. We call this the rising tide of performance, which is achieved through the Systems Approach for Workforce Performance.

Quality measurements are built into the overall process. Management will receive the following assurances:

1. The employees will like the courses and assignments.
2. The students will learn their lessons and acquire their skills.
3. The employees will apply the lessons and skills from the performance system to their jobs.
4. The performance system will have a positive impact on operating and financial measurements.

Many progressive organizations are also benchmarking the performance of their major job categories against other organizations to ensure that their employees are superior performers.

Justification for This New Approach

New methods are used to justify the expense of developing a performance system for every major job category. Figure 20.2 showed how entry-level employees often achieve mastery of performance in half the time and at half the cost. Of course, each job category has a different cost associated with its training, which must be justified by the kind of results that are expected.

Required New Executive

Restructuring or reengineering a traditional training organization into a function that focuses on workforce performance is a major undertaking. If a CEO or senior management team wants to achieve a strategic breakthrough in workforce performance, they need to hire or appoint a leader who has a proven record for creating and managing change. This new executive position can be given one of these titles:

- Chief Training Officer (CTO).
- Chief Learning Officer (CLO).
- Chief Performance Officer (CPO).

Skeptics will ask why a new executive position is needed in a time when companies and government agencies are trying to reduce their headquarters staff. The answer is quite clear: Virtually every successful organization, Big-Six accounting firms, Motorola,

SUN Microsystems, Intel, McDonald's, Southern Company, Sprint, GTE, Coca-Cola, GE, and many others, have an executive in charge of training and learning who reports directly to someone on the senior management team. There is proof of the concept based on the successes of the past ten years. The title varies, but the job description does not. The CTO is responsible for transforming a traditional training organization into one that increases workforce performance through leading-edge performance systems.

Line executives simply do not have the time to become experts on needs and task analysis, instructional-design methods, course-delivery systems, education technologies, measurement systems, authoring systems, performance-management systems, and communication networks. Someone has to lead this effort, and that executive must have specialized knowledge.

Required Leadership from Senior Executives

Senior and line executives are becoming increasingly interested in the training department because of the following reasons:

- The cost of each employee (payroll, benefits, and basic support) increases annually. There is no such thing as an inexpensive employee.
- Companies' and government agencies' expectations of technology are more realistic. They now know that employee performance is equally as important as computer performance.
- Jobs are more complex. Organizations expect their employees to know more and to do more.
- Intense competition exists in every organization and industry, and workforce performance can be a differentiating factor.
- There is now and will continue to be a shortage of qualified entry-level workers in the United States.
- Public-school reforms are not achieving learning breakthroughs, so company training programs are of necessity teaching remedial courses.
- Workforce performance is one of the last areas in which an organization can achieve a strategic advantage.
- Improved performance leads to greater productivity and increased earnings.

The Systems Approach works in any industry, whether large, intermediate, or small. It has worked in organizations with 100 employees as well as those with over 400,000 employees. The system has been successful in commercial companies, government agencies, and not-for-profit enterprises. It works whether the organization is centralized or decentralized. In summary, an organization really has no excuse for not having such a basic management system to increase workforce performance.

Here is a list of questions that senior executives, including the CEO, should be asking their training departments:

1. Does the training department have a mission statement that clearly states that it must develop a performance system for the critical jobs within the organization?
2. Have all the major job categories been identified, and do line executives concur with this list?
3. Does our organization have a management system such as the Systems Approach for Workforce Performance?
4. Has the training department established a formal working partnership with line management to design and develop a performance system for each major job category?
5. Have we established detailed performance requirements for each major job category, and do line executives concur with these requirements?
6. Do we have a professional group that knows how to buy, modify, or develop the required courses, design on-the-job training assignments, develop basic support systems, and assign personal-development tasks to achieve low-cost and successful performance systems?
7. Do we have a delivery-system strategy that ensures that our organization uses the most cost-effective methods?
8. Are we using all four quality-control measurements within each performance system?
9. Does our performance-management system aim for mastery of learning and performance, rather than for the obsolete bell-shaped curve?
10. Is there a formal change-management system that continuously updates our courses, on-the-job training assignments, and support systems?

11. Do we need an integrated electronic performance support system within any of our major job categories?
12. Are we on target with our reward and recognition programs?

Summary of the Book

Senior executives must ask penetrating questions to determine the need for action. This book contains a complete plan of action for restructuring a training department so that it can be managed as efficiently as manufacturing, operations, or marketing. Accordingly, the Systems Approach will have a major impact on the success of all quality and reengineering programs.

It requires very little of the senior executives' time to achieve the advantages discussed in this book. It is not a matter of time or cost, but of leadership.

A few years ago, the CEO of Xerox made the following comments at the national ASTD convention:

> I believe that training and development clearly has come of age in transforming itself from a function that was around the edge to a major strategic weapon. The challenges of this competitive economy require fundamental and systemic change. Workforce performance must become a strategic priority.

This is a bold statement. Unfortunately, too many organizations continue to tinker around the edges of training rather than focus on achieving breakthroughs in workforce performance. Change within most training departments has been both modest and incremental. This book provides a complete road map for reengineering the training department to achieve measurable improvements in workforce performance that will greatly improve an organization's operating and financial results.

A typical reaction of a senior executive after reading this chapter is, "Let's bring a spotlight to bear on this subject to ensure that we have a *well-trained, low cost,* and *competitive workforce* for future years."

References and Suggested Reading

ASTD (1996) Benchmarking forum report. *Training & Development.* November 1996.

ASTD (1995). Study on international organizations.

Bassi, L., Gallagher, A., & Schroer, E. (1996). *The ASTD training data book.* Alexandria, VA: ASTD Press.

Bennis, W. (1989). *On becoming a leader.* Reading, MA: Addison-Wesley.

Blake, R., Mouton, J., & Allen, R. (1987). *Spectacular teamwork.* New York: John Wiley.

Bowsher, J. (1989). *Educating America.* New York: John Wiley.

Camp, R. (1989). *Benchmarking.* Milwaukee, WI: Quality Press.

Carnevale, A., Gainer, L., & Villet, J. (1990). *Training in America.* San Francisco: Jossey-Bass.

Carnevale, A. (1991). *America and the new economy.* San Francisco: Jossey-Bass.

Champy, J. (1993). *Reengineering management.*

Covey, S. (1989). *The 7 habits of highly effective people.* New York: Fireside Books.

Craig, R. (1996). *ASTD training and development handbook.* New York: McGraw-Hill.

Csoka, L. (1994). "The Human Performance Gap." The Conference Board.

Deming, W.E. (1986). "Crisis." Cambridge MA: MIT Center for Advanced Engineering Study.

Dertouzos, M., Lester, R., & Solow, R. (1989). *Made in America.* Cambridge, MA: MIT Press.

Dick, W., & Reiser, R. (1989). *Planning effective instruction.* Englewood Cliffs, NJ: Prentice Hall.

Dick, W., & Carey, L. (1990). *The systemic design of instruction.* Glenview, IL: Scott Foresman.

Drucker Foundation. (1996). *The leader of the future.* San Francisco: Jossey-Bass.

Drucker, P. (1995). *Managing in time of great change*. New York: Truman Talley Books/Dutton.

Estes, R. (1996). *Tyranny of the bottom line*. San Francisco: Berrett-Koehler.

Filipczar, B. (December, 1996). "Who owns OJT?" *Training Magazine*.

Fingleton, E. (1995). *Why Japan is still on track to overtake the U.S. by the year 2000*. New York: Houghton Mifflin.

Frame, R.M., Hess, R.K., & Nielsen, W.R. (1982) *The OD source book*. Jossey-Bass/Pfeiffer.

Fuller, J. (1997). *Managing performance improvement projects*. Jossey-Bass/Pfeiffer.

GAO report. (February, 1995). Multiple Employment Training Programs.

Gartner Group report. "Do You Know Where Your PCs Are?" *BusinessWeek*, March 6, 1995. pp. 73–74.

Gery, G. (1987). *Making CTB happen*. Boston: Weingarten Publications.

Gery, G. (1991). *Electronic performance support systems*. Cambridge, MA: Ziff Institute.

Gilley, J., & Boughton, N. (1996). *Stop managing: Start coaching*. Burr Ridge, IL: Irwin Professional Publishing.

Gorden, D. (1996). *Fat and mean*. New York: The Free Press.

Hacker, C. A. (1996). *The costs of bad hiring decisions & how to avoid them*. Delray Beach, FL: Lucie Press.

Hamel, G., & Prahalad, D. (1994). *Competing for the future*. Boston: Harvard Business School Press.

Hammer, M., & Champy, J. (1993). *Reengineering the corporation*. New York: Harper Business.

Hanna, D. (1988). *Designing organizations for high performance*. Reading, MA: Addison-Wesley.

Harless, J. (1980). *An ounce of analysis is worth a pound of objectives*. Newnan, GA: Harless Press.

Harless, J. (1997). *Analyzing human performance: Tools for achieving business results*. Alexandria, VA: ASTD. *Harvard Business Review*, October.

Heisebein, F., Goldsmith, M., & Beckhard, R. (1997). *The organization of the future: The Drucker foundation*. San Francisco: Jossey-Bass.

Horton, T. (1992). *The CEO paradox*. New York: American Management Association.

Hunter, J.E. "Individual Differences in Output Variability as a Function of Job Complexity." *Journal of Applied Psychology* (95).

Huselid, M. (June, 1995). "The Road to High Performance." *Training and Development Magazine*.

Jacobs, R.L., & Jones, M.J. (1995). *Structured on-the-job training*. San Francisco: Jossey-Bass.

Johnston, W. B., & Packer, A. E. (1987). "Workforce 2000." Hudson Institute Report (June).

Juran, J. (1992). *Juran on quality by design: The new steps for planning quality into goods and services.* New York: The Free Press.

Kanter, R. (1989). *When giants learn to dance: Mastering the challenge of strategy, management, and careers in the 1990s.* New York: Simon & Schuster.

Kanter, R. (1993). *The views from the 1990s: How the global economy is reshaping corporate power and careers.* New York: Basic Books.

Katz, D. (1987). *The big store.* New York: Viking Press.

Kaufman, R. (1991). *Strategic planning plus.* Glenview, IL: Scott Foresman.

Kaufman, R., Rojas, A., & Mayer, H. (1993). *Needs assessment: A user's guide.* Englewood Cliffs, NJ: Educational Technology Publications.

Kaufman, R., Thiagarajan, S., & MacGillis, P. (Eds.) (1997). *The guidebook for performance improvement.* Jossey-Bass/Pfeiffer.

Kay, J. (1997) "Shareholders Aren't Everything." *Fortune.*

Kearns, D., & Nadler, D. (1992). *Prophets in the dark.* New York: Harper Business Books.

Kearsley, G. (1984). *Training and technology.* Reading, MA: Addison-Wesley.

Kirkpatrick, D.L. (1996). *Evaluating training programs.* Alexandria, VA: ASTD Press.

Kotter, J. (1990). "What Leaders Really Do." *Harvard Business Review* (May–June).

Kotter, J. (1996). *Leading change.* Boston: Harvard Business School Press.

Kouzes, J., & Posner, B. (1987). *The leadership challenge: How to get extraordinary things done in organizations.* San Francisco: Jossey-Bass.

Lee, C. (May 1996). *Training Magazine.*

Mager, R., & Pipe, R. (1984). *Analyzing performance problems.* Belmont, CA: Lake.

Malcolm, S.E. (1992). "Reengineering Corporate Training." *Training Magazine.*

McKenna, R. (1989). *Who's afraid of big blue?* Reading, MA: Addison-Wesley.

Meister, J. (1994). *Corporate quality universities.* Burr Ridge, IL: Irwin Professional.

Michael, M. (1996). *Building the learning organization.* New York: McGraw-Hill.

Nelson, B. (1994). *1001 ways to reward employees.* New York: Workman Publishing.

Orlin, J. (1988). *Training to win.* New York: Nichols Publishing.

Peoples, D. (1992). *Presentations plus.* New York City: Wiley.

Pepitone, J. (1995). *Future training.* Dallas, TX: Add Vantage.

Phillips, J.J. (1994). *Measuring return on investment.* Alexandria, VA: ASTD Press.

Reichheld, F. (1996). *The loyalty effect.* Cambridge, MA: Harvard Business School Press.

Robinson, D.G., & Robinson, J.C. (1989). *Training for impact.* San Francisco: Jossey-Bass.

Robinson, D.G., & Robinson, J.C. (1995) *Performance consulting: Moving beyond training.* San Francisco: Berrett-Koehler.

Rosow, J., & Zager, R. (1988). *Training: The competitive edge.* San Francisco: Jossey-Bass.

Rossett, A. (1987). *Training needs assessment.* Englewood Cliffs, N.J.: Education Technology Publications.

Rossett A., & Gautier-Downes, J. (1997). *Job aids.* Jossey-Bass/Pfeiffer.

Rothwell, W.J., & Kazanas, H.C. (1994). *Improving on-the-job training.* San Francisco: Jossey-Bass.

Rothwell, W.J., Sullivan, R., & McLean, G.N. (1995). *Practicing organization development: A guide for consultants.* Jossey-Bass/Pfeiffer.

Rothwell, W. (1996). *ASTD models for human performance improvement.* Alexandria, VA: ASTD Publishing.

Rummler, G., & Brache, A. (1995). *Improving performance: How to manage the white space on the organizational chart.* San Francisco: Jossey-Bass.

Schohl, J.T. (1991) *Achieving excellence through customer service.* Englewood Cliffs, NJ: Prentice Hall.

Senge, P. (1990). *The fifth discipline: The art and practice of the learning organization.* New York: Doubleday.

Shandler, D. (1996). *Reengineering the training function.* Delray Beach, FL: St. Lucie Press.

Slater, R. (1993). *The new GE.* Homewood, IL: Irwin Professional Publishing.

Spendolini, M. (1992). *The benchmarking book.* New York: American Management Association.

Stewart, T.A. (January, 1996). "Taking on the last bureaucracy." *Fortune.*

Stolovitch, H.D., & Keeps, E.J. (1992). *Handbook of human performance technology: A comprehensive guide for analyzing and solving performance problems in organizations.*

Svenson, R., & Rinderer, M. (1992). *The training and development strategic plan workbook.* Englewood Cliffs, NJ: Prentice Hall.

Swanson, R. (1994). *Analysis for improving performance.* San Francisco: Berrett-Koehler.

Thurow, L. (1992). *Head to head.* New York: William Morrow.

Tichy, N., & Devanna, M. (1986). *The transformational leader.* New York: John Wiley.

Tichy, N., & Stratford, S. (1993). *Control your destiny or someone else will: How Jack Welch is making General Electric the world's most competitive corporation.* New York: Doubleday.

U.S. Department of Education. (1983). "A Nation at Risk."

U.S. Department of Labor. (1994). "Nine characteristics of high-performing workplaces."

Walton, M. (1986). *The Deming management method.* New York: Perigee Books.

Weiss, T., & Hartle, F. (1996). *Reengineering performance management.* Delray Beach, FL: St. Lucie Press.

Whiteley, R., & Hessan, D. (1996). *Customer centered growth.* Reading, MA: Addison-Wesley.

Wilcox, J. (Ed.) (1994). "Road to High-Performance Workplaces: A Guide to Better Jobs and Better Business Results." *The Business of Training* (ASTD newsletter).

Wilson, T. (1994). *Innovative reward systems for the changing workplace.* New York: McGraw-Hill.

Winslow, C., & Bramer, W. (1994). *Future work.* New York: The Free Press.

About the Author

Jack E. Bowsher, formerly IBM's chief training officer, has worked extensively since his retirement as a teacher, course developer, consultant, and executive within the areas of training and workforce performance. For more than twenty-five years, he has been a leader in the development of new programs and management systems that achieve breakthroughs in workforce performance. Mr. Bowsher is also leading the drive for corporations and government agencies to adopt the new standard-mastery of learning and performance. Mr. Bowsher led the restructuring of employee-training programs in over one hundred education centers and one thousand learning centers, bringing instructional-design methods into the world of employee training and performance. He earned an MBA from the University of Chicago and has additional training and experience in accounting, information systems, marketing, and personnel administration. Also the author of *Educating America: Lessons Learned in the Nation's Corporations*, he previously served as a member of the Board of Governors at ASTD and on the Business Advisory Board for NSPI. Mr. Bowsher resides in Westport, Connecticut, and San Diego, California, where he continues working as a guest lecturer and consultant on restructuring training organizations and improving job performance.

Index

"Quick and dirty" course development, 107
Quick-fixes, in public school system, 85

R

Reactive training, 4
Real-time conferencing, 134–135
Recognition, 174–175; in Systems Approach, 49, 167–176. *See also* Reward and recognition systems
Recognition programs, creation of, 90
Recruiting costs, in workforces with some training, 14
Recruitment of training personnel, 35–36
Reengineering of basic processes, 80, 84–86
Reengineering of performance-management systems, 179–182
Reengineering Performance Management (Weiss & Hartle), 178
Reengineering the Corporation (Hammer & Champy), 79, 84
Reference books, 152
Regulatory requirements, in Systems Approach, 44–46
Reinforcement of training, by executives, 66
Reliability, of training-evaluation tests, 192
Repetitive tasks, on-the-job training for, 144
Requirements: for training courses, 72. *See also* Competitive requirements; Customer requirements; Performance requirements; Regulatory requirements
Resources, for job training, 28, 66, 72–73
Responsibility: for justification of training costs, 223–224; for training courses, 71–72
Restaurant industry, 116–117
Results. *See* Evaluating results; Negative results
Resumes, 207
Return on investment (ROI), measuring, 198–199, 221–222

Revenue reduction, in workforces with some training, 15
Reviews: of performance, 152–154; of training programs, 65–66; of workforce performance, 68–69
Reward and recognition systems, 167–176; bonuses in, 173–174; compensation in, 169–170, 170–171; formal awards in, 175–176; informal awards and recognition in, 174–175; need for, 167–168; negative results in, 169–170; organizational objectives and, 168–169; paying for knowledge through, 171–172; paying for performance through, 172; successful elements of, 170
Rewards, in Systems Approach, 49, 167–176
Ritz Carlton, workforce training of, 26
Robinson, Dana Gaines, 81, 94
Robinson, James C., 81, 94
Rojas, Alicia, 100
Rossett, Allison, 100, 110–111, 241
Rothwell, William J., 140
Rummler, Geary A., 81, 82, 98

S

Sales personnel, costs and productivity of, 218–221
Schank, Roger, 110–111
Secretaries, Systems Approach applied to training of, 50–51, 225
Self-directed teams, 91–92
Self-paced individual courses, 130
Self-paced individual learning delivery systems, 120, 122–127
Senior executives. *See* Executives
Service awards, 175
Service tasks, on-the-job training for, 144–145
Siemens, on-the-job training at, 145–146
Silo phenomenon, 82
Six Sigma definition of quality, 24, 69
Skill-based pay, 171–172
Skills: evaluating application of, 193–195; required of performance consultant, 93; responsibility for